IMAGES OF EDUCATIONAL CHANGE

IMAGES OF EDUCATIONAL CHANGE

EDITED BY
HERBERT ALTRICHTER
AND
JOHN ELLIOTT

Open University Press
Buckingham • Philadelphia

This book is dedicated to Barry MacDonald and Peter Posch both of whom, over the last three decades, have contributed enormously to our understanding of educational change and whose work has been a source of inspiration to many of the contributors to this volume.

Open University Press
Celtic Court
22 Ballmoor
Buckingham
MK18 1XW

e-mail: enquiries@openup.co.uk
world wide web: http://www.openup.co.uk

and
325 Chestnut Street
Philadelphia, PA 19106, USA

First Published 2000

A catalogue record of this book is available from the British Library

ISBN 0 335 20188 1 (pb) 0 335 20189 X (hb)

Library of Congress Cataloging-in-Publication Data
Images of educational change/edited by Herbert Altrichter and John Elliott.
p. cm.
Includes bibliographical references (p.) and index.
ISBN 0-335-20188-1. – ISBN 0-335-20189-X
1. Educational change. 2. School management and oganization.
3. Education – Social aspects. I. Altrichter, Herbert.
II. Elliott, John, Dip. Phil. Ed.
LB2805.I415 2000 99-44710
371.2–dc21 CIP

Typeset by Type Study, Scarborough, North Yorkshire
Printed in Great Britain by Biddles Ltd, Guildford and King's Lynn

Contents

Notes on contributors

HERBERT ALTRICHTER was born in 1954 in Vienna, Austria. He received a PhD from the University of Vienna in 1978. Between 1980 and 1991 he was a lecturer at the University of Klagenfurt. From 1991 to 1996 he was Professor of Business Education at the University of Innsbruck, and he is currently Professor of Education and Educational Psychology and Head of Department at the Johannes-Kepler University of Linz. He is the author of *Teachers Investigate Their Classrooms* (1994).

J. MYRON ATKIN, Professor of Education at Stanford University and a science teacher for seven years at elementary and secondary school levels in New York, also served on the faculty of the University of Illinois at Urbana-Champaign. At both Illinois and Stanford, he also was Dean of Education – from 1970 to 1979 at Illinois and from 1979 to 1986 at Stanford.

MARIE BRENNAN is Associate Professor and Associate Dean (Postgraduate Education) and coordinates the Master of School Management for the Faculty of Education at Central Queensland University, Australia. She has been involved as researcher and facilitator for action research projects with educators and students in a variety of settings for almost twenty years.

JOHN ELLIOTT has directed and coordinated a number of nationally and internationally recognized research projects aimed at engaging teachers with and in pedagogical research. Two early trend-setting projects involving local teachers in schools in the UK were the Ford Teaching Project (Ford Foundation 1973–5) and the Teacher–Pupil Interaction and the Quality of Learning Project (funded by the Schools Council 1980–3). The former project resulted in the formation of the Collaborative Action Research Network (CARN), which evolved into an international professional network to support the development of practitioner-based action research. Over the years John Elliott has coordinated a number of ESRC-funded action research projects, including 'A study of teachers' jobs and lives', 'The use of microcomputers to foster autonomous learning' and 'A study of teachers as researchers in the context of award bearing courses'. He has played a leading role as a pedagogical consultant for the OECD (CERI) Programme on the Environment and School Initiatives (ENSI). His central role has been to support teachers in constructing a knowledge base about their attempts to change the culture of teaching and learning in schools to foster action learning in relation to local environmental issues. He has written a number of influential books and papers on teaching as a research-based practice, including *Action Research for Educational Change* and *The Curriculum Experiment: Meeting the Challenge of Social Change*.

CHRISTINE FINNAN is an assistant professor at the College of Charleston in South Carolina and the director of the South Carolina Accelerated Schools Project and the Center of Excellence in Accelerating Learning, both located at the College of Charleston. She received her PhD from Stanford University in Education with a minor in anthropology in 1980.

SUSAN GROUNDWATER SMITH is a research consultant based in Sydney, having worked previously at the University of Technology, Sydney and at Sydney University. She is currently a research fellow in education at the University of East Anglia. Her most recent book, with Robyn Cusworth and Rosie Dobbins, is *Teaching: Challenges and Dilemmas*. She is also the author, with Vivienne White, of *Improving our Primary Schools: Evaluation and Assessment through Participation*.

ERNEST R. HOUSE is a professor in the School of Education at the University of Colorado at Boulder. His interests are evaluation and policy. He has been a visiting scholar at UCLA, Harvard and New Mexico, and in England, Spain, Sweden, Austria and Australia. Books include *The Politics of Educational Innovation, Survival in the Classroom* (with S. Lapan), *Evaluating with Validity, Jesse Jackson and the Politics of Charisma, Professional Evaluation, Schools for Sale* and *Values in Evaluation and Social Research* (with K. Howe). He is recipient of the Lasswell Prize for the article contributing most to the theory and practice of the policy sciences in 1989 and of the Lazarsfeld Award for Evaluation Theory, presented by the American Evaluation Association in 1990.

LAWRENCE INGVARSON is an associate professor in the Faculty of Education at Monash University. He formerly taught science in Australia and the UK and lectured at the University of Stirling in Scotland. His main research interests are teachers, work, professional development and relationships between policy and practice. He is currently editing a book on the work of the US National Board for Professional Teaching Standards over its first ten years.

HENRY M. LEVIN is the David Jacks Professor of Higher Education and Economics at Stanford University and the Director of the Accelerated Schools Project, a movement of over 1000 elementary and secondary schools in 40 states that is in its twelfth year. He is a specialist in the economics of human resources and educational policy.

BARRY MACDONALD is an evaluation specialist who, over three decades in this role, has studied change in the social services of the UK and elsewhere, particularly with respect to education and training. He pioneered a case study approach to evaluation, and has contributed generally to qualitative enquiry and the politics of research.

SUSAN E. NOFFKE was a teacher of elementary and middle school aged children in Wisconsin, USA, for ten years. She is currently Assistant Professor of Curriculum and Instruction at the University of Illinois-Urbana/Champaign, where she teaches pre-service elementary teachers and works with experienced teachers in graduate programmes. She has worked for over ten years with various aspects of action research. Her publications include 'Professional, personal, and political dimensions of action research' in the *Review of Research in Education* and she is co-editor (with Robert Stevenson) of *Educational Action Research: Becoming Practically Critical.*

CHRISTINE O'HANLON is a senior lecturer at the School of Education, University of Birmingham. She began her career as a teacher, then transferred to higher education and has now been a teacher educator for many years. She writes about inclusive education, action research and, more recently, higher degree supervision and research issues in universities. She has always been interested in the process of change, which forms the basis of her practice, which is ultimately to improve the professional practice of teachers and other educational professionals, with the aim of benefiting children's and young people's learning through schooling. At present she is trying to change the 'research' culture in universities to enable teachers to feel more in control of what they do in their professional lives. She has published in an international context and has extensive experience of working with teachers in Europe.

ANGEL PÉREZ GÓMEZ is a full professor of curriculum and teaching method in the University of Málaga. He has academic degrees in education and psychology (PhD 1976). He has been Vice Chancellor of the University of Málaga, Vice Dean of the Faculty of Education at the University of Málaga and Head of Department of Curriculum and Teaching Methods at the Universities of Salamanca, Complutense, Madrid and Málaga. He has been a consultant to the Ministry of Education. He won the top national award in educational research in 1994. He has been, and still is, a member of the different national and regional committees of research and evaluation on education, and of the editorial committee of a number of educational journals. He has written ten books and more than a hundred papers on curriculum research and innovation, educational evaluation, teacher training and professional development, school culture and political determination. Since 1982 he has been one of the initiators of the growing tradition of action research in Spain, leading many projects of curriculum change and professional development, teacher training and school innovation. He has been involved in important projects of educational evaluation at a national level.

PETER POSCH has teaching degrees in English and geography, and PhDs in education and psychology. He has conducted studies and research activities at the Universities of Innsbruck and Constance and the Vienna School of Economics. He has been Professor of Education at the Institute of Education at the University of Klagenfurt in Austria since 1976, and was Visiting Professor at the School of Education of Stanford University in 1992.

STEFAN SALZGEBER is a lecturer in human resource management at the Department of Business Education and Human Resource Management, University of Innsbruck. His research is on constitutional theories in the field of organization theory and human resource management. One of his current research projects is the coaching of the succession process in five family companies.

JOHN SCHOSTAK is a professor at the Centre for Applied Research in Education at the University of East Anglia, and is interested in researching education, the processes of 'knowing' and the production of 'knowledge' in schools, the clinical areas of the health professions, the practices of business organizations, the media and more broadly in any area of everyday life.

BRIDGET SOMEKH worked at CARE from 1987 to 1995, after 14 years as a secondary English teacher. During the same period she was coordinator of CARN (the Collaborative (formerly Classroom) Action Research Network). She is well known for her research and evaluation work in information and communication technology in education, which she regards as a particularly interesting field in which to study change. Her publications include *Teachers Investigate Their Work* (co-authored with Herbert Altrichter and Peter Posch) and *Using IT Effectively in Teaching and Learning* (co-edited with Niki Davis). In 1994–6, while Deputy Director of the Scottish Council for Research in Education, she coordinated the Management for Organisational and Human Development Project, funded by the European Union across six research centres in Austria, Spain, Italy and the UK. She is currently Dean of the School of Education and Professional Development at The Manchester Metropolitan University.

ROB WALKER is at the University of East Anglia and currently has interests in information technology and education especially in relation to higher education. More information is available at http://www2.deakin.edu.au/e&c/dcec/members/walker.html

Introduction

HERBERT ALTRICHTER

A man who had not met Mr Keuner for a long time welcomed him with the words: 'You have not changed at all.' – 'Oh!' said Mr Keuner and grew pale.

(Bertolt Brecht)

Change is ubiquitous, and so is talk about 'changes'. 'Change' and its family of 'change-words', such as 'progress', 'improvement', 'evolution' and 'development', are among the key concepts of modernity (see de Mul and Korthals 1997: 245). A few theorists believe that the notion of 'change' has lost importance in recent times, or that even history will come to its end (see the discussion of this argument by Elliott in Chapter 14 of this volume), but most analysts would argue that we see an intensification, a speeding up, an increased complexity of change processes (see, for example, Posch in Chapter 4 of this volume).

This is nowhere more true than in education. While many European countries experienced a period of stagnation in their education systems in the 1980s – as a backlash to the period of educational reform during the late 1960s and the 1970s, in the 1990s and beyond the idea of change has once again become central to educational discourse. Everywhere we see 'innovation', 'reform', 'development', 'improvement' etc. with respect to school governance, teacher education, teaching methods, school inspection, school financing, evaluation etc. in many educational systems of the Western world – and we hear even more talk about it.

'Change' is not uniform, and a variety of concepts of 'educational change' compete for the attention of policy makers, practitioners and the wider public. For example, 'change' may be used to argue for more autonomy in order to allow and enhance self-management of schools or for stricter central surveillance, accreditation and evaluation, or for both; it may be used to argue for more room for market forces or for more parent participation in the governance of schools. 'Change' shapes up differently in different discourse contexts, and appears to be infinitely contestable and inherently unstable.

The aim of this book is to explore the range and variety of contemporary 'images of change' which inform educational discourse, and to evaluate their potential and consequences for shaping educational thought and practice. We have asked authors working on educational change issues in a number of countries and variety of contexts to explore 'change' within their field, to give examples of 'change' in order to help readers to understand the origin, possible uses and practical consequences of the 'change' concepts implied in the practical work and proclaimed in the programmatic ideas which govern this work.

In the remaining sections of this introduction, I want to identify a number of different possible meanings and uses of 'change' concepts, and provide an overview of the chapters in this volume by identifying the main issues which they discuss.

Gazing through the kaleidoscope: dimensions of change

Change is ubiquitous, and so is the concept of 'change'. However, the meanings of both, of the concept and of the practices referred to, seem to oscillate. Images of change processes vary widely in the scope and emphases of meanings conveyed. It is like gazing through a kaleidoscope. The image changes quickly when the instrument is turned around, held at varying angles or pointed to different backgrounds. So let us play around with the kaleidoscope for a while, trying to distinguish several possible dimensions of the concept of 'change' (see van Haften 1997).

Most obviously, 'change' may refer both to a *process* and to a *product* (of such processes). While the features of products and processes of specific 'changes' are usually intricately linked, it is not often possible to deduce one from the other. Furthermore, educational discourse seems to become more and more interested in processes not only of individual, but also of group, macro-group, organizational and societal development.

Second, the verb 'change' may be used *intransitively* (a situation changes) or *transitively* (I change the situation). In the first case, we tend to assume natural, even necessary, developments according to immanent laws, while in the second case we are inclined to search for 'agents of change'. Or we look for structural factors in the widest sense (such as demographic trends or natural catastrophes). A key issue stems from the question: are change processes conceived as mainly driven by *internal* or *external* forces (of an organism, a social entity etc.)? And where does the locus of control lie?

Third, we may attribute changes to *intentional processes* or we may see them as a result of *unintentional consequences* of other processes and actions (some of which may have been 'intentional', however, with respect to other goals). Similarly, the term 'change' is used both for processes which the main actors are *aware* of, and for those of which they are *unaware*.

This difference has gained some importance in recent theories of organizational change. While this field has been dominated for a long time by concepts of rationally planned organizational development, these have been called into question by observations that real changes very often do not conform to the neat designs of organizational planners, but are contested and resemble political struggles (see, for example, Ball 1987). Recent approaches search for a new relationship between intentionality and unintended consequences, which implies that they are also searching for a new relationship between agency and structure (see, for example, Altrichter and Salzgeber in Chapter 8 of this volume). For instance, Ortmann *et al.* (1997: 333–5) argue that even if reorganization is intended, this does not imply that its results are necessarily those which had been intended. Lévy-Strauss's (1981) image of *bricolage* provides a better concept of organizational innovation processes than the rationalist step-by-step innovation models to be found in various versions in different textbooks. Change in this view is productive action with a limited 'toolbox' of measures and resources, rather than a plan to be realized as written. Limited rationality of action is its typical feature; a type of work which is only partially moulded by overarching goals, but the objectives of which shift according to the opportunities provided by the tools and resources available. However, the metaphor has its limits: restructuring of an organization is the work not of a lonely *bricoleur* but of a political process. Those who are resisting change are using resources and rules provided by the existing structure of organization in order to uphold the routine games that are the same as those the innovators have available to orchestrate their innovation games.

Once we have abandoned the image of a rationally planned and orchestrated reorganization, it seems that social Darwinist concepts of unintended *evolution* may save the threatened rationality: if it is not sensible innovators who elaborate rational forms of organization fit for survival, then environment, selection and/or adaptation will do the job. However, human beings make their history – and their organizations – not independently of all external contingencies, but knowing their history and their organizations. They are reflexive creatures and they change their history and their organizations in relationship to their knowledge. Society and organizations cannot be conceived as basic evolutionary entities which may be delineated unequivocally and independently of the course of history. When we are talking about organizational change we have to expect contingency, necessity *and* chance. The concept of path dependence aims to depict the strange mixture of chance and necessity: small events considered to be ephemeral may nevertheless provide the basis for later moves which lock in some 'changes' in typical organizational tracks. The winner is not always the protagonist of the universal principle of efficiency – as the concept of the survival of the fittest would have us expect. Organizational change often sees lucky winners, who came very close to losing it all, but who, once having won, have the means to build up and substantiate their win – gradually to extend the efficiency of their programme – and to rewrite the history and the success criteria of the organization in such a way that their win can be viewed as a new triumph of efficiency (see Ortmann *et al.* 1997: 333–5).

This brings us to a fourth difference: the concept of 'change' may be used in the same way to refer to *individuals* or to *collectives*. Fifth, we may use the word 'change' for results which differ *profoundly* or only *partially* from the prior situation. The product may be *'more of the same'* or *qualitatively different* – and it is still change.

Sixth, the very idea of change situates an instance in a trajectory, since it implies that there has been at least one prior situation. Some images of change imply an idea of a *pattern of stages*, while elsewhere it is 'just changes'. Furthermore, this developmental pattern may be conceived as *locally and temporally* or as *universally valid* (sometimes offering a good outlook on the future which is conceived as the next stage of this pattern of changes). A change pattern may be seen as *fixed* or *historically flexible*. It may be seen as *reversible* or *irreversible*. And the transitions from one stage to the next may be conceptualized as *smooth*, more or less *gradual*, or as *abrupt* and connected with *crises*.

From this set of distinctions and differences we may conclude that a 'change' argument has at least two levels (see van Haften 1997: 23; see also Figure 1): to talk about 'changes' implies that some time has passed with respect to the observed phenomenon and that the entity under discussion has altered its structure in some respect. Thus, a 'change argument' refers, on a time level, to dynamic processes which are always irreversible, while on a 'structural' level a 'change argument' reconstructs temporal development as transitions between different stages and conditions, which need not necessarily be irreversible.

Finally, 'images of change' may be *reconstructive*, in that they purport to describe and interpret observed transitions. On the other hand, they may be *evaluative* when they aim to identify progress, stagnation or decay. There is much 'crypto-normativism' among change theories when some *telos*, some fixed end or mature stage, underpins the reconstructions of transitions. 'Almost every developmental theory has therapeutic claims and implications, even as it proposes a fixed sequence of stages leading to a final stage. The theory is written to improve the . . . situation' (Korthals 1997: 165).

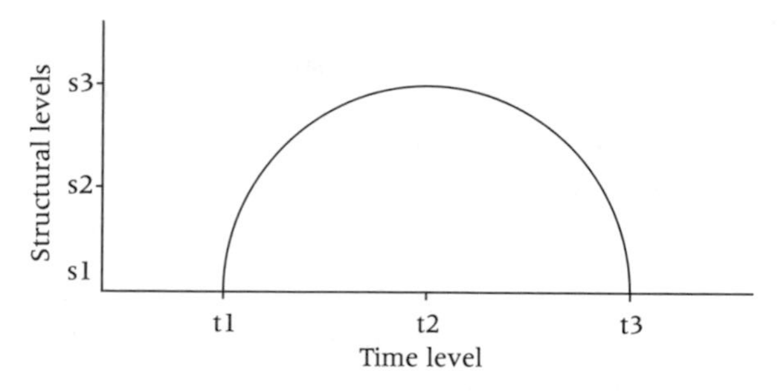

Figure 1 Levels of a change argument

'Development' may be a conceptual amoeba but, on the other hand, the term – just like other concepts from the family of 'change words', such as growth, evolution and maturation – has a specific overtone which is heard irrespective of the context of use, as Esteva (1993: 96) argues: 'In some way, it always sounds like wished-for change, like steps in the right direction, from the simple to the various and complex, from the inferior to the superior, from the worse to the better, as if an improvement is meant, a movement . . . directed to a desirable aim.' Esteva (1993) exemplifies this claim in his brilliant essay on the invention of 'development policy', and thereby gives a perfect example of Foucault's concept of 'power–knowledge complexes' *(dispositives)*.

Foucault (1986) argued that knowledge is connected not only with specific interests, but also with certain social practices. Knowledge supports practices that change reality, and these practices, in turn, produce knowledge. Thus, knowledge is not an independent representation or even reproduction of reality, since reality is produced by power–knowledge complexes. In particular, for 'modernist' developmental theories, Foucault has argued that there is 'an inherent connection between progress, the new idea of segmenting in stages, and the disciplining of the body', and that these concepts, therefore, 'have intrinsic disciplining effects' (de Mul and Korthals 1997: 252).

I think these ideas are appropriate when one is working with educational change theories. What are the implicit evaluative claims underlying an 'image of change'? And what 'power–knowledge complexes' are associated with the change theory analysed?

To sum up: if someone talks about changes this can mean a lot – and a lot of different things. Quite a range of 'meanings of change' may be implicitly transported by virtue of this 'kaleidoscopic character' of the term. As we know from processes of educational and organizational change in schools, undefined language has potential for approaching new issues and for developing new perspectives, but it can create ongoing misunderstanding in situations where some concerted effort and synergy is necessary.

Our book does not aspire to 'change' this situation by proposing *one* concise and comprehensive definition of 'educational change'. However, we want to fuel the discussion about educational change theories by bringing together a variety of contemporary 'images of change', which should allow readers to evaluate their explanatory power for the fields they have been originally developed for, and also by comparing and contrasting them to explore their potential and consequences for other areas of educational change.

The organization of this book

Part I of this book concerns the relationship between 'educational change and policy formation'. In Chapter 1, 'Economic change, educational policy formation and the role of the state', Ernest House shows how policies are formed and how they change again: 'streams' of social problems, political concerns, and policies evolve somewhat independently of each other. Sometimes these streams interconnect and open up 'windows of opportunity' in which problems become connected to policies. Most of the time educational policies do not work, are even counter-productive, and House develops an *error theory* in order to explain why. He also emphasizes the increasing importance of the role of policy entrepreneurs in the process of policy formation, who develop attractive and marketable 'policy ideas'.

House's chapter is followed by Barry MacDonald's complementary and provocative analysis of educational policy making in the UK during the Thatcher years and beyond. Ironically entitled 'How education became nobody's business', the chapter depicts a 'pathology' of policy formation in a particular national context in terms of consequences which render education, conceived as preparing all students for active citizenship in a democratic society, literally 'nobody's business'.

In the third chapter, entitled 'Developing under developing circumstances', John Schostak outlines contemporary politics where 'schooling' – understood as 'processing of children and adults for social purposes' – is cleansed from all 'education' which can only be negatively defined as 'not playing the game'. Policy makers and researchers work on 'high reliability schools', and the paranoid curriculum 'is essentially about control for the purposes of "rational" purification; that is, the construction of an order in the name of which individuals submit to reason and reject all that is inessential to reason.' It is a scenario of externally engineered changes for the worse within which – nevertheless – personal and social development for the better (i.e. 'education') still seems possible to the author. It begins with the education of judgement, which is moulded after MacDonald's 'democratic evaluation' paradigm. When we ask what the agents of these favourable changes are, 'no grand narrative' is provided. Instead, we are pointed to the child, to 'the individual, at whatever age, [who] must be included as a decision-making partner in the [curricular] process', and to principles such as 'diversity, dialogue and a mutuality of relationships', which introduce a multitude of players into the change processes.

Part II brings together three chapters on the theme of 'the relationship between social and educational change'. In 'Community, school change and strategic networking', Peter Posch identifies two 'external' societal processes – increasing individualization and fragmentation of work conditions – as posing major challenges for change to schools. New 'dynamic competencies' are needed both for work life and for constructive use of times of unemployment. Strategic networking and alliances of schools with cultural and economic institutions or – even more radically – the integration of schools into community affairs can help schools to cope with these challenges. Posch introduces an example from an Austrian secondary school in order to discuss two points: in what way is the concept of learning altered in dynamic networks of this kind; what can we learn from the characteristics of dynamic networks (as opposed to hierarchical structures of communication) for the organization of schools?

Despite rapid changes in our political, social, cultural and economic environment, not everything has changed. 'Older as well as emergent ways of organizing social life exist side by side, interacting with and interrupting one another . . . offering a wider range of resources for individual and community identity formation.' What appears to be a site of conservatism may also be a basis for resistance. In 'Social change and the individual: changing patterns of community and the challenge for schooling', Marie Brennan and Susan Noffke explore such tensions of school change by examining two reform projects centred on an image of change as a 'community of enquirers'. They use the supposed dichotomy of individual and community to put forward an argument which is also central to systemic approaches to change (see, for example, Luhmann 1988). They emphasize that the differences, the sometimes painful tensions that change processes point to, may be a resource for constructive development. But it is only when such difference is not denied, but 'accepted and worked with, that shared and worthwhile products are derived from the effort put into them.'

In 'Social change, subject matter – and the teacher', J. Myron Atkin provides us with a specific example of the way in which social change impacts on the conception and organization of knowledge in society and presents new curricular tensions and challenges for schools and teachers. He notes that changes in perceptions as to what constitutes a desirable science education have reflected changes in the social status and in the uses of science from the nineteenth century onwards. Atkin goes on to argue that such images of subject matter are a core element of teachers' beliefs and assumptions about teaching and also about themselves. Theories of changes must account for this. Strategies of educational change must 'recognize just how deeply projected changes in subject matter itself can challenge the images teachers have of *themselves* as the custodians and proponents of their disciplines.'

Part III comprises three chapters that are specifically concerned with 'conceptualizing school change processes'. Christine Finnan and Henry M. Levin's contribution, 'Changing school cultures', is organized around the concept of culture. 'Culture' is seen as involving artefacts, processes and basic beliefs and assumptions. Culture is both conservative (in that it gives us old answers to new questions) and ever-changing (since it is adapting all the time to new influences). However, most educational change is, as the authors argue, at the somewhat superficial level of artefacts and processes: 'Real, sustained change, however, does not occur unless basic beliefs and assumptions also change.' Finnan and Levin identify five critical components of the basic beliefs and assumptions that shape school culture and that must be addressed in order 'truly to change school culture': the school's expectations for children, children's expectations for their own school experience, expectations for adults, opinions about acceptable educational practices and assumptions about the desirability of change. Although they argue that school cultures are unique and can be changed through 'local initiatives', they acknowledge the way in which a societally defined culture of schooling interacts with and shapes, without determining every aspect of, those cultures.

In traditional micro-political theories change is endemic to organizations. It results from the organization members' power struggles for various types of gratification and for autonomy and influence. But why is it that many of us experience organizations as rather stable? Starting from case material concerning the integration of a new teacher into the staff of a 'reform school', 'Some elements of a micro-political theory of school development' are discussed in Chapter 8, by Stefan Salzgeber and myself. Organizations are understood as webs woven from concrete interactions of (self-)interested actors. They acquire some spatial-temporal stability through the actors' use and reproduction of games. The 'game' is the point in which the analytically divided elements of 'agency and structure', of 'individual and organization', meet. The interlocked character of the games and the large number of routine elements in social practices are major reasons for the relative stability of organizations.

Starting with her own experiences as a teacher researcher, Bridget Somekh explores 'Changing concepts of action research' as a model for involving teachers in educational change within schools. In her view, much of the early action research was individualistic and, thus, based on a model of change of limited value: 'it is only suited to a few "super-persons" (workaholics); second, it can only focus upon a small field of study, such as a single classroom, because that is the domain of the individual concerned.' She perceives a 'relentless suspicion of management-led, whole-school action research projects', and advocates a group and multi-level approach to action research, in which as many organization members as possible are drawn into the process of change management.

The contributions in the fourth and final part of the book focus on 'preparing teachers for creative engagement with educational change'. In 'Reflective education and school culture: the socialization of student teachers', Angel Pérez Gómez discusses the results of case studies of the *practicum* experiences of Spanish student teachers. His evidence shows that the *practicum* powerfully socializes novices into the dominant school culture. Thus, this type of practical training of student teachers appears to be 'more of an obstacle than a tool' for educational change, since the education of future teachers must strive, as the author argues, to encourage reflective professionals.

In 'Case study and case records', Susan Groundwater Smith and Rob Walker examine a possible way of counteracting the kind of socialization into conservative practices that Pérez Gómez depicts. The idea of the 'Hathaway Project' was to create a case record of a school that could be used in teacher education programmes. The authors discuss the original intentions of this piece of work, the background of their knowledge, which is rooted in shared work experiences with Lawrence Stenhouse and Barry MacDonald, and what they have learned from the uses students made of this case material in order to explore the development of their thinking about case studies, case records and their possible formats and uses.

In the context of debates about the continuing professional development of teachers, Christine O'Hanlon asks how 'Experts of the future' can be educated. This will not result from mere immersion in practice and its traditions, but calls for a process of critical reasoning in which practical arguments are taken seriously, by listening to them, examining them and deconstructing them 'to find the contradictions and disparities which inevitably arise'. Deconstruction and change go side-by-side, and a collegial structure is a necessary precondition for critical reasoning.

Lawrence Ingvarson takes up the 'quality theme', which is to be heard in the educational debates in so many countries, and gives it a fresh treatment. In 'Teacher control and the reform of professional development', he argues that current policies for quality development, which are focusing on schools, not on the profession, overestimate the effectiveness of managerial models of change through the control over teachers' work (a point also made by Somekh). He advocates a strategy that links educational change with the reform of the professional development system and the development of teaching as a profession. A central role in this strategy is awarded to standards formulated by the profession itself. These standards signal to fellow teachers what their profession expects from its members. And they demonstrate that 'the profession has the capacity to lay down its own directions and goals for the professional development of its members.'

In a final overview chapter, John Elliott makes his own personal voyage through the various images of educational change presented in this book, in search of some kind of synthesis, seeking to construct something like a synoptic understanding and vision of education change in advanced industrial societies for the twenty-first century. An over-ambitious aspiration? Even a misguided one? He and I will leave the reader to judge.

References

Ball, S. J. (1987) *The Micro-politics of the School.* London: Routledge.

de Mul, J. and Korthals, M. (1997) Developmental philosophy and postmodernism. In W. van Haften, M. Korthals and T. Wren (eds) *Philosophy of Development.* Dordrecht: Kluwer, pp. 245–60.

Esteva, G. (1993) Entwicklung. In W. Sachs (ed.) *Wie im Westen so auf Erden.* Rororo: Reinbek, pp. 89–121 (English edition under the title *The Development Dictionary.* London: Zed Books, 1992).

Foucault, M. (1986) *The History of Sexuality,* Volume 1. New York: Pantheon.

Foucault, M. (1991) *Discipline and Punish: the Birth of the Prison.* London: Penguin.

Korthals, M. (1997) Societal Development. In W. van Haften, M. Korthals and T. Wren (eds) *Philosophy of Development.* Dordrecht: Kluwer, pp. 163–81.

Lévy-Strauss, C. (1981) *Das wilde Denken.* Frankfurt am Main: Suhrkamp.

Luhmann, N. (1988) *Soziale Systeme.* Frankfurt am Main: Suhrkamp.

Ortmann, G., Sydow, J. and Windeler, A. (1997) Organisation als reflexive Strukturation. In G.Ortmann, J. Sydow and K. Tuerk (eds) *Theorien der Organisation*. Opladen: Westdeutscher Verlag, pp. 315–54.
van Haften, W. (1997) The concept of development. In W. van Haften, M. Korthals and T. Wren (eds) *Philosophy of Development*. Dordrecht: Kluwer, pp. 13–29.
van Haften, W., Korthals, M. and Wren, T. (1997) (eds) *Philosophy of Development*. Dordrecht: Kluwer.

PART I

Educational change and policy formation

1

Economic change, educational policy formation and the role of the state

ERNEST R. HOUSE

We live in an age of economic productivity, during a time in which the dominant concerns in all our countries are expanding the economy, raising personal income and increasing the standard of living. No government in liberal democracies can long survive without economic expansion, whether the country is run by conservatives, social democrats or socialists (or apparently communists either). This concern for productivity is manifested in a drive for greater efficiency and has special implications for education. In fact, it is the source of most educational policy at the national level.

Although productivity is a dominant concern in all industrial countries, it results in somewhat different educational policies in each. Britain, the oldest industrial economy, is different from the ageing economy of the United States, which is different again from the mature economies of Japan and Germany, or the relatively young economy of Spain. One national educational system expands, while another contracts painfully. None the less, in most countries educational policies appear to be formulated primarily with regard to the national economy and without sufficient regard for educational practice.

Of course, other factors, like culture and history, influence educational policies as well. For example, racial politics permeates everything in the USA and is not duplicated elsewhere, though some countries show signs of catching up. Britain clings to its eternal class structure, which manifests itself throughout British society. And Spain nurtures a virile traditionalism which suffuses its lifestyle. None the less, despite these differences, in all these countries economic concerns influence educational policy more strongly than anything else at the current time (Wirt and Harman 1986).

I am *not* saying that economic policies necessarily influence educational *practices*. Educational practices (everyday teaching and learning patterns of teachers and students) have many influences other than government policies; in fact, practices frequently run counter to government policies (MacDonald and Walker 1976). Furthermore, policies have effects opposite to what is intended. I am *not* advancing a functionalist explanation of educational change in which education and work mirror each other (a contested topic in the neo-Marxist literature, e.g. Bowles and Gintis 1976; Apple and Weiss 1983; Carnoy and Levin 1985; Liston 1988). Nor am I proposing that policies and practices mirror each other faithfully. They do not.

Rather, my contention is that national leaders formulate educational policies primarily in response to national economic concerns – without sufficient understanding or appreciation of educational institutions. This overdrawn focus causes educational policies to be mismatched to practices. Policies intended to increase productivity often decrease it. It is as if suggestions for improving productivity in the auto industry were made without detailed knowledge of how cars are assembled. In Sarason's words, 'those outside the system have nothing resembling a holistic conception of the system they seek to influence. In principle . . . ignorance need not be lethal, although it almost always has been' (Sarason 1990: 27).

Nor do government leaders do this deliberately with foreknowledge that their policies will fail. Instead they are mistaken in their initiatives because they are too far removed from educational work, too wedded to powerful interests, too imbued with misleading ideologies and simply misinformed. Thus, educational policies dissolve into ineffectiveness, to be replaced by other mistaken and ineffective policies. So my analysis is an 'error theory' of policy which explains why we have the policies that we do and why these policies fail, to be replaced by other policies that also fail.

The influence of economics

There are at least four ways in which economic concerns influence educational policies. First, economic conditions strongly influence educational policies. For example, government budgets constrain educational spending. The expansionist policies of the 1950s and 1960s cannot be repeated in the 1990s, even if one wanted to, because budget surpluses do not exist in most countries. Furthermore, economic policies have consequences, such as increasing income inequality or increased immigration, with which the schools must contend.

Second, educational policies are frequently formulated to reduce costs and increase the productivity of schools. This pressure is more than a budget consideration. The market forces of advanced capitalism work to increase the efficiency and productivity of all institutions, as they have done already in agriculture and car manufacture. It may be education's turn for economic rationalization. At other times, considerations such as defence, caring for the disabled or assimilation of immigrants prevailed as concerns.

Third, education and economic development are presumed to be closely linked. It is assumed that more or better education leads to improved technological capabilities and better jobs. This connection is taken for granted for the most part, and provides the rationale for much educational policy proposed by educators and non-educators alike, although this relationship is less straightforward than one might think. There is the distinct possibility that education is led by jobs, rather than the other way around (Carnoy and Levin 1985).

Fourth, economic concepts and metaphors permeate educational thinking (McCloskey 1990). For example, the concepts and imagery of markets and productivity have been applied to schools. Educators are urged to create and respond to markets (Chubb and Moe 1990). Corporate structure is taken as a model for school governance. And this intellectual influence extends deep into the social sciences, so that even when one analyses from a political perspective, one may be using economic concepts that have migrated there (Boyd *et al.* 1994).

Corresponding to these influences are four types of errors: misunderstanding the economic system; misunderstanding the educational system; misunderstanding the fit between the two; and misapplying economic concepts. All four errors are abundant in education, which is not to say that economic concepts cannot be productively applied. In fact, educational institutions share key features with economic institutions, and many educational reforms would be seen as foolish if similar reforms were attempted in business. The mistake is not one of applying economic concepts to education but of applying them badly, without understanding the effects they are likely to have.

One of the anomalies of educational reform is that educators and students are not treated like other people. That is, economics treats investments in education as rational responses to a calculus of expected costs and benefits (Becker 1993). Yet teachers and students themselves are often not accorded this same calculative rationality that is used to justify educational expenditures in the first place. Assumptions of altruism, incompetence and obedience are no more valid in schools than elsewhere.

Although each country is unique in its policy dynamics, there are strong similarities. Economic rationalism is pervasive in Britain, Australia, New Zealand, the Netherlands and many advanced countries (Pusey 1991; Kelsey 1995). In my view, the United States is following a pattern similar to that of Britain (Barberis and May 1993). The situation is not one of historical cycles but of similar forces at work. In both countries the educational systems are undergoing retrenchments and reforms in governance closely related to (relatively) declining economies. For example, in the next decade US higher education will undergo retrenchment, as has occurred in Britain, even as other countries, such as Sweden and Finland, expand higher education. Although education is tied to economic development in most countries, each country stands at a different place.

Policy formation

I take policy formation in US education to be similar to that in other domestic areas, though with its own peculiarities (Wirt and Kirst 1975; Kingdon 1984). 'Streams' of problems, politics and policies evolve somewhat independently of each other. Major problems appear and disappear from public attention; politics shifts between liberal and conservative; and policy solutions are shaped by 'policy communities'. Social problems arise, only to remain unsolved and disappear; political concerns shift without solving problems; policies are offered without political takers or connections to the problems.

Sometimes these streams interconnect. 'Windows of opportunity' appear in which problems become connected to facilitative politics and policies, often through the services of policy entrepreneurs, who persistently advocate their favourite policies from politically advantageous positions. An opportunistic melding of problems, politics and policies sometimes results in government action, which may be more or less effective in solving problems. Public attention is then focused on other issues.

Such a policy formation process contrasts to either a fully rational policy process, in which problems are defined and appropriate policies invented (Lasswell 1971), or an incrementalist process, in which policy drifts in small steps over periods of time, with policy makers 'muddling through' (Braybrooke and Lindblom 1970). Although these other models sometimes characterize policy action, the overall pattern is neither fully rational nor irrational. Unfortunately, problems often are not solved. In fact, there is a mismatch. The policies adopted do not do the job.

In this process policy entrepreneurs play key roles (Krugman 1994). Entrepreneurs present ideas that appeal to politicians even when these ideas will not work, and this mismatch occurs in economic as well as educational policy, as the notorious 'supply-side' policies of the Reagan administration illustrate:

> The ideas embraced by the Reagan administration were, however, anything but deep. To the astonishment of the serious conservatives, the real winners of 1980 turned out to be the supply-siders – ideologues whose economic concepts were cartoonlike in their simplicity, who dismissed conventional economics because they could not be bothered to understand it.
>
> (Krugman 1994: 281)

The Laffer curve would have been a laugher, except for the national debt that followed its application. But if 'voodoo' economics has been an albatross of conservatives, liberals have also advanced ineffective policies. In understanding how productivity is improved, for example, some have miscast the role of foreign competition. Something similar has occurred with prescriptions drawn from international educational comparisons meant to improve educational competitiveness in the service of the economy.

'Marketing' policy ideas aggressively has taken on new importance in the past few decades. Ideas have emerged increasingly from a concentrated policy elite, mostly from think tanks in Washington or London or whatever capital, funded by non-educational sources (Ricci 1993).

> It has become barely possible to draw the line between the disinterested scholar – more accurately, the scholar wrestling honestly with the biases and preconceptions that inevitably cloud any research effort – and the intellectual advocate who earnestly marshals evidence to bolster an unshakable political position. All research begins to look like advocacy, all experts begin to look like hired guns, and all think tanks seem to use their institutional resources to advance a point of view.
>
> (Smith 1991: 231)

No doubt somewhere there is an analysis of idea propagation that takes the auction as the model. In any case, the economics advanced by the policy institutes is not the same as that endorsed by academic economists, who tend to be more equivocal, qualified and less assertive. But, then again, their ideas are unlikely to be seized upon by politicians and transformed into legislation.

Why productivity?

In recent years the open window of opportunity in education policy has been productivity, a central concept of economic thinking. Economists play influential roles in domestic and foreign policy, raising questions such as 'How does this policy increase productivity?' or 'Can productivity be improved?' Economic productivity – increased production for the same or less cost – is closely tied to the standard of living. Heightened concern for productivity is integral to advanced capitalism. Unless productivity improves, one group's standard of living improves at another's expense. As a political economist noted,

> Yet another characteristic of a market economy is a tendency to incorporate every aspect of society into the nexus of market relations. Through such 'commercialization', the market generally brings all facets of society into the orbit of the price mechanism. Land, labor, and other so-called factors of production become commodities to be exchanged; they are subject to the interplay of market forces . . . Stated more crudely, everything has its price and, as an economist friend is fond of saying, 'Its value is its price.' As a consequence, markets have a profound and destabilizing impact on society because they dissolve traditional structures and social relations.
>
> (Gilpin 1987: 20)

One can add education to the factors of production. Put another way, the deterioration of traditional social institutions – the family, community and church – has led to social disarray, thus increasing the urgency of providing the population with even more material benefits. The legitimacy of the government itself rests on improving the material well-being of its citizens. In fact, governments cannot survive without doing so. As market relations destroy communal and traditional bases of support, the government must rely on material means of securing compliance. This means government becoming more dependent on business enterprises, which produce the wealth in capitalist societies. A British anthropologist put the situation bluntly:

> Industrial society is the only society ever to live by and rely on sustained and perpetual growth, on an expected and continuous improvement. Not surprisingly, it was the first society to invent the concept and idea of progress, of continuous improvement. Its favoured mode of social control is universal Danegeld, buying off social aggression with material enhancement; its greatest weakness is its inability to survive any temporary reduction of the social bribery fund, and to weather the loss of legitimacy which befalls it if the cornucopia becomes temporarily jammed and the flow falters.
>
> (Gellner 1983: 22)

The modern capitalist state and its politicians find themselves caught in the vice of the markets, often portrayed as representing natural law, but in any case apparently the only way to produce wealth for societies that increasingly depend on material prosperity, even as the markets disrupt other aspects of social life.

> [If] we ask what is the immediate central political issue in capitalism – the issue that takes on an often obsessive prominence in every capitalist nation – there is no question where to look. It is the relationship between business and government, or from our more distant perspective, between the economy and the state.
>
> (Heilbroner 1993: 68)

As an empirical matter, government policies are usually (but not always) counter-productive. Frequently, they do not result in better education or improved productivity. A series of educational failures litters the reform path. None the less, misguided policies continue to be advanced and to secure high-level support. Policy should be based on the way educational institutions actually function if there is to be hope of better and more productive schools. Yet there is little sign of this happening, though there are many excellent guides to how to improve practice based on how the schools and teachers actually function (e.g. Elliott 1991; Altrichter *et al.* 1993).

References

Altrichter, H., Posch, P. and Somekh, B. (1993) *Teachers Investigate Their Work: an Introduction to the Methods of Action Research*. London/New York: Routledge.

Apple, M. and Weiss, L. (eds) (1983) *Ideology and Practice in Schooling*. Philadelphia, PA: Temple University Press.
Barberis, P. and May, T. (1993) *Government, Industry and Political Economy*. Buckingham: Open University Press.
Becker, G. S. (1993) *Human Capital*, 3rd edn. Chicago: University of Chicago Press.
Boston, J., Martin, J., Pallot, J. and Walsh, P. (1996) *Public Management: the New Zealand Model*. Oxford: Oxford University Press.
Bowles, S. and Gintis, H. (1976) *Schooling in Capitalist America*. New York: Basic Books.
Boyd, W. L., Crowson, R. L. and van Geel, T. (1994) Rational choice theory and the politics of education: promise and limitations. *Journal of Education Policy*, 9(5/6), 127–45.
Braybooke, D. and Lindblom, C. E. (1970) *A Strategy of Decision*. New York: Free Press.
Carnoy, M. and Levin, H. M. (1985) *Schooling and Work in the Democratic State*. Stanford, CA: Stanford University Press.
Chubb, J. E. and Moe, T. M. (1990) *Politics, Markets, and America's Schools*. Washington, DC: Brookings Institution.
Clark, D. L. and Astuto, T. A. (1990) The disjunction of federal education policy and educational needs in the 1990s. In D. A. Mitchell and M. E. Goertz (eds), *Education Politics for the New Century*. London: Falmer Press, pp. 11–15.
Elliott, J. (1991) *Action Research for Educational Change*. Buckingham: Open University Press.
Elmore, R. F. and McLaughlin, M. W. (1988) *Steady Work: Policy, Practice and the Reform of American Education*. Santa Monica, CA: Rand Corporation.
Gellner, E. (1983) *Nations and Nationalism*. Oxford: Basil Blackwell.
Gilpin, R. (1987) *The Political Economy of International Relations*. Princeton, NJ: Princeton University Press.
Heilbroner, R. (1993) *21st Century Capitalism*. New York: W. W. Norton.
Kelsey, J. (1995) *The New Zealand Experiment*. Auckland: Auckland University Press.
Kingdon, J. W. (1984) *Agendas, Alternatives, and Public Policies*. New York: HarperCollins.
Kozol, J. (1991) *Savage Inequalities*. New York: Crown Publishers.
Krugman, P. (1994) *Peddling Prosperity*. New York: W. W. Norton.
Lasswell, H. (1971) *A Preview of the Policy Sciences*. New York: Elsevier.
Liston, D. (1988) *Capitalist Schools*. New York: Routledge.
McCloskey, D. N. (1990) *If You're so Smart: the Narrative of Economic Expertise*. Chicago: University of Chicago Press.
MacDonald, B. and Walker, R. (1976) *Changing the Curriculum*. London: Open Books.
Pusey, M. (1991) *Economic Rationalism in Canberra*. Cambridge: Cambridge University Press.
Ricci, D. M. (1993) *The Transformation of American Politics: The New Washington and the Rise of the Think Tanks*. New Haven, CT: Yale University Press.
Sarason, S. B. (1990) *The Predictable Failure of Educational Reform*. San Francisco: Jossey-Bass.
Smith, J. A. (1991) *The Idea Brokers: Think Tanks and the Rise of the New Policy Elite*. New York: Free Press.
Wirt, F. M. and Harman, G. (eds) (1986) *Education, Recession, and the World Village*. London: Falmer Press.
Wirt, F. M. and Kirst, M. (1982) *The Politics of Education: Schools in Conflict*. Berkeley, CA: McCutchan.

2

How education became nobody's business

BARRY MACDONALD

The New Right Project (1979–1997)

The fragility of British democracy, in the face of dictatorial intent, was the last thing on my mind when, some twenty years ago, I concluded a critical review of the accountability movement with these words: 'I believe that power over the English school is so effectively distributed that it can only be effectively changed by consent, between legislature and executive, between teacher and pupil, and between school and community' (MacDonald 1979).

That same year Margaret Thatcher led the Conservative Party to the first of four successive victories in the general election, the last one under John Major after she had been persuaded to step down reluctantly from the leadership. Now we live in a different country, made by Thatcher, maintained with increasing difficulty by Major, inherited by Tony Blair's revamped Labour Party. The spell of Messiah Maggie may be a fading memory, but the wreckage remains. Every state school in England is a testament to her inglorious achievement.

The New Right Project, hatched and honed during her years in opposition, was of course not just about or even mainly about schooling. It was about wealth creation, with redistribution relegated to a drip-down assumption. The strategy was twofold: first, to increase the size of the private sector by the privatization of state assets and responsibilities, and to unfetter it from regulatory constraints ('rolling back the state'). Second, to curb welfare state expenditure by a combination of internal marketization, more managerial control, contracting out and performance indicators, all of that to be accompanied by an all-out attack on the 'dependency culture'.

How, one might ask, could she possibly expect to succeed with such a revolutionary enterprise in a stable, developed democracy where power and influence were sufficiently distributed to constitute checks and balances? The answer was simple – the legislative supremacy of Parliament. No body outside Parliament enjoys constitutional protection. She used her dominance of her own party and therefore of Parliament to restore the authority of the state and to draw the teeth from all organized opposition. The Thatcher decade was marked by a seemingly inexorable concentration of civic power in the hands of central executive government, to an extent not previously seen in peacetime. Countervailing and mediating interest groups, such as local government, labour unions and professional associations, the judiciary, the universities, even the civil service and Parliament itself, were seriously weakened by the onslaught of New Right ideology, though we had to wait until 1996 for the Scott Report[1] to reveal the widespread abuse of political and administrative power at the heart of Conservative government. In a remarkably short period of time, substantive democracy was residualized to the franchise, the assumed bulwark against tyranny, but one over which Thatcher managed to exercise almost magical control with her personalized conviction politics ('There is no other way'). No other way meant the reappearance of destitution on the streets and lanes of our urban and rural ghettos. Wealth creation meant that in 1992 Britain overtook the USA in boasting the widest gap between rich and poor of all the developed countries. It began to look as if democracy was just another way of maintaining power and privilege. At the beginning of a new millennium, and in a book aimed at an academic readership, it may be worth asking: was not mass education, now a century old, meant to change all that, and was not social science, of similar age, expected to supply the blueprint?

Before dealing with those issues, and for the benefit of readers who may be unacquainted with the transformation of the school system under the new ideology, I had better outline the main features. Heralded in the Government's election manifesto in 1987, the Education Act of 1988, in the remaining teeth of professional and political opposition, introduced major changes in the management, status and content of the state schools. Finance was devolved to the individual school, rather than the local education authority, with schools having the option, on the basis of a parental vote, of opting out entirely from local control. A National Curriculum, prescribed in detail, and compulsory for all schools, supplanted the longstanding tradition of professional judgement. A system of attainment targets and test-based performance measures was introduced, the results to be published for each school in its locality as an aid to consumer choice in the new, internal market. The highly respected, professional and independent schools inspectorate was decimated, its function of monitoring schools largely taken over by a new, *ad hoc* inspectorate chosen from a centrally approved list and paid daily rates to carry out periodic evaluations of individual school compliance and performance. Thus failing schools would be identified, publicly shamed and threatened with closure, much like a bankrupt business. Needless to say, the Secretary of State for Education assumed unprecedented powers under the Act.

It would be difficult to overstate the extent to which these reforms constituted a repudiation of the values, aspirations and organizations which had hitherto powered the post-war expansion and modernization project. It was the final verdict on the Schools Council,[2] on the progressive movement, on the comprehensive school, on the very notion of curriculum development. Moreover, in holding teachers to account for only the quantifiable elements of their output, the reforms fatally undermined that balance between academic and humanistic development on which their claim to be truly educative institutions rests.

The new National Curriculum, to the horror of the education establishment, which had at least expected a strong vocational element, turned out to be a fundamentalist restoration of the traditional grammar school syllabus. In essence it could have been borrowed from the archives of the Victoria and Albert Museum. For secondary schools it meant the marginalization of personal, social and anything remotely conducive to civic or political education. For primary schools it meant a narrow concentration on basic skills, reinforced by the extension of test-based accountability for delivery.

Such a curriculum, combined with school autonomy in other respects, league tables and consumer choice, was calculated to lead to a rapid stratification of schools by social class, and in the course of the past decade we have seen the process of differentiation evolve to a point where it could be claimed that the former organization of secondary schooling by selection has been restored. In such matters it is always difficult to distinguish between unintended effects and unacknowledged intentions, but outcomes on this scale can hardly be denied.

Some will maintain that nothing has changed, that what Goodson (1988), following Bernstein, calls 'the deep structure of curriculum, differentiation linked to a social base', has merely been made more transparent. This is true as far as it goes. The traditional route to higher education has been maintained for those whose expectations, aspirations and stomach fit them for the climb: for the rest, basic skills plus the rudiments of patriotic history, parochial geography and socially sanitized science. But the 'plus ça change' conclusion is insufficient. What the government did in dismissing the Schools Council for 'mediocre' performance was to dismiss its mission. That was, in general terms, to prepare for the raising of the school leaving age (to 16 in 1972) by making the curriculum and pedagogy, particularly of the secondary school, more engaging and more relevant to the life of the average pupil. That involved a more liberal reinterpretation of subject matter, thematic integration of disciplines around human issues, more enquiry-based learning, more child-centred approaches. It was not the conservatism of individual teachers that frustrated the full realization of these efforts, but the conservatism of their own, and their governing, institutions.

What was dismissed in this transformation of schooling was the problem of pupil motivation. Flugel, writing in the 1930s, offered from a psychoanalytic perspective this distinction. 'The older education, relying on coercion and the doctrine of formal training, and insisting on the performance of unpleasant tasks in order to cultivate the 'will', usually held – implicitly if not explicitly – that it does not matter what a child is taught so long as he hates it. The newer education would rather take the view that only what arouses a child's interest can be satisfactorily and profitably taught' (Flugel 1933). As examples of the latter he pointed not to normal schools, but to re-educative institutions for juvenile offenders, such as Homer Lane's Little Commonwealth, from which those elements of 'hate and sadism' in the scholastic tradition had been expunged.

Embarking in the 1990s on programme implementation, a deprofessionalized and demoralized teaching force faced a formidable problem of pupil resistance to a bread and water diet, and the need for a more coercive regime than most of them aspired to. Drained of all enterprise other than marketing, deprived of support from local education authorities largely reduced to commercializing their remaining services, inundated by detailed directives from government agencies and faced with a laughably undertrained and unpredictable militia of government evaluators, they looked around for help, help they could afford on, for most schools, tight budgets. Continuing professional education, formerly financed by local authorities, was already in steep decline. Even advice from university-based educators and teacher centres was subject to market disciplines. What was readily available, at a price, was the so-called effective schools movement, and the schools improvement service, both academically led, managerially oriented 'solutions' to the problem of achieving government-set targets. Many schools signed up for these offerings, only to find that the wrappings of the curriculum could not for long disguise the poverty of the merchandise. As we reached the end of the decade the problems mounted. They began with a rush of early retirements on the part of teachers and demands by headteachers for greater powers of exclusion over recalcitrant and alienated pupils, and they ended with a crisis of teacher recruitment.

Looking back on this period as a project of the New Right, it is possible to see the demolition as a deliberate piece of social engineering, a prelude to privatization, perhaps along the lines of those city administrations in the United States which had already handed over the running of their school systems to private companies. Perhaps the far right critics of curriculum control underestimated the ingenuity of the executive. Or perhaps not. In the context of government promises that the new regime would raise standards, I recall two politically significant responses to the publication of the results of the first national tests of attainment, by 11-year-olds in English and mathematics. The first was by the then Secretary of State for Education, Gillian Shephard. Given her totalitarian control over all school-related matters, I was puzzled by her rather flustered reaction to the 'shocking' news that half the pupils had turned in below standard performances. Didn't she know? After all, they were her tests, commissioned and custom-built to her requirements. There is no independent standard. The first thing that a competent technologist of attainment tests asks of the customer is, 'What percentage of the testees do you want to fail?' Only on that basis can the technologist proceed with confidence to construct the tests and deliver the required result. Did the test people get it wrong, I asked myself? Was she really flustered, or did she have in mind a more generous cut-off point the following year for a pre-election performance boom? Testing is a dangerously flexible instrument when it falls under direct political control.

I preferred then, and still do, a cock-up rather than a conspiracy explanation, a view reinforced at the time by my second significant response, from David Blunkett, then opposition spokesman on education, now New Labour's Secretary of State for Education and Employment. During a radio phone-in programme following up the bad news about the tests, he hesitated only once. That was when a caller asked, 'Where do we get this standard from, then?' There followed an atypical pause, at the end of which Mr Blunkett muttered something about 'comparison with other countries'.

That might have sounded reasonable, were it not for the fact that for many years the educational economists in the OECD had been tearing their hair out trying, and failing, to establish a valid basis for such international comparisons (see OECD 1992, for a non-progress report). This difficulty, of course, does not inhibit our politicians, who increasingly invoke bogus international comparisons to bolster their arguments about a construct, 'standards', that neither they, nor the public, understand in terms of how it is now applied to the success or failure of schooling. In this context, buying yourself a psychometrist is like buying yourself an accountant. They can do amazing things for you, without breaking any rules.

Broadening the focus to include the whole package, let us consider how the Conservative Government contrived to sell this pup to the public. In the first place, it helped considerably that New Labour, give or take a cavil here and there, bought it, thus confining fundamental opposition to the dispossessed, the so-called 'educational establishment', an imaginary Goliath of which our previous Prime Minister, John Major, boldly declared he was unafraid. Now, apart from anything else, it is the duty of the opposition to oppose, so that the public can make up its mind at least partially on the basis of alternative scenarios. In this case there was a massive dereliction of that duty. As far as education was concerned, the 'breath of fresh air' that Blair promised to bring to government was almost entirely composed of air freshener. Labour in the 1990s continued to believe that education is an issue of quantitative provision.

In the second place, it helped that, from the beginning of the 1970s, the public became increasingly aware of living in an economically failing society. In such circumstances schooling is invariably scapegoated. From that point on, successive governments relentlessly plugged deficit models of the schools, the teachers, the pupils, the workforce. During the Thatcher years a very special contempt was levelled at the 1960s, a contempt so venomous at times that it is not enough simply to point to the fact that Labour was in office for most of the decade. It is tempting to add, following Flugel, that there was a decade in which hate and sadism plumbed unacceptably low levels, and some quite ordinary people danced rather than slept on the pavements. Ah, the sins of the fathers.

These attacks destabilized public opinion and professional confidence, distracted attention from contracting resources and paved the way for the legislation of the 1980s. As the National Curriculum was unveiled, and with it the means of mobilizing economic bias in the conception, delivery and control of schooling, the Government made its sales pitch, directly to the public. The appeal was couched in simple, clear terms – it was an appeal to the public's 'common sense'. So it was 'common sense', in the name of equality of opportunity, to have a National Curriculum. The same for all, what could be fairer than that? And a familiar one, so parents could help kids with the homework. Targets, benchmarks, objective tests to keep kids and teachers up to the mark – common sense. Parental choice of schools, rather than bureaucratic allocation – common sense. As the Government warmed to its theme, more 'common sense' made an appearance – segregation by ability, whole-class teaching, larger classes. Sorry, delete that last one, there's only so much mileage in any slogan. And it didn't do any harm that the media, down to the last editorial, fell sheepishly or mindlessly into line behind the Thatcher crusade.

Now where, I asked myself, had we heard this before? Ah, yes. In 1986 the Reagan administration published a 65-page document (US Department of Education 1986), titled *What Works: Research about Teaching and Learning*, which instantly became an unprecedented bestseller in the field of education. It claimed to summarize a century of scholarship and empirical research in 41 findings of practical significance. It also claimed that these findings could be culled from the thoughts of the great educational thinkers of all time. In the preface to the document the President wrote of the 'renewed trust in common sense' emerging from the summary, which indeed argued that the findings were consistent with what experience and intuition would suggest. The reaction to the publication was instant. It was celebrated in the media and applauded by many leading educational researchers across the land, presumably in the hope that this vindication of the utility of their profession would release in the aftermath a flow of federal funds.

Within a year Gene Glass published a masterly refutation of *What Works*, ridiculing its conservative selectivity, pointing to the many 'overlooked' studies that contradicted the findings, particularly the many researches that had found in favour of open rather than traditional organization of learning, collaborative rather than competitive learning and smaller classes (Glass 1987). He also pointed to the ideological congruence of the document with established Reaganite policies, in particular its maintenance 'that the only needed reform in schooling is a change in the ethos of the school and classroom – a change in the way teachers and parents think about and act towards children – not a change in the level of resources invested in education. Noting successive cuts in the federal research budget for education during the Reagan years (other than for statistics), Glass ended his analysis by quoting Chester

Finn, principal author of *What Works* and Assistant Secretary for Research and Improvement. In an interview some months after the publication, Finn declared that the restoration of the quantitative database for American education was now his highest priority, with 'new research' relegated to fourth place.

By the end of the 1980s, on both sides of the Atlantic, the installation of deeply conservative thinking about the means and ends of schooling was complete, and under political control, centralized in the UK and devolved to state level in the USA. Two nations, divided by a common language, united by common sense. Bad news for educational research, in systems dedicated to the production of a static commodity, bad news for anyone who looked to schooling for a response to a profoundly changing world, or to the real needs of children growing into an unfathomable twenty-first century. Some years later, more recently under new political management, the cracks in the factory walls are showing, but the government prefers to shore them up with sticking plaster rather than engage with any fundamental review. Even Thatcher didn't threaten parents with a £1000 fine for persistent truancy on the part of their children, as Secretary of State Blunkett has recently done. Politicians do not seem to understand that if you propose to incarcerate children for fifteen thousand hours in order to set them free, you must first persuade them of your case. I am reminded of the prison governor who, when asked if the food was good, replied 'It has to be, otherwise the guests wouldn't stay.'

Democracy and education: the plan

It has to be said that this wasn't in the plan. It wasn't in the plan that politicians could still, at this stage of the game, pick and mix from our knowledge store according to taste. What plan? Let me give you a hint by again crossing the Atlantic, to listen to a lament by a prominent American researcher, commenting on the decline of educational research and development as a feature of the policy landscape just a few years after *What Works*.

> Research and Development advocates envisioned an eventual outpouring of new instructional processes and products that would make education less of an art and craft and more of a science. Schools, through the adoption of new scientifically developed techniques, were to be transformed into productive institutions contributing to a powerful national economy and capable of breaking the cycle of poverty.
>
> (Guthrie 1990)

He concludes that, after 25 years, 'the inability of research to contribute a visible scientific basis for instruction has rendered schooling increasingly vulnerable to reform fads.' And, we might add, to political sequestration.

Now you remember the plan. It was hatched in the nineteenth century by the great encyclopaedic minds (Comte, Spencer, Durkheim, Weber) for implementation in the twentieth. It was called a science of society, a science that, as it matured, would assume a corresponding authority over social policy and social action. For Comte, sociology would become the 'queen' of science, while for Spencer all sciences would become as one. Narrowing the frame to late Victorian England (and wishing we had had Weber rather than Spencer for inspiration), we find the cult of science at its height and, amidst the rampant greed of the new capitalists and the squalor of their casualties, hopes of a better world to come, a more just and more rationally ordered society. Mass education was under way, mass democracy around the corner.

How did we get from there to the end of the twentieth century, indeed the end of the millennium, these accomplishments being only remarkable for the fact that we, along with the termites and a few other species, have survived, and that the poor will pay for the fireworks from the National Lottery? Obviously I can't tell the whole story, only one bald summary with specific interests in mind. Looking back, we can see that what social research inherited from the Victorian reformists, in order to carry out the mission of justice through rationality, was a methodological poisoned chalice, what O'Connor (1957) called a 'Chinese box'. Some of us, who do fieldwork in the 'swamp of important human concerns' (Schon 1987), are still struggling to escape, while others, as we have seen, are likely to press on. The poison was, of course, the notion ('imperative' might be more accurate) that sciences of mind and of social organization, based on a model devised for prediction and control, would automatically serve the aims of individual and social emancipation. The view of science as a benevolent, even 'noble', activity, yielding technologies that enhanced the quality of life, was firmly established in the visionary mind. Why not harbour the same hopes by adopting the same methods for a science of life?

For some this entailed a belief that the book of nature, material and human, would ultimately prove to be a single volume, written in mathematics. Physics was the ascendant paradigm, mechanism the buried treasure, mathematics the decoding procedure. The order of the established sciences was the order of their assumed numeracy, a rating scale bequeathed to their social progeny.

So what happened? Briefly, something like this. In the first place, capitalism won just about everything. In the second place, Marx, Freud and Galton had more influence on our thinking than the founding fathers of sociology. In the third place, the book of nature was torn apart by specialization, and became a paper chase, pursued by what Ortega y Gasset referred to as the 'learned ignoramuses' who had replaced the encyclopaedic minds of the previous era (Ortega y Gasset [1930] 1950). In the fourth place, the public image of science changed, as the physical and biological sciences became industrialized, bureaucratized and militarized, caught 'helplessly' in the rising cost of their own technology. The public image started with Rutherford in a Manchester cellar, commending his small group of students for their improvised adaptation of discarded tobacco tins to manufacture the apparatus of experimental physics (Andrade 1965). It moved from there through Oppenheimer and the Manhattan Project to Star Wars, a conspiracy (yes, conspiracy) between government, science and its associated industries to defraud a scientifically illiterate public of $30 billion. At the present time it is estimated that almost half the world's scientific/technological workforce is engaged in the death industry ('defence' if you're squeamish, but most of it is exported). But now a new image has taken precedence, that of the bio-engineer queuing up at the patent office to lodge a blueprint for a new life form. The icons of yesteryear are today's fallen idols, perhaps tomorrow's *condottieri* (see Nowotny 1985). And no one has the slightest idea what to do about it. The scientists (a few of them) call for more education, but we can't do much from an ice floe.

What about the social sciences, rational control and all that? Well, really there's not much to say. Economics has done well in the corridors of power, despite an early warning from Albion Small, founder of the first graduate school of sociology in the world, in Chicago (Small 1907). An admirer of Adam Smith, he noted the increasing divorce of economic reasoning from its roots in moral philosophy, castigated the 'new' economics as a 'grammar without language' and warned that the celibate social science was doomed to sterility. Perhaps the message didn't cross the ocean but (*pace* Tawney, Keynes, Will Hutton in our own day) sterility certainly pays the bills in a society where, as the news magnate Northcliffe predicted at the launch of the twentieth century, 'Everything counts, and nothing matters.'

As for sociology, well, slow to get started and reluctant to get metric is the story, at least in the UK. A visiting American sociologist, as late as the mid-1960s, was so shocked by the lack of mathematical competence in the professors she met, and this, she said indignantly, in the birth place of psychometrics and social survey, that she was moved to propose they attend a summer school in the States, so that they might, as she put it, understand the articles in the leading journals (Selvin 1965). As for the slow start, for the first half of the century sociology was resisted by the conservative universities, as was psychology to a lesser extent. Philosophy and social anthropology were entrenched, and unwilling to roll over. It wasn't until the welfare state got well under way that sociology flourished, and not until the late 1960s and early 1970s that it 'discovered' curriculum as a key to social and economic maintenance (Young 1971). Not much since then. Whitty (1985) sees a need to 'retrieve the radical promise of a sociology of the curriculum' through oppositional politics on a broad front. Let us hope that the ever-expanding market for social survey can keep it in business until then.

Psychology is yet another story, and my last one. Unlike sociology, its utility was immediately grasped, or at least that part of it on which I have already focused. In the context of the development of schooling as a sorting and selection process for a modernizing society characterized by an expanding bureaucracy, the growth of the professions and the proliferation of specialized occupational skills, its success was assured. Central to that success was the quantitative, mathematical character of psycho-statistics, on which the mental testing movement was based. Mental testing, the most widely used social technology of the twentieth century, went on to have a huge influence across the whole of society, not least upon the determination of life chances via the credentialling functions of educational provision. The story of its uses and abuses is well known (see, for instance, Karier 1973). I would just point to its evolution as a technology increasingly detached both from its parent discipline and from its original moorings in educational values. Driven by a combination of its internal logic and the conditions of its marketability to pursue precision rather than span, it has in global terms become, despite or arguably because of its limitations, big business, in both the public and the private sectors. Its values can be hidden, its stochastic processes are inaccessible to all but a few but its products have the appearance of simplicity, transparency and fairness.

So, take away the psycho-statistic machinery, and what have you got left? To educators looking around for some authoritative support from our own and related research, the answer must be 'Not a lot.' Subjective assertion, argument, persuasion based on suggestive evidence. No more. During the 1970s and 1980s we discarded the disciplines and initiated a methodologically patchwork effort to build a new and holistic theory from the study of practice (the 'swamp' referred to above). We could claim that it worked, that it was cumulative and that it served policy needs. But those were the needs of an open, dynamic system and a process of continuous change. Now we face a hostile state and a closed system, whose only acknowledged needs are for management and surveillance. The business of the schools is no longer a business we want to be in.

Even if we did, government funding of educational research has now for many years been conditional upon our disavowing ownership of its products and vowing silence with regard to their contents or how government makes use of them. Invoking Rothchild's principle, never intended by him to be applied to social research, such knowledge has now been commodified and privatized for the discretionary use of the executive and its agents. There has been no fuss about this from our employers, the universities. There is room for us under the shroud of secrecy that already marks the incorporation of the ivory towers in the business of government and industry. The pressure to sell or be damned is something we are all acutely aware of in an increasingly competitive environment. Publish and be damned is its corollary.

The stifling of dissent and the control of new knowledge have been key features of government over the past twenty years. By a combination of gagging clauses in the contracts of social service employees and veto powers over the publication of research findings, dissent has been largely muted. Surely, you may ask, the new Government will change all that? Let us see.

The Blair inheritance and the Blair vision

In 1997, with the Conservative Government of John Major having committed political suicide by prioritizing its internal wranglings about Europe over growing public concern about the future of the Health Service, Tony Blair's New Labour Party romped home in the May general election. What was 'new' in the party was more identifiable by what was absent from its manifesto than by what was present – mainly the ditching of socialist doctrine in favour of a more 'inclusive' (unspecified) view of society. Most of us didn't know what kind of government we had voted for, but were certain about what kind of government we had voted out. It was said that a gorilla could have won the election. Perhaps one did. We still don't know.

Arguments continue about whether Blair is a reconstructed socialist, a one nation Tory, a nineteenth-century liberal or just a man for all seasons. What we do know is that Mr Blair is not only the most powerful person in the country but, in the eyes of many commentators, the most powerful prime minister in democratic history, the envy of the political world. What he inherited was a democratic wasteland, a residual democracy from which all opposition had been expunged. There was still the vote of course, and that had to be managed. It is an idiosyncrasy of our electoral system that, as in this case, a quite narrow victory can deliver an overwhelming majority. At the same time, those who had long awaited a victory for the Left in order to right the wrongs perpetrated by their predecessors were well aware of that fragility and in no mood to provide succour to the defeated enemy.

Blair promised constitutional change, but so far has shown no constitutional vision. Changes yes, lots of them – devolution in Scotland, something less in Wales, something fragile in Northern Ireland, elected mayors in the cities, removing the voting rights of hereditary peers in the House of Lords, incorporation of the European Convention on Human Rights, a Freedom of Information Act (already under heavy dilution), a whistleblowers' protection Act – lots of bits and pieces, but bits and pieces of what? There is no overview relating these changes to one another, no way of knowing whether this rather cautious, minimalist approach will sooner or later eventuate in some kind of constitutionally protected balance of powers and responsibilities.

In education, and very specifically with respect to schooling, Mr Blair had made known his views well before the election by publically endorsing in virtually every detail the Thatcher reforms, leaving us with constitutional reform as the main hope for educational leverage. At the time, some of us found it hard to believe that such an apparently intelligent and compassionate man could find no fault with the system, but only had some enhancements and minor corrections to offer. Since he appeared to be well informed, why was there no outrage at the way, for instance, special needs children had been discharged like sewage into a school market in which they had negative value, why could he not see that we might value some outcomes of schooling more than those we can measure, or that a curriculum originally designed for gentlemen in the nineteenth century might need to be rethought for mass education in the twenty-first, or that such a curriculum was destined to even more effectively reproduce the economic order?

These questions remain unanswered. The public school, albeit with additional resources for building repairs, smaller infant classes and more books, is still locked into an accountability model that prioritizes quantifiable pupil attainment and yields a rank order of schools that, in denying complexity, denies justice. This is a crude piece of malevolent social engineering on the part of a right-wing government. Why on earth would a Labour government, however 'New', subscribe to such a model? Why did Tony Blair go out of his way to commit his party to its continuity before the general election?

There is no single answer to that, but there are several. In the first place, as I wrote above, the National Curriculum and its machinery of compliance had massive public and media support, and the new Government is a populist government. Minimally, this could be phrased as 'Let sleeping dogs lie.' The Government had enough on its legislative programme, and the nation's teachers were sick and tired of change *per se*. In the second place, the 'skills before frills' emphasis in the core curriculum, given official figures for functional illiteracy as one in every six adults, had widespread appeal to the egalitarian spirit of party members, and offered grounds, as it had done in the USA, for more close control and direction of schools to secure at least minimal levels of basic accomplishment for all pupils. Whether schools, now devoted to the production of examinees, will deliver that social good, and if so at what price, must remain in some doubt for some time, though what evidence we have, from both universities and schools, already suggests that Campbell's Law (Campbell 1977) is in no danger of refutation. That law states: 'The more any quantitative social indicator is used for social decision making, the more subject it will be to corruption pressures and the more apt it will be to distort and corrupt the social processes it is intended to monitor.'

Let me move to a third reason, one that places the school in the broader context of the management of public expenditure. In this context the school, historically accustomed to the role of scapegoat in times of discontent, may be seen as the prototype of a more generalized and inclusive approach to resource accountability (setting on one side the give-away anomaly that school inspectors are not allowed to consider school resources when assessing their performance). This is not limited to replications of the school accountability scheme across the social services, although we are promised league tables of hospitals, police forces, local authorities and other claimants on the public purse. It will not for long be a case of Whitehall commanding compliance while itself claiming exemption. What was not declared in the baggage of the incoming government was a plan to make its own spending departments subject to output and performance assessments with regard to economy, efficiency and effectiveness; and, what's more, to publish these assessments. Although efforts such as these to bring public sector expenditure under rational control have a long and undistinguished history (see Heclo and Wildavsky 1974), this one goes further than any predecessor in requiring results-based evaluation and offering process transparency to Parliament and public alike. To call this 'revolutionary' is no overstatement. It blows away the traditional structure of central administration as a federation of departments, each minding its own business and boundaries as it competes with others for Treasury favour. The notorious secrecy of British government owes much to this structure, as does the longstanding difficulty of constructing a Cabinet overview of the executive machine.

Good news or bad news? Well, that depends. Good in principle, but in practice? On the face of it none would argue with the promotion of effective, democratic and accountable government, but it was that very rationale that underpinned the extinction of liberal education from our schools, alienating teachers and pupils alike. What can we expect when government policies and programmes are accompanied by performance targets and evaluation of results and costs? Will we see league tables of departments, will the Prime Minister be called upon to name and shame underperforming ministers, just as the Secretary of State for Education urges local authorities to do with underperforming schools? Will departmental missions be contracted out to the predatory private companies now buzzing with anticipation of school and local education authority take-overs? This last possibility, though logically consistent with Whitehall's adoption of private sector accounting procedures and market disciplines, would be difficult to reconcile with democratic intent, or even accountability, since the National Audit Office is legally barred from monitoring the private sector. In any case, the history of performance contracting is littered with examples of Campbell's Law. We shall see.

The adoption of RAB (resource accounting and budgeting) may constitute in the UK a radical departure from command-administrative techniques, but it is in line with international trends, particularly those monitored and promoted by OECD's Public Management Service (PUMA), which is particularly keen on programme evaluation. So is the European Commission, which recently announced a policy of no appropriation without independent evaluation. Should we take the Commission's example as an augur of what is to come, we could be forgiven some cynicism. In practice what that policy means is that programme operational managers are given funds to employ independent evaluators, but are not required to pay them until they consider the evaluation report to be acceptable. Some independence. The Commission is (surprise, surprise) opposed to any outside scrutiny of its own performance.

Here, there can be little doubt that the Treasury means business. Value for money is no mere mantra. Expenditure must be justified, *ante* and *post*. Little doubt either that the initial response of departments will be cautious. The distinction between performance indicators and performance terminators has so far been noticeable by its absence in those sectors where they are now established. The result has been defensive teaching, defensive policing and, increasingly, defensive health care. No-trust comes with a high price tag. We can expect departments not to set their aims too high, and perhaps to avoid, or at least postpone, dealing with problems they know they can't solve, or areas of intervention where evidence of attainment is not susceptible to statistical formulation. We can also expect them, for reasons of cost and risk, to keep the evaluation function in-house, a function delegated to their own economists. This accountability model virtually demands econometric evaluation, which is only comfortable with discrete programmes yielding quantifiable results. But here is the rub. Part of the reasoning behind the reforms, the need for a Cabinet overview, is the government's commitment to what it calls 'joined-up policy making', policies which cross departmental boundaries in an effort to mount a holistic attack on persistent social problems such as typically disadvantaged communities in the inner city. How will econometric evaluation cope with the complexity inherent in such initiatives? Let me return to the USA for a compelling cautionary tale.

Evaluations of evaluations are rare, but one of the few is Bob Stake's meta-evaluation of the Cities-in-Schools programme (CIS), a collection of urban youthwork projects which had grown up in the 1970s under generous and varied sponsorship, including federal support. It was also personally endorsed by President Carter, which gave it political clout. It was evaluated by an independent, eminent research group, led by Charles Murray, between 1977 and 1981, with federal funding from the National Institute of Education. We should note that by the time the final report of Murray was delivered, Carter had given way to Reagan.

The goal of CIS was to identify disaffected youngsters from the urban ghetto and bring them back into the mainstream. To achieve this, in the three large cities chosen to represent the programme, the various social agencies were integrated by a process of outstationing some of their members to work intensively and personally with estranged youngsters. As Stake was pointedly to observe, it was more of a movement than a programme, with an evolving, organic character typical of such social initiatives.

Murray's approach was cost–benefit: how big a band did the government get for its buck? His conclusion was that CIS had failed. He went further, saying that all such programmes were futile and doomed to failure. Despite vociferous outrage expressed by local stakeholders, he held to this view and extended it in a widely read book, *Losing Ground*, published in 1984, arguing for the dismantlement of federal social programmes. There can be little doubt that Murray's evaluation of an expensive, high-profile programme made a significant contribution to Reagan's war on welfare in the 1980s. The National CIS Office was closed, the National Director of Urban Initiatives retired and was not replaced, the National Institute of Education was threatened with termination, and only survived in reduced and precarious form. Stake was invited by the National Institute of Education, somewhat bravely in the circumstances, to revisit the scene and offer a commentary. His case study of the evaluation, published in 1986, was called *Quieting Reform*, which encapsulates his major generalization – that evaluations of the Murray kind, which seek to quantify social benefit in elusive and complex areas of social action, have the effect of undermining such action.

Had Murray's evaluation been abnormal in approach, such a generalization could be seen as unsafe, but no, it was and remains typical of the dominant form of such evaluations in the USA. Stake writes:

> The program people agreed to demonstrate their effectiveness nationally, in fact asked for the opportunity to do so. But many of them did not understand that effectiveness is an econometric term. They did not understand what constitutes a demonstration. But they wanted the money for growth so they accepted the language of the evaluators, even finding it amusing and not without meaning. But they did not realize how compelling would be the science-technology metaphors of effectiveness, productivity and impact – pre-empting their own practitioner metaphors and valuings. They thought their stories – of services rendered, clients engaged, hurts mended, would count as evidence of accomplishment. They didn't – in the end the program was failed because it couldn't produce student gain scores.

As our new management machine swings into action, we have to hope that our governors will take from its experience a different message, that the achievement of social goals calls for a more responsive, more interactive, more encompassing and more developmentally oriented approach to evaluation than either our psychometrists or our econometrists can provide. The cost may well be uncertainty, but the cost of precision is infinitely higher.

I was going to conclude this review on an optimistic, if ironic, note, one that takes me back to the problem of school evaluation. It concerns the fate of one of the world's most famous schools: Summerhill, A. S. Neill's enduring beacon of the century's progressive movement. It is of course a private school and therefore exempt from the National Curriculum, but still subject to government inspection and approval. Recently, following such an inspection and after many years of threats to close it down, the headmistress received a letter from the Department of Education assuring her of its survival. Part of the letter reads: 'Attainment and progress ought not necessarily to be considered purely from the value-added but should also encompass the values-added and the extent to which the school was impacting on pupils' personal, social, moral, spiritual and cultural development.' A department spokesman subsequently commented, 'We are working towards a way to assess levels of progress in a school that has a different philosophy.' Most parents are unfortunately under the illusion that these added values are part and parcel of the institutionalized care of their children.

This (individual?) deviance from orthodoxy on the part of the department did not go unnoticed. Following another inspection of Summerhill in March 1999, the Secretary of State announced his intention to order the closure of the school within six months unless it changes its ways. The end of Summerhill, the end of the century. From here on it's all uphill for those who will not accept that the value of children's education can be measured, costed and stamped on their foreheads like the price tags in a supermarket.

Should we fail at all levels to resurrect pluralism, we may have to concede irrecoverable ground to those, and they are always with us, who believe that Aristotle got it right about slavery, and Plato about democracy.

Notes

This chapter is a substantially revised, enlarged and updated version of an article originally published, under the same title, in the *Cambridge Journal of Education*, volume 26, number 2, 1996. Permission to draw upon the original matter is gratefully acknowledged.

1 *Inquiry into the Export of Defense Equipment and Dual-use Goods to Iraq and Related Prosecutions*, Sir Richard Scott, London, HMSO 1996.

2 The Schools Council for Curriculum and Examinations was a tripartite agency (national and local governments, with teacher union representation as *primus inter pares*) set up in 1964 to animate and oversee the modernization of schools. It was closed down in 1982, despite a favourable verdict by a government-chosen evaluator.

References

Andrade, C. da (1965) *Rutherford and the Nature of the Atom*. London: Heinemann.

Campbell, D. T. (1977) Keeping the data honest in the experimenting society. In H. W. Melton and D. J. H. Watson (eds) *Interdisciplinary Dimensions of Accounting for Social Goals and Social Organizations*. Columbus, OH: Grid Inc.

Flugel, J. C. (1933) *A Hundred Years of Psychology*. London: Duckworth.

Glass, G. (1987) What works: politics and research. *Educational Researcher*, April, 5–10.

Goodson, I. (1988) *School Subjects and Curriculum Change*. Brighton: Falmer Press.

Guthrie, J. W. (1990) Education R & D's lament, and what to do about it. *Educational Researcher*, March, 26–34.

Heclo, H. and Wildavsky, A. (1974) *The Private Government of Public Money*. London: Macmillan.

Karier, C. (1973) *Roots of Crisis: American Education in the Twentieth Century*. Chicago: Rand McNally.

MacDonald, B. (1979) Hard times: educational accountability in England. *Educational Analysis*, 1(1), 23–44.

Murray, C. (1984) *Losing Ground: American Social Policy, 1950–1980*. New York: Basic Books.

Nowotny, H. (1985) Does it only need good men to do good science? In M. Gibbons and B. Wittrock (eds) *Science as a Commodity: Threats to the Open Community of Scholars*. Harlow: Longman.

O'Connor, D. J. (1957) *The Philosophy of Education*. London: Routledge and Kegan Paul.

OECD (1992) *The OECD International Education Indicators, a Framework for Analysis*. Paris: OECD.

Ortega y Gasset, J. ([1930]1950) *The Revolt of the Masses*. New York: Signet Books.

Schon, D. E. (1987) *Educating the Reflective Practitioner*. London: Jossey-Bass.

Scott, Sir Richard (1996) *Inquiry into the Export of Defence Equipment and Dual-use Goods to Iraq and Related Prosecutions*. London: HMSO.

Selvin, H. (1965) Training for social research, the recent American experience. In *Penguin Survey of the Social Sciences 1965*. Harmondsworth: Penguin.

Small, A. W. (1907) *Adam Smith and Modern Sociology*. Chicago: University of Chicago Press.

Stake, R. F. (1986) *Quieting Reform – Social Science and Social Action in an Urban Youth Program*. Urbana: University of Illinois Press.

US Department of Education (1986) *What Works: Research about Teaching and Learning*. Washington, DC: US Department of Education.
Whitty, G. (1985) *Sociology and School Knowledge*. London: Methuen.
Young, M. F. D. (ed.) (1971) *Knowledge and Control*. London: Collier-Macmillan.

3

Developing under developing circumstances: the personal and social development of students and the process of schooling

JOHN SCHOSTAK

The key educational issue is how to get people to go off the rails. If a formal curriculum is imagined as being like a chariot race where competitors go round and round in circles until some arbitrary finishing point is reached, then deliberate crashes, derailings or simply stopping and not playing the game become the only real challenges to the system. In this chapter I explore a paradoxical view of education which is founded upon not playing the game; or, at least, playing it by rules other than those officially sanctioned and hence derailing the players.

Regarding schools, colleges and universities as construction sites is a precondition for doing this. They look finished, solid, as if we all know what they are for and what goes on there. However, schools are merely specific material sites where many different kinds of things occur. There has long been a distinction between overt, official forms of curricula and the hidden curricula (e.g. Jackson 1968) where children are divided into pro-school and anti-school factions (Hargreaves 1967; Lacey 1971), where working-class children learn to fulfil the expectations of teachers as to whether they are clever or not (Rosenthal and Jacobsen 1968), or learn to adopt working-class expectations and attitudes and careers (Willis 1977), learn how to resist authorities ritually (Hall and Jefferson 1975) and act within schools maladjusted to their needs and interests (Schostak 1983); where they generate a violent imagination appropriate to surviving in and accommodating to society's demands (Schostak 1986) and to learning the social narratives required to be an active – whether compliant or creative – member of a social group (Schostak 1991).

Somewhere within this complex of competing processes and orientations there grew in the 1960s a multiplicity of demands for creative, liberatory, revolutionary forms of educational action in schools, colleges, universities, media and workplaces. There was a sense of the need for new ideas and cultural forms for new times and new challenges. The question was: how might one facilitate the development of individuals to meet a radically new world of cultural and technological achievements? There were many different kinds of response: there was Bruner's 'Man: a course of studies', and Carl Roger's (1969, 1983) facilitative approaches, alongside Freire's (1970) more obviously politically cultural action for adult literacy and Illich's (1971) vision of a deschooled society. There was the investigative journalism of a John Pilger covering Vietnam and the powerful documentary style dramas like *Cathy Come Home*, or the radical folk music of Bob Dylan. Schools were not the only sites that called for educational action. The vision encompassed the whole of society. To say that vested interests were worried is an understatement. The history of the 1980s and 1990s was a reaction to the 1960s and 1970s, with both the USA and the UK retrenching into a neo-conservativism calling for a move 'back to basics', a focus on 'family values' and a denigration of so-called 'trendy' or 'progressive' forms of education and politics (Schostak 1993). Even with the landslide victory of a Labour government in the UK in 1997, there is still a timid obeisance towards conservative ideals in a wide range of political, economic, health, welfare and particularly educational policies. It was not schooling that was under attack but education, and it remains under attack. Schools were, and still are, to be cleansed of educational action. Where education challenges the prevailing order, schooling reinforces it. How, then, were individuals to be schooled to meet the needs of a society rapidly changing under the impact of a revolution in information technologies?

It is no accident that the school efficiency 'movement' came to dominate political discourses of schooling in the 1990s, since the political definition of mainstream schooling is all about the engineering of children as raw materials to fit the needs of economic and administrative powers. Its language is one of benchmarking, standards, standardization, comparisons with competitors and engineering children in ways similar to those for the engineering of aircraft, in the words of David Reynolds, to prevent crashes:

> The High Reliability Schools Project is an attempt to move beyond the goal of relatively successful schools towards the creation of schools which are absolutely successful and which have eradicated failure. Using the latest information from the study of highly reliable organisations such as air traffic controllers and nuclear power plants and from school effectiveness and school improvement programmes, an innovatory programme has been designed that aims to ensure high quality educational outcomes for all, in schools which set ambitious targets and which relentlessly push for success.[1]

It is most certainly not about education. It is about strategies to engineer highly reliable forms of schooling which stand in angry opposition to what it sees as the *laissez-faire* learning through play attitudes of 'progressive education'. But it is not a defence of progressive education that I want to pursue here. I have elsewhere discussed much of what counts as progressive education in terms of its conservative orientations; that is, in terms of its nature as schooling rather than as education. In order to make a decisive turn away from the various forms of schooling – whether traditional or progressive or some other technicist version – I want to focus upon a key theme: that seems to me to run subversively through Barry MacDonald's research career: the potential for personal and social development or change through the adoption of a radical democratic methodology of applied research. I want to discuss this in terms of the distinction I have begun to develop between schooling and education.

Schooling subjectivity

Schooling is the general name I give to the processing of children and adults for social purposes. Since there is not a single social purpose agreed by all, school is a place of contested, multiple schoolings that lie in angry opposition or perhaps in ironic play with each other. Policy makers in the UK are currently attempting to engineer politically a dominant definition of schooling that will act as a 'standard'. This is being engineered through the mechanisms of a national curriculum, national testing and inspections. In general, it can be said that a considerable amount of resource appears to go into trying to school people of all ages to follow certain pathways, which are variously called 'courses' or 'curricula', and thus counteract those paths considered subversive, deviant or simply frivolous. It results in what I call the paranoid curriculum, which will be described more fully below.

Laing (1967), perhaps not too facetiously, wrote that we were better at driving children mad than we were at educating them. The important point here is to think clearly about how the subjective experiences of others are manipulated within the formal and informal processes of an institution. In its broadest sense, I regard a curriculum as a process through which cultural subjectivities emerge. By this I mean that any society needs to organize the subjective states of a given individual in relation to other individuals. What it means to say that such subjective states are 'mad', 'bad' or 'educated' I leave open at this point. To develop further the idea of schooling subjectivities, a point of comparison may be made with Kant's purpose in the *Critique of Pure Reason*.

Here Kant remarked that his own 'Copernican revolution' was to identify the limits of reason, showing that the thing-in-itself cannot as such be experienced directly and known, but can only be known in ways which are mediated by the senses and by the *a priori* ways in which the mind itself works to organize experience and thinking. What is being dealt with is always that which appears to consciousness rather than the thing itself (Kant [1781]1966:

36). All that we have of the world about is through subjectivity; that is, how things appear to our minds when mediated through the senses and acted upon by our minds. How subjectivity gets to be organized is absolutely critical to how our world is constructed as being 'real'. The organization of subjectivity is in the form of 'courses'; that is, a sense of being directed towards objects in the world for particular purposes.

This is how schooling is ultimately and intimately linked to the exercise of power. Real power resides in how 'reality' itself gets to be manufactured in the minds of subjects, and hence how subjectivity itself is organized for a variety of cultural and personal purposes. Schooling, with its mechanisms of control over what counts as knowledge in terms of what is worth knowing and worth doing for which 'subjects', is at the heart of a curriculum through which political power is itself constructed and exercised; that is, it is the way in which the course of power is shaped in the lives of people. Elsewhere I have defined curricula as involving courses of reflection on experience, expression and action. Such a process is fundamental to building up a sense of a world and a biographical identity with others. How this process is managed in terms of the degree of critical reflection that can take place to generate the possibilities for independent and creative action is crucial to any notion of freedom of thought and expression, as well as the development of a political framework conducive to the expression of freedoms. How does one know about the world except by the ways in which subjectivity itself is organized through the courses of reflection, expression and action set in motion by one's family, community and politically ordered institutions of society? Anderson (1983) described how the press constructed for the nineteenth-century British a sense of empire and through that a sense of belonging to a community which was essentially imaginary. The distant reaches of the Empire were experienced by most only, at best, second hand through textually mediated accounts. Reflection on experience was then only experienced as already processed through journalistic accounts. Similarly, contemporary schooling largely proceeds by reflection upon highly processed secondary, tertiary, *n*-iary sources of 'experience' as formulated by textbooks and routinized 'experiments' for the purposes of 'passing' a 'course'. In this sense, school curricula are the means by which children are inducted into imaginary communities and their 'knowledges' and other 'cultural riches', which then constitute their 'world'. In the light of these musings, what can 'effectiveness' mean?

Developing this line of thought, one of the pioneers of school effectiveness has to be Schreber. He is perhaps not a name to spring immediately to mind – if at all – since it is his son Judge Schreber who is better known, and then largely in psychoanalytic circles for having written a book on his own mental illness, which in turn became the famous subject of analysis by Freud and others. Judge Schreber's father, however, was a German educationist of international fame during the nineteenth century. Without going into too much detail, he advocated the use of harnesses to ensure the body remained in a desired posture, exercise to control eye and head movements, and feeding babies according to a strict regimen. These methods drove one son mad and another to suicide, and his daughters were regarded as somewhat odd (Schatzman 1973). This is not to say that contemporary forms of school effectiveness are of such an obvious extreme, merely that the methods have a certain affinity with the aim of producing children who fit a standardized ideal. Schreber serves as a caricature and, like most caricatures, focuses attention upon what is most absurd in ordinary, accepted behaviour. Unlike caricatures, however, the educational tracts of Schreber were taken very seriously by educators of the time. The general features of his method are described in the next section.

As a preparatory step to critiquing the method and seeing the pertinence to contemporary strategies for facilitating the personal and social development of individuals, rather than focusing upon the cruder tools for moulding and fashioning the body and the mind, the attention may be turned to language as a tool. Here language underpins or is the infrastructure for the organization of subjectivity and for orienting the 'subject' to a world which becomes its object both as a fantasy for the fulfilment of desire and as a 'real', or 'objective', world which is claimed to be independent of the whims and fantasies of the subject.

Many contemporary studies have shown how people are socially positioned by the images routinely deployed by both professional and wider cultural discourses (e.g. Davies and Harré 1990; Schostak 1993). Language may be thought of as a way not only of cutting up reality but also of coming to recognize one's self as an object of the language acts of others and as a subject and agent in the world. By simply being called 'boy' or 'girl' one is positioned into a given category that has associated with it a range of other categories. Crudely, the gender associations have typically traditionally been dichotomized in a manner like the following:

Boy	*Girl*
Hard	Soft
Strong	Weak
Dominant	Submissive
Aggressive	Docile
Active	Passive
Abstract	Feeling
Rational	Irrational

Pushing an individual into one category rather than another can be seen as either 'natural' and the fulfilment of a biological and social destiny, or reductive, repressive and suffocating. The engineering of masculinity and femininity has been the subject of furious debate for much of the twentieth century. Rather than rehearse this debate, I want to indicate that a category or the naming of some difference has two effects central to my argument: (a) framing an identity which is then imposed upon an individual; (b) excluding aspects of the experience of the individual from the named category as being 'superfluous' or 'wrong' or 'waste'. For example, in the above crude categorization of 'boy' the individual's experience of say 'softness' or 'weakness' would have to be excluded if the individual were to recognize his self as 'male' with respect to the list. The experienced 'softness' or 'weakness' can be regarded as a waste product in the process of engineering a child, or, say, a soldier, to present himself as a pure representation of the 'real man', or 'macho' individual. This can be done for a whole range of other categories where, in order to 'fit in', experiences, behaviours, thoughts, expressions or actions have to be 'purified'. In this process of 'purifying' – that is becoming a good representative of a given category – a waste product then emerges and has to be dealt with in some way as a rejected aspect of experience which can find no acceptable place within the subjectivity of the individual. Unfortunately, what is 'left out' does not simply go away, but returns as a politics of the 'left out', the residual. Perhaps the major lesson of contemporary discussions in the associated fields of psychoanalysis, feminism and cultural studies is that the process of engineering individuals always leads to a politics of resistance which draws its energies precisely from what has not been admitted into the standardizing categories of 'excellence' and 'acceptability'. Through the adoption or rejection of such processes of categorization, the image that one has of one's self, one's powers of agency and the objects of one's public/private world is systematically constructed either in conformity to a given process of schooling or as a resistance to it. Even the resistance itself generates a counter set of discourses of courses to be followed, a forbidden discourse (Schostak 1993) which underpins, or provides a subterranean course for, alternative visions (or perhaps nightmares) of the 'real' that cling or hover around the official or acceptable visions acting as a dark escape or as a fearful abyss for the individual. Looking into the abyss constructed from the residual, the waste products of schooling, the paranoid curriculum emerges as a safety rail to guide the personal and social development of individuals through the uncertainties created by developing circumstances.

The paranoid curriculum

We are born into worlds, the shape of which, the scenery of which, the elements of which must be formed into relationships, perspectives, ways of seeing. This is accomplished through the process of learning a language/culture. Language in its broadest sense in this case refers to that repository of codes, lexicons, discourse repertoires and signifiers through which all attempts at representing a world for a self and a self for a world must pass. The mirror has long been used as a metaphor of this process of 'reflecting/re-presenting a world, a self'. Mead and Cooley in the 1930s both talked of the self being formed through the ways the other responds to the self, thus re-presenting the self through the agency of the other. Cooley talked in particular of the looking glass self. Lacan (1977) wrote of the mirror stage of child development. At around 7–18 months old, the visual acuity of the child develops faster than the ability to coordinate the limbs of the body. Looking into a mirror (generalized as the Other-as-mirror) somehow fixes and gives shape to the body, which is at odds with the sense of inner incoherence or clumsiness from not being able to control the bodily movements and sensations. Similarly, as the child develops, language and culture provide a means of 'fixing' or giving shape to all the unknowns, the uncertainties, the flux of life. Cultural products provide mirrors, selves are fixed by the self's own gaze into the mirror/cultural matrix. This matrix provides a means of establishing a sense of identity, position with regard to others, ways of behaving with others and what constitutes the ground rules of the world. In this sense the Other-as-mirror becomes easily conflated with the Other-as-truth (seeing is believing) or the Other-as-authority (whoever controls the system of mirroring both authors and authorizes the 'truth' about the world – hence the power of the news and entertainments media), which in turn generates the Other as the legitimating source of all reason. This conflation results in what I call the paranoid curriculum. The paranoid curriculum is essentially about control for the purposes of 'rational' purification; that is, the construction of an order in the name of which individuals submit to reason and reject all that is inessential to reason. Reason is defined, like God, as a final court of judgement, and reason itself is whatever is defined as such by the voice of reason. Reason here is whatever is ordered by the Dominant Other.

In the paranoid curriculum, derived from a reading of Schreber's experiences (Schreber 1955, 1988; Schatzman 1973), the gaze is organized[2] to produce a particular kind of curriculum, a particular kind of learning relationship, between a dominant individual/group (Pd)[3] defined as possessing the voice of reason and an Other, a subordinate or inferior individual or group (Os) who must be inducted into the ways of reason. Pd has a conceptual framework which defines Os along the dimensions of:

1 Identity.
2 Conduct.
3 Potential for becoming/growth.
4 Use and value.
5 Social position and function.

Simultaneously, Pd's framework defines how Pd should behave towards Os to realize particular goals and intentions. This framework is applied in terms of a specific regimen, and is in turn defined as rational by Pd. Pd applies this regimen (R) to Os. The principles and procedures which define R are directed towards a systematic control of:

1 Os's beliefs about Pd's intentions and knowledge.
2 Os's conduct and behaviour.
3 Os's presentation of Self in terms of such dimensions as posture, speech, dress.

4 Os's interpretations of bodily experiences, awareness of bodily experiences and formation of body image.
5 Os's beliefs concerning the extent to which Pd knows/sees into Os.
6 Os's knowledge of Self and World.
7 Os's experience of Self and formation of self identity (where identity is a function of the Other).

In addition, records and reports about Os are made and continually reported; this was what Judge Schreber referred to as the 'writing down system' (Schreber 1955: 188). Some are (a) behind the scenes, and some are (b) as a continual reminder to Os. In each case, Os knows someone – or something – is always watching and recording. The contemporary obsessions with auditing, national attainment testing, cross-cultural comparisons of performance, benchmarking, personality profiling and behavioural regimens to control classroom behaviour (e.g. Rogers 1990) are symptoms of the demand by the paranoid curriculum for a totalizing 'writing down system' through which the lives and activities of individuals are turned into 'records of achievement', 'case records', government computer files and market research profiles.

Fortunately, not all fathers and institutions are as systematic as was Judge Schreber's father. For the Judge and his brothers and sisters it would seem that the only real option was to go mad to varying degrees or to commit suicide. Most people experience a respite from the insanity of such schooling, where home values and support networks may be far more human and creative. Indeed, schools themselves may often mitigate the worst aspects of a paranoid curriculum. However, there is a sufficient history of school studies to indicate the power and pervasiveness of a paranoid curriculum (e.g. Holt 1969; Willis 1977; Schostak 1983) in producing unhappiness, a sense of failure and a sense of aggressive rebellion (Schostak 1986) for us to look sadly and anxiously at contemporary reproductions of its worst aspects in the lives of both children and their teachers (Jeffrey and Woods 1996). The paranoid curriculum can thus be read in many different ways. It may refer to the daily regime where children are placed under the watchful eyes of the teacher. It may refer to teachers under the watchful eyes of Ofsted or some other surveillance agencies of a government's choice. Or, more generally still, it may be read as referring to the ways in which business organizations deal with their employees. In any of these cases, where Os is not privy to Pd's framework, or to Pd's goals and values, Os's options are:

1 Have complete Faith in Pd (a fundamentalist religious or cult solution).
2 Adopt an attitude which leads to the continual search for signs upon which to found interpretations of Pd's behaviour in order to inform Os's own reactions to Pd's actions and presumed intentions (a kind of hermeneutic solution).
3 Choose to take recourse to counter discourses (the radical/revolutionary/subversive solution) which (a) have no access to Pd discourses, (b) have

covert access to Pd discourses or (c) derive from the 'revelations' of those who have been but are no longer Pds.

4 Choose complete or limited submission (the 'I won't do it unless I can get away with it' solution).
5 Choose 'a quiet life' of apparent submission (the 'mask', 'disguise', 'camouflage' solution resulting more in apathy than in real social change).
6 Choose hidden rejection (the 'underground movement' solution).
7 Choose open rejection (the open 'guerrilla', 'civil war' solution).

Because Pd anticipates Os's alternatives to complete Faith and complete submission, Pd's possible strategies for the application of R are:

1 Adopt a discourse of love, care and a benign vocabulary which categorizes all Pd acts as being 'in your best interests'; such a discourse screens or veils and is very common in the 'caring professions'.
2 Use force, threats, terror.
3 Use privation (by denying access to opportunities and rewards) in conjunction with (1) and a discourse of opportunity, and merit (a common ploy in market economies controlled by powerful vested interests unwilling to give up the conditions under which the continual accumulation of wealth is inevitable for them).
4 Generate a discourse of self-blame for all failure, and self-praise for all success, as a covering discourse. This has the effect of creating a sub-discourse enjoyed by the 'winners' in the system, who achieve a sense of self-responsibility and autonomy, together with a sense of well earned wealth. The failures have, of course, only themselves (and perhaps luck) to blame. Hence the system is immune from any attack.

The most subtle of strategies would use all of the above within a discourse structure that disguises or diverts attention from the real source of any threats and privations, and which permeates all discourse with 'love', 'care' and a vocabulary of 'in your best interests'. Its overall effect is the corruption of judgement in the interests of maintaining the structures of domination by the few over the many. As a process of the corruption of judgement, it is a certain kind of framework to bring about a required personal and social development. However, it is one which has the ultimate purpose of 'purifying' and 'freezing' the individual to be a 'fitting' member of a given socially desired category. The outcome is 'subject/ion' rather than a creative free flowing subject-as-agent. What is the alternative course?

Personal and social development: changing courses

Paul Virilio (1996: 15) has coined a useful term which facilitates the discussion to be raised in this section. It is 'dromocratic', from the Greek *dromos*, which means 'course'. Society is organized according to courses, paths to be travelled to attain goals at ever greater speeds. The notion of speed is useful to add to the discussion so far, because pushed to its limits it cracks open the rhetorics of the carefully ordered societies of the global enterprise. For him, 'power is always the power of controlling a territory by messengers, the means of transport and of transmission.'[4] Think now of school as a mechanism of transforming teachers into messengers, with lessons as a means of transmission. As the electronic means for the processing and transportation of messages ever faster increases, so too the control over what pupils know/reproduce and what teachers teach increases. I have elsewhere variously defined the curriculum in terms of a course, like a chariot race, which covers paths of reflection, expression and action (Schostak 1983). To return to the initial premise of this chapter, how does one go about derailing the chariot as people manically pursue the goals of the race set out by governments and employing organizations of all kinds? How is personal and social development in these times possible? It begins, I think, with the education of judgement.

The education of judgement starts with a critical challenge to the structures of compliance to the images projected by official curricula underlying programmes initiated by policy makers, whether we are here speaking of schools, businesses or the institutions of government and social welfare. In this respect, MacDonald (1974, 1987) described three distinct stances that evaluators can adopt with respect to policy makers (or the sponsors of a given evaluation), only one of which I regard as an education of judgement as distinct from a schooling of judgement. The three are:

1 Bureaucratic evaluation.
2 Autocratic evaluation.
3 Democratic evaluation.

Where bureaucratic evaluation locates dominance with the policy maker, autocratic evaluation locates it with the evaluator. In each case the service is to the policy maker. The bureaucratic evaluator unconditionally 'accepts the values of those who hold office, and offers information which will help them to accomplish their policy objectives.' This is a clear description of Ofsted inspections, for example. The autocratic evaluator provides 'a conditional service to those government agencies which have major control over the allocation of educational resources.' It is conditional because its 'values are derived from the evaluator's perception of the constitutional and moral obligations of the bureaucracy.' With respect to the paranoid curriculum, the bureaucratic evaluator is in the position of Os and adopts a position of complete faith and submission to the policy maker, whose desire has to be satisfied if success is to be attained. The position of the autocratic evaluator is more complex. It is a position of 'stand-off', where one Pd (government) confronts or is confronted by another Pd (the academic community of researchers). To judge the viability of this stand-off, one must ask who is likely to win any showdown with regard to the power to act and the allocation of resources to implement policy recommendations. MacDonald's (1996) answer is clear:

> government funding of educational research is now conditional upon disavowing ownership of its products and vowing silence with regard to their contents or how government makes use of them . . . such knowledge has now been commodified and privatised for the discretionary use of the executive and its agents. There's been no fuss about this from our employers, the universities. There is room for us under the shroud of secrecy that already marks the incorporation of the ivory towers in the business of government and industry. The pressure to sell or be damned is something we are all acutely aware of in an increasingly competitive environment.
>
> As for the future, there is one lesson. The government divided and rules, we divided and lost.

In these circumstances, what chance is there for MacDonald's third form of evaluation, the democratic? Here the evaluator acts as an information broker, facilitating its exchange between all members of an organization or system so that the power relations between the dominant (Pd) and the subordinates (Os) are suspended for the purposes of educating judgement through a representation of voices, and hence encouraging a rational dialogue, with all having access to the 'facts'. This approach, placed alongside its running mate, Stenhouse's Humanities Curriculum Project (HCP), provides an early attempt at transforming the curriculum and the processes of teaching and learning. The democratic impulse was sown by HCP through a radical undermining of traditional teacher/knowledge authority patterns by the instigation of the concept and practice of the 'neutral chair'. In the position of the 'neutral chair' the teacher would set the rules for rational debate but could not provide the content for that debate. Rather, children were to discuss, employing evidence, key controversial issues: law and order, race, sex and so on. In this way, opinions were raised, challenged and debated in ways which set people into relations of equality rather than dominance and submission. HCP and the processes of evaluation that were developed by MacDonald to be appropriate to it thus provide a challenging alternative to the paranoid curriculum and its contemporary variations.

There is one last question which I consider key to any notion of personal and social development in these fast changing times. Who decides on the curriculum? Under the paranoid curriculum the answer is clear: whoever is the most powerful. In a democratic curriculum the answer is less clear. If a key principle of education is to include a sense of mutuality and equality of access to the means, products and processes of cultural action, then the individual, at whatever age, must be included as a decision-making partner in the process. Simply, the child contributes to any agenda through which a curriculum is framed. Including the child as a decision-making partner whose claims are equal to those of any other individual in an arena of debate and cultural action is something rarely considered (Schostak and Logan 1984). In this image of what it means to follow a process of education the child is not locked on to a track but located at the 'points', the place where multiple tracks arise, some already laid out for choice, others only emergent and yet others indicated simply as territory that remains to be explored. The child is at the point of decision where tracks may be switched, where it is always possible to challenge and pursue alternatives.

As we face the changes of a new millennium, like many other countries, Britain chooses to look back to a golden age of 'basics'. Ahead are the postmodern tracks of information flows so fast that they not only cut up the world into domains battled over by federations and coalitions of states and multinationals, but striate the world, making changing alliances hard to focus on, let alone try to control. What sort of world is this? What are its curricula? How may individuals best organize their access to information flows and knowledge capital in order to participate creatively and constructively?

Personal and social development at the end of time

When things change so quickly that their duration can no longer be adequately counted in terms of the human heart beat, time itself no longer means anything. The global electronic mechanization of information flows and decision making raises more urgently still the question of what principles should underpin the educational development of people so that they can challenge policies and institutional mechanisms and insert themselves into a democratic process of decision making. It is surely not too hard to work out some of the underlying principles that can inform educational debate about appropriate curricula for personal and social development in this postmodern world.

There can be no grand narrative concerning what is 'good for all'. Standardization and its surveillance techniques to create *the* curriculum are patently absurd in a context of change that is so fast, so diverse and so technologically and culturally creative. A forward looking curriculum for personal and social development requires principles that facilitate diversity, dialogue and a mutuality of relationship. Such a curriculum cannot have personal meaning unless time is brought into the ambit of an individual's lifetime, an individual's life course; nor can it have social meaning unless there is a community of regard where time is defined as the time to meet, to interact and to develop through dialogue.

I have elsewhere developed some insights into the processes of curricular design constituted through personal and social reflection upon experience (Schostak 1991). These are where the narratives of personal and social development intersect in a creative deconstruction of biographies, identities, events and the stages which frame the performances of everyday lives. It is through such a process that individuals in the company of others can free themselves of the constrictions of their lives by first formulating the structures which constrain them and then problematizing them in order to re-create themselves. MacDonald, throughout the times we have worked together on various projects, has always drawn attention to the examination of problem structures and the exploration of opportunity structures. Any given situation has its problem structure. Individuals and organizations have to attend to certain problems in order to function. The more successfully they understand and resource themselves intellectually, emotionally, socially (through appropriate cultural practices) and materially to meet their problem structure, the better they achieve their goals. Any intellectual, critical exploration of a problem structure defines a curriculum that meets the exigencies of everyday life. Furthermore, any problem structure can be defined in terms of the opportunity structures either offered or denied by a given way of meeting it.

Any child is already positioned within a problem structure that defines his or her life at a given moment: how to deal with parents, how make friends, how to handle the confusing demands of social life, how to make life with others, how to contribute in ways that others respect, how to get to grips with the fast paced exciting and daunting world about.

The denial of opportunities for educational development in the UK and other countries pursuing similar contemporary forms of schooling is not merely a tragedy but points to the shame of a profession of educationists which has abandoned education to the engineers of politically imposed practices. The words of Noam Chomsky, speaking of his intellectual and academic critics, can hardly be bettered in this context. He was interviewed by John Pilger on *The Late Show* (BBC 2, 25 November 1992). Reporting the interview in the *Guardian*, Pilger wrote:

> I said, 'But they often describe you as an extremist.'
>
> 'Sure,' he replied, 'I *am* an extremist, because moderate is anyone who supports Western power and an extremist is anyone who objects to it. Take for example, George Kennan (the post-war American cold war strategist). He was one of the leading architects of the modern world and is at the soft or dovish end of the US planning spectrum. When he was head of the policy planning staff he quite explicitly said – in internal documents, not publicly of course – that we must put aside vague and idealistic slogans about human rights, democratisation and the raising of living standards and deal in straight power concepts if we want to maintain the disparity between our enormous wealth and the poverty of everyone else. But it is rare that someone is that honest.'
>
> I said, 'You've had some spectacular rows. Arthur Schlesinger accused you of betraying the intellectual tradition.'
>
> 'That's true, I agree with him. The intellectual tradition is one of servility to power, and if I didn't betray it I'd be ashamed of myself.'

What does it take to build a curriculum for personal and social development that genuinely provides the opportunity structures for making available democratic powers for all? It takes time, the time to allow people to reflect upon their own situation, their own purposes and their own problems, and to investigate their own opportunities in a climate of mutual support. Is it too much to write in these terms? Won't the professionals in schools of education supporting the intellectual tradition label it hysterical? Probably. However, millions of children leave school all over the world each day no better able to engage in democratic action and make changes in their communities to meet their needs than when they entered. Rather than a curriculum that constructs subjectivities around failure, around 'knowing one's place', around complacent disregard of the misfortunes and experiences of others, around an apathetic acceptance that 'things can't change', around a meritocracy that disowns its underclass, the chance always exists for education to construct curricula for challenge, for change, for the development of people and not the engineering of employees. MacDonald (1996) quotes with approval Berliner (1993), commenting within the US context:

> by the year 2000 we should be number one in the world in the percentage of eighteen year olds that are politically and socially involved. Far more important than our mathematics and our science scores is the involvement of the next generation in maintaining our democracy and helping those within it who need assistance – the young, the ill, the old, the retarded, the illiterate, the homeless and the hungry. Schools that cannot turn out politically active and socially helpful citizens, should be identified and their rates of failure announced in the newspapers.

In order to know why after the major developments in educational theory and practice in the UK during the 1960s and 1970s this is far from being the case we would have to begin at the beginning and, with MacDonald (1996; and Chapter 2 of this volume), consider how education became nobody's business.

Notes

1 From a signed letter by David Reynolds sent to publicize 'The High Reliability School: Theory and Practice' conference,' London, 7 March 1997.
2 In all aspects of life, it seems, people are being progressively turned into cyphers. The paranoid curriculum, of course, delights in league tables, in classes, in labels. Individuality is always reduced to being a representative individual of a group. Hence, the schema that I detail here mimics this cypherization. If relentless abstraction is uncomfortable to read, it is certainly more uncomfortable to live. Yet children are routinely placed into the abstract matrices of schooling, in their best interests, regardless of their individuality. I hope the ironic structure, while displeasing to some to read, may at least emphasize the point.
3 May be read as 'dominant person'. This may be the 'person' of a single individual like a father, a teacher, police officer; it may be the legal sense of 'person' that an institution possesses in law; or it may be some ineffable 'person' that is worshiped as a god, or feared as 'them'.
4 My translation.

References

Anderson, B. (1983) *Imagined Communities. Reflections on the Origin and Spread of Nationalism*. London and New York: Verso.

Berliner, D. C. (1993) Educational reform in an era of disinformation. *Education Policy Analysis Archives*, 1(2), 1–43.

Davies, B. and Harré, R. (1990) Positioning: the discursive production of selves. *Journal for the Theory of Social Behaviour*, 20(1), 43–63.

Freire, P. (1970) *Cultural Action for Freedom*. Harmondsworth: Penguin.

Hall, S. and Jefferson, T. (eds) (1975) *Resistance through Rituals: Youth Subcultures in Post-war Britain*. London and Melbourne: CCCS, University of Birmingham and Hutchinson University Library.

Hargreaves, D. H. (1967) *Social Relations in a Secondary School*. London: Routledge & Kegan Paul.

Holt, J. (1969) *How Children Fail*. Harmondsworth: Penguin.

Illich, I. (1971) *Deschooling Society*. London: Calder and Boyers.

Jackson, P. W. (1968) *Life in Classrooms*. New York: Holt, Rinehart & Winston.

Jeffrey, B. and Woods, P. (1996) Feeling deprofessionalised: the social construction of emotions during an OFSTED inspection. *Cambridge Journal of Education*, 26(3), 325–43.

Kant, I. ([1781]1966) *Critique of Pure Reason*, trans. F. Max Müller. New York: Doubleday Anchor (originally published 1781).

Lacan, J. (1977) *Écrits. A Selection*. London: Tavistock/Routlege.

Lacey, C. (1971) *Hightown Grammar*. Manchester: Manchester University Press.

Laing, R. D. (1967) *The Politics of Experience and the Bird of Paradise*. Harmondsworth: Penguin.

MacDonald, B. (1974) Evaluation and the control of education. In B. MacDonald and R. Walker (eds) *Innovation, Evaluation, Research and the Problem of Control*. Norwich: CARE, UEA.

MacDonald, B. (1987) Evaluation and the control of education. In R. Murphy and H. Torrance (eds) *Evaluating Education: Issues and Methods*. London: Harper and Row.

MacDonald, B. (1996) How education became nobody's business. *Cambridge Journal of Education*, 26(2), 241–9.

Rogers, B. (1990) *'You Know the Fair Rule: Strategies for Making the Hard Job of Discipline in School Easier*. London: Longman.

Rogers, C. (1969) *Freedom to Learn*. Columbus, OH: Merrill.

Rogers, C. (1983) *Freedom to Learn for the 80s*. Columbus, OH: Merrill.

Rosenthal, R. and Jacobsen, L. F. (1968) *Pygmalion in the Classroom*. New York: Holt, Rinehart & Winston.

Schatzman, M. (1973) *Soul Murder. Persecution in the Family*. London: Allen Lane.

Schostak, J. F. (1983) *Maladjusted Schooling: Deviance, Social Control and Individuality in Secondary Schooling*. London: Falmer.

Schostak, J. F. (1986) *Schooling the Violent Imagination*. London: Routledge & Kegan Paul.

Schostak, J. F. (ed.) (1991) *Youth in Trouble. Educational Responses*. London: Kogan Page.

Schostak, J. F. (1993) *Dirty Marks. The Education of Self, Media and Popular Culture*. London: Pluto.

Schostak, J. F. and Logan, T. (eds) (1984) *Pupil Experience*. London: Croom Helm.

Schreber, D. P. (1955) *Memoirs of My Nervous Illness*, trans. I. Macalpine and R. Hunter. London: Dawson. Second revised edition, Cambridge, MA: Harvard Belknap (1988).

Virilio, P. (1996) *Cybermonde, la politique du pire,* entretien avec Phillippe Petit. Paris: Les éditions textuel, Diffusion Le Seuil.
Willis, P. (1977) *Learning to Labour*. Farnborough: Saxon House.

PART II

The relationship between social and educational change

4

Community, school change and strategic networking

PETER POSCH

Introduction

In this chapter I discuss the view that major challenges which schools are facing are not 'home-made' but effects of developments in the larger society. Two megatrends in society and their implications for schools are outlined. One of the emerging answers to social change is the development of 'dynamic networks' linking schools and communities and providing opportunities for an extension of the traditional concept of learning, to include the production of local knowledge and joint ventures between students, teachers and community agencies to shape the conditions of life. They provide opportunities for the young to act on their environment in a responsible and constructive way and understand that they 'matter' in society. An example of such a network is elaborated. The final section provides some theoretical reflections on the character of dynamic networks and on their strengths and potential problems.

Trends in society and implications for schools

The process of individualization

There are hardly any differences of opinion about the global process of individualization. 'The individual moves out of historical social structures and bonds and loses traditional securities with respect to knowledge in action, to beliefs, and to guiding norms' (Popp 1996). This is one side of the coin. Helmut Fend (1990) expresses the other side. For him the programmatic claim of the Enlightenment has become a realistic claim in our days: 'The right, the duty and the opportunity to use one's mind without being led by somebody else, and to shape one's life at one's own terms is only now becoming a widely held claim and emerging reality.' Beck (1992: 90) also points out the double face of individualization: on the one hand the liberation from traditional ties raises expectations for a life of one's own, free from industrial and administrative interference in the personal sphere. On the other hand, the individual increasingly becomes dependent on the labour market and on the standardized ways of life that support its operation, such as education, consumption, product offers.

The trend towards individualization is closely related to the destabilization of traditional social networks and of social control. Centralized power structures, such as governments, political parties, churches and unions, appear to be less and less able to keep the multiplicity of social influences under control and to guarantee security and stability (see, for example, Handy 1995). The social units which have to find their own strategies to cope with complexity appear to become smaller and smaller, down to the smallest possible social unit, the individual.

The process of individualization can also be traced to changes in the structure and function of families. Authority relations in families have been changing in the past few decades. What is allowed and not allowed is less an authoritative parental decision and more negotiated. An increasing number of children even grow up in a *laissez-faire* situation and do not experience any leadership from their parents.

The individualization process is also related to a shift from an ethic of personal obligation and responsibility to an ethic of personal development. The meaning of life is increasingly seen in terms of self-fulfilment, of the realization of one's own abilities, interests and aims. It has promoted tendencies to seek short-term satisfaction of needs and to instrumentalize other persons.

This trend has enormous implications for schools. If social control and structures of responsibility outside school lose stability and legitimization, and if the young are no longer embedded in seemingly self-evident social relationships, these structures have to be actively constructed and schools are increasingly expected to provide the necessary social continuity.

Children and young people have become more independent and more difficult at the same time, because rules from adults are less and less accepted without question. Activities that are not experienced immediately as meaningful will be opposed by many children. Increasingly schools are expected to deal with the meaning of learning and its connection with the personal life situation and future perspectives of the young, and to cope constructively with the conflict between the ethic of self-fulfilment and an ethic of responsibility.

Individual demands to shape one's life have increased enormously. At the same time there is a growing discrepancy between expectations and what can actually be achieved. Increasingly schools will be expected to provide opportunities for the young to participate in shaping their learning situation (aims, methods, quality standards) and to experience themselves as persons who can leave constructive traces in their environment and who feel respected.

The fragmentation of conditions of work

Working conditions have become increasingly fragmented. The percentage of part-time contracts and temporary work on low wages grows rapidly. Increasing numbers of citizens are unlikely to have careers in the future, but will become 'portfolio people', having to sell their skills on a temporary contract basis. In addition, they will have to modify and reconstruct their 'portfolios' continuously through retraining, because skills will become rapidly redundant. According to Charles Handy (1995: 9), productivity in liberal economies means 'ever more and better work from ever fewer people.' The effects of this philosophy of economic progress are burnout, early retirement and long-term unemployment for many.

Decreasing job perspectives meet with increasing job demands. Demands on employees have grown in several respects (see European Round Table of Industrialists 1994):

- In a theoretical sense: to understand complex relationships.
- In a technical sense: to deal with program-controlled working tools.
- In a social sense: to cooperate in teams.
- In an organizational sense: to be able to cope with a spectrum of organizational, executive and evaluative tasks.
- In an emotional sense: to identify with work and develop personal work-related motivation.

Both developments have implications for schools. If unemployment becomes a 'normal' feature of industrialized societies, an increasing number of young people cannot be convinced of the exchange value of educational qualifications. Besides preparation for work, schools are increasingly requested to provide competences and concrete experiences to enable constructive use of times of unemployment for socially respectable but (generally) unpaid work, such as neighbourhood help and community work. The traditional task of schools – to prepare the young for a satisfactory life in society – will have to be reinterpreted to cope with both the increasing demands for professional careers and the qualifications and experiences needed for survival in a 'do-it-yourself economy' (Handy 1995). Many of the competences needed for both perspectives are quite new:

- to take initiative in responsibly shaping the conditions of one's life;
- actively to create satisfactory relationships;
- to engage in meaningful activities even without integration into a 'proper job';
- to generate, test and utilize knowledge;
- to pause and reflect on the stream of events and to deal constructively with time pressure and with information overload.

Elliott (1996: 15) has highlighted three implications for educational policy derived from these trends:

- the delegation of curriculum decisions to schools;
- the construction by schools of social networks with agencies, groups and individuals in the local community;
- increasingly differentiated and diverse provision of curricula within and between educational institutions, to cater for a range and variety of individually and locally determined learning needs, but located within a framework of shared educational goals and values, (within) a common vision.

Strategic networking and alliances of schools with cultural and economic institutions in society can provide important contributions to these new tasks: they offer a wealth of competences and information, they provide opportunities for the young to influence their conditions of life and they offer early experiences with the 'significance value' of learning to complement its 'utility value' (Tenbruck 1975).

Strategic networks linking schools and communities

One of the emerging answers to these two megatrends in industrialized societies is the development of links between schools and communities and – more radically – the integration of schools into community affairs. The emergence of these links has implications for the concept of learning, which can include the production of local knowledge and activities to shape the conditions of life. The following example of a school–community network emerged in the context of the Environment and School Initiatives project (OECD 1991, 1995; Elliott 1995), but has already gained independent status and is developing its own dynamics. Its development over a time span of about six years shows an important shift of the centre of gravity from the school to the community (see also Posch and Mair 1997).

In a secondary school in Austria, a biology teacher (Gottfried Mair) started an 'energy project' with a group of 14-year-old pupils (Mair *et al.* 1992; personal communication). In a pilot phase they began to study the use of energy in their school building and in their own homes. A year later they tackled a major task: to analyse the use of energy in four small villages (the home communities of most of the pupils). The first step was the construction of a questionnaire with 50 questions and – supported by an energy expert – an intensive learning phase to gain an understanding of the issues and to master the theoretical and social demands involved in collecting the necessary data. Through role plays possible reactions of inhabitants were anticipated and discussed. Then groups of two or three students went from house to house with their questionnaire, informed people about their intentions and offered assistance in filling it in. Nearly 70 per cent of the households completed the questionnaire.

The students processed the data at school and produced a comparative analysis of the use of energy for each house and for each village, and of possibilities for using renewable energies (such as bio-gas, wood and solar energy).

The teachers involved and their students kept 'research diaries' to facilitate reflection on the progress of work. The results were presented by the students at a public event. The students played out sketches to illustrate experiences and conflicts during data collection. The main part was the presentation and discussion of findings and proposals.

Two months after the event a few pupils, with their parents, started to build sun collectors for their own houses. This stimulated the foundation of a local association for renewable energy, and within two years 700 installations for solar water-heating were built in the whole region. A number of other investments followed. In one village, for example, the school building was insulated to reduce energy consumption.

In this project a number of relationships were established:

- contact with an energy expert to receive professional assistance in the design of the questionnaire;
- cooperation with a teacher of computer science in order to get classroom time and assistance in processing the data for comparative analysis and for presentation to the public;
- contact with the mayors of the communities to get the support of the community councils and financial assistance.

The project showed students and teachers that with only moderate effort a considerable amount of energy could be saved and public approval could be gained. The next step appeared to be a logical consequence, i.e. to link up with other schools and to find solutions for a number of new questions: how to inform schools, how to identify persons and institutions who would provide financial, political and other kinds of support etc. A first issue of a network newspaper was published, in which the project was described and support was offered (advice by teachers and students, computer software, the questionnaire for data collection etc.). The project was also presented at several fairs and exhibitions and a number of schools reacted and invited teachers and students for short introductory courses to get familiar with the ideas, the logistics and the computer software, which had been continuously improved.

In a school in a larger community, for example, the two teachers and a group of students were invited to act as expert advisers on launching a major energy project involving several teachers and several forms. One piece of strategic advice was to involve political actors and to inform the public from the very beginning of the project. As a result, the school organized public evenings to inform the community, initiated discussions in the community council, held press conferences to involve the regional media etc. Students were involved in most of these activities; for example, they held the first press conference and produced articles for the local paper.

More and more schools and local authorities became interested and were given the opportunity to learn about the concept on site and/or be visited. In subsequent years the logistics were continuously improved, involving local enterprises (such as chimney sweepers and plumbers) as well. From

1991 to 1994, almost 30 schools had taken on the idea of contributing to the development of an energy policy in their communities. This created an enormous demand for advice and external support and communication across schools. Most of it was accomplished by informal contacts, presentations in school conferences and the regular network newspaper.

The teacher who had initiated the energy network gained a fine reputation, won with his students a number of national and international awards and was offered financial and infrastructural support through the authorities. The regional government provided the funds for the production of the newsletter and central government provided resources for part-time secondment and operational money for the energy network.

In 1994 an interesting shift of emphasis occurred. The teacher was convinced that in order to stabilize the energy network it had to have many 'fathers and mothers'. In other words, understanding had to 'grow' in the local population that the saving of energy was both a valuable and a feasible endeavour. The question was how such a consciousness and feeling of collective ownership could develop. His strategy was that all persons and institutions with influence, vested interests or know-how in energy matters should be involved in the design and implementation of initiatives. For the first time he moved beyond school initiatives to community initiatives. The network newspaper (originally school-based) became a newspaper on community environmental projects. The teacher's main interest became the creation of local groups, with broad participation and a strong emphasis on the training of local coordinators. Schools (teachers and pupils) were still (and in some cases heavily) involved but the community projects were no longer fully dependent on their participation.

In 1996 the teacher was invited to speak about his concept of an energy network at a meeting of mayors of 37 communities in a rural region. Twenty-eight communities decided to develop an energy concept, with the strong involvement of local enterprises and schools, and asked him for assistance. Four communities have taken the first steps, and have involved schools from the very beginning. In one community a teacher who already had some know-how in energy matters made the first step. With his pupils he carried out an analysis of energy use in the school building and contacted a local architect for advice. The results showed an extremely wasteful use of energy. The architect became interested and offered cooperation in carrying out a similar analysis in a few other communal buildings and in calculating the potential for saving energy and costs. A small group was formed, comprising the architect, the teacher and members of the community council. One of their proposals was the development of a local heat supply through a heating system using chopped wood.

In another community where the council had also decided to develop a local energy concept, the mayor asked the head of the local school to involve teachers and pupils in this endeavour and promised financial support for necessary investments. The head organized an afternoon seminar for his teachers. The seminar was led by the teacher who had originally raised the energy network idea. The main issues were the design of energy projects with pupils. A group of teachers decided to cooperate, prepared with their pupils an analysis of the energy situation of the school and presented the results at a public event. Teachers and pupils participated in other initiatives of the community as well, e.g. building a demonstration model for solar energy.

In the meantime, regional initiatives emerged. A bank and 14 regional companies formed a buying cooperative to provide members of the participating communities with a package comprising price reductions on necessary materials (e.g. for insulation), free energy analysis and advice, assistance in applying for subsidies, guidelines for installation and an evaluation of the effects after some time. Jobless people were trained to act as advisers and to assist communities and schools in collecting and analysing data. These people act on demand from the communities involved in the network.

A characteristic of these networks is that schools are integrated in long-term community activities (intended to last for five years). They are actively involved in a network that goes far beyond schools and has its centre of gravity in organizational structures which have manifold roots in the public, economic and private domains. The pupils (most are 13–15 years old) are involved in areas to which they can contribute in a serious and respected way, but are still not misused in being made to to do other people's work. The children participate in the collection and analysis of data and in the improvement of the energy situation of their immediate environment: the school, their homes and their relatives' homes.

So far there has not been any systematic evaluation of the effects of the energy network on participating schools. There are, however, a number of informal observations which provide indications of impact. It appears to have created a new awakening among several teachers who were already suffering from resignation and burnout-like symptoms. For them – most of them aged from 40 to 45 – major reasons for their involvement were being able to participate in shaping the conditions of their work, to open routes for more satisfactory work with the children and to gain respect in their communities. Other indications were the high participation rate of pupils and their involvement in relatively complex activities (such as writing reports, contributions to press conferences and presentations in public).

A number of supportive conditions appear to have been of paramount importance for the development of the energy network:

- A strong emphasis on training: seminars for employees of enterprises (e.g. in solar technology), evening presentations for local citizens (often organized by teachers) and special seminars for teachers (e.g. on project design).
- The systematic use of 'good examples': contacts were established with teachers of schools outside the region who could offer practical experience of local energy networks.
- The search for a variety of financial supports: apart from local and regional

public support, private sponsors such as banks and private companies increasingly participated in financing training and communication activities.
- The traditional involvement of some teachers in local agencies, such as adult education or community politics: these teachers had already developed a responsibility towards the community and were familiar with the local micropolitical scene. Both facilitated the first steps of integrating school initiatives into the community network.

The energy network idea and the emerging logistics have attracted considerable attention from other communities and there is a growing interest on the part of the provincial government in finding ways of systematically supporting its further development.

Dynamic networks: a theoretical perspective

Networks and 'joint ventures' between communities and schools are international phenomena, and in part result from increasing complexity in industrialized societies. To be able to cope with complexity and uncertainty, institutions and individuals are stimulated to create active relationships with each other. These 'dynamic' networks (Ochsenbauer 1989) complement and to some extent even replace the traditional 'hierarchical' relationships that have characterized the infrastructure of social life in the past (Posch 1994).

Dynamic networks are answers to specific situational characteristics:

- The situations are relatively unstructured: neither the problems nor the aims are 'given' but are in need of being defined by negotiation of the parties concerned.
- The necessary knowledge ('situational understanding') can to some extent be generated only *within* the situations and by those persons who through their action (or non-action) are elements of it (Elliott and Rice 1990).
- The knowledge is not applied instrumentally to solve the problems but expresses itself holistically in actions comprising cognitions, value orientations and feelings.

These three characteristics are well expressed in the philosophy underpinning the work of the teacher who initiated the energy network described above (Mair, personal communication). Communication and joint reflection on shared values, on the situation and on feasible improvements are at the centre of his approach. Saving energy is not regarded merely as a matter of technical solutions and expert services but primarily as a matter of reflection on one's life conditions and on personal communication and negotiation. It seems that the tangible effects of these activities are not results of any 'personality changes' in the participating persons. They are results of the values embedded in the social structures which these people have participated in creating and feel they are part of.

Dynamic networks differ in several respects from hierarchical structures of communication (Fischer-Kowalski 1991; see also Clary 1993: 27):

- The relationship between the persons involved is not one of sub- and superordination but is relatively symmetrical.
- There is a good cost–benefit ratio for each participant. Each person gets at least as much out of the interaction as she or he invests in it.
- Dynamic networks are constituted by ongoing communication and exchange processes (e.g. by comparing, learning, planning, influencing). Personal relationships of mutual trust and informal contacts are the breeding ground for dynamic networks. 'Ideas move along the social network of personal acquaintance' (House 1974: 10).
- Dynamic networks do not develop along pre-specified routes but are stimulated by the perception of shared interests. Dynamic networks, in this sense, have a micro-political dimension (Altrichter and Posch 1996). The decision to participate is a matter of negotiation between the parties concerned. Relationships can develop quite spontaneously.
- The duration of dynamic networks can vary. If complex tasks are tackled, they tend to have a relatively stable long-term character.
- Each participant in a dynamic network can be involved in a potentially unlimited number of interactions. New relationships can be developed without the existing ones having to be abandoned. This contrasts sharply with a hierarchical structure in which new relationships have to be defined by another rank (e.g. by a new boss) and in general replace the old ones.

Dynamic networks are specific ways in which people share their abilities for joint enterprises and for mutual learning and assistance. They contradict one of the traditional assumptions of schooling: the assumption of a separation of school and society. If dynamic networks develop it is difficult to say where the educational organization ends and where society and its abundance of personal and institutional relationships begin.

Dynamic networks can have a number of advantages for schools. They introduce a horizontal division of labour. According to Ernest House (1974), 'the features of such a horizontal division of labour might mean shorter, less alienating development cycles where participants can see and understand what is going on and have immediate control. This would mean more self-reliance and the utilisation of the local, indigenous expertise and resources at hand.' Dynamic networks create contexts necessary for cooperation. Cooperation, in general, does not evolve if a task can also be accomplished without cooperation. However, if initiatives 'are aimed at solving real problems, in a real situation, a partnership with decision-makers, local authorities or non-governmental organisations is essential' (Clary 1993: 16). They can allow teachers and students to do what they can do best and still be effective in actively influencing the conditions of life, here and now:

- through the generation of local knowledge and their active involvement in

change in areas which are physically, intellectually and emotionally accessible to the young;
- through the documentation and presentation of experiences in public;
- through their provision of critical, reflective and creative elements to joint enterprises in a community or region.

Community-based dynamic networks need not have the compensatory character of traditional community education (see Popp 1996: 60), but can be steps to a new phase of regional economic and social development in which schools become respected and reliable partners.

References

Altrichter, H. and Posch, P. (eds)(1996) *Mikropolitik der Schulentwicklung.* Innsbruck: Studienverlag.

Beck, U. (1992) *Risk Society: towards a New Modernity.* London: Sage.

Clary, M. (1993) *OECD/CERI ENSI Project: National Report.* Aix en Provence, mimeo.

Elliott, J. (1995) Reconstructing the environmental education curriculum. In OECD, *Environmental Learning for the 21st Century.* Paris: OECD/CERI, pp. 13–29.

Elliott, J. (1996) *Environmental Education and School Initiatives: Implications for the Curriculum in Basic Education.* Norwich: University of East Anglia.

Elliott, J. and Rice, J. (1990) The relationship between disciplinary knowledge and situational understanding in the development of environmental awareness. In M. Pieters (ed.) *Teaching for Sustainable Development: Report on a Workshop at Veldhoven, Netherlands, 23–25 April 1990.* Enschede: Institute for Curriculum Development, pp. 66–72.

European Round Table of Industrialists (1994) *Education for Europeans: towards a Learning Society.* Brussels: ERT Education Policy Group.

Fend, H. (1990) Bildungskonzepte und Lebensfelder Jugendlicher im sozialhistorischen Wandel. In L. Leitner (ed.) *Wie öffnet sich die Schule neuen Entwicklungen und Aufgaben?* Vienna: Bundesverlag, pp. 42–66.

Fischer-Kowalski, M. (1991) Das pyramidale und das unbegrenzte Netz. In A. Pellert (ed.) *Vernetzung und Widerspruch: zur Neuorganisation H Von Wissenschaft.* Munich: Profil-Verlag, pp. 165–94.

Gössling, H. J. (1985) Schulwelt und ausserschulische Bildungswelten. *Pädagogische Rundschau,* 39(1), 599–610.

Gstrein, J. and Krabacher, O. (1995) In Karrösten gehen die Uhren vor. *Gemeinde-Netzwerkzeitung,* October, 10–11.

Handy, C. (1995) *The Empty Raincoat.* London: Arrow Books.

House, E. (1974) *The Politics of Educational Innovation.* Berkeley, CA: McCutchan.

Mair, G. (1997a) Öko-Modell Ausserfern. *Gemeinde-Netzwerkzeitung,* February, 7, 7.

Mair, G. (1997b) Öko-Modell Ausserfern. *Gemeinde-Netzwerkzeitung,* June, 10–13.

Mair, G., Mallaun, K. and Montibeller, R. (1992) *Projekthandbuch Energie.* Imst: Bundesrealgymnasium.

Ochsenbauer, C. (1989) *Organisatorische Alternativen zur Hierarchie.* Munich: GBI-Verlag.

OECD (1991) *Environment, Schools and Active Learning.* Paris: OECD.

OECD (1995) *Environmental Learning for the 21st Century.* Paris: OECD/CERI.

Popp, R. (1996) Psychotherapie und Sozialplanung: Anmerkungen zur Entwicklung der sozialstaatlichen Leistungen im Spannungsfeld zwischen Individualisierung und Gemeinwesenorientierung. In R. Hutterer-Krisch, V. Pfersmann and I. S. Farag (eds) *Psychotherapie, Lebensqualität und Prophylaxe: Beiträge zur Gesundheitsvorsorge in Gesellschaftspolitik, Arbeitswelt und beim Individuum.* Vienna: Springer, pp. 49–66.

Posch, P. (1994) Networking in environmental education. In M. Pettigrew and B. Somekh (eds) *Evaluation and Innovation in Environmental Education.* Paris: OECD/CERI, pp. 61–87.

Posch, P. and Mair, G. (1997) Dynamic networking and community collaboration: the cultural scope of educational action research. In S. Hollingsworth (ed.) *International Action Research: a Casebook for Educational Reform.* London: Falmer, pp. 261–74.

Tenbruck, F. (1975) Der Fortschritt der Wissenschaft als Trivialisierungsprozess. *Wissenschaftssoziologie*, 18, 19–47.

5

Social change and the individual: changing patterns of community and the challenge for schooling

MARIE BRENNAN AND SUSAN E. NOFFKE

The pressures of the globalizing economy and its infrastructures significantly altered political, social and cultural patterns of advanced capitalist countries in the last quarter of the twentieth century. Yet this does not mean that everything has changed: older as well as emergent ways of organizing social life now exist side by side, interacting and interrupting one another (Luke 1996), offering a wide range of resources for individual and community identity formation. The schooling sector provides an excellent example of these contradictory and ambiguous tendencies at work. On several continents, school systems are required to provide more and more standardized accountability information, along lines familiar since the introduction of mass schooling. Simultaneously they are required, under devolutionary state policies, to take up more local responsibility. In this way, schools are part of a globalizing shift which pairs homogenization and local differentiation tendencies (Appadurai 1990). They are under increased pressure to change, while at the same time they are expected to provide a stable and relatively enduring institution around which identity and community can be formed.

Yet alongside, and perhaps because of, the glut of interventionist policies in the field of education (for example, the 'standards' and 'charter schools' movements in the USA), strident accusations are made by governments and communities and through the media that schools are too slow to change. Within the confines of increased surveillance and control mechanisms, the capacity to alter state schooling at the local level is severely circumscribed, more so than it has been in the past half century, we suggest. At the same time, many people in and around schools are continuing their longstanding and active concern with changing these institutions to become more socially just, future-oriented and responsive to the articulated needs of their communities. They are pushing the edges of self-management policy rhetorics in ways which open up new spaces for school reform. In this chapter, we explore two of the many projects which exhibit the tensions of attempting to change through taking on the consequences of the 'big picture' at local schooling levels. Both projects have now finished, with mixed success. Yet each provides ways to explore the issues of school change and reform, and the capacity to develop new forms of social practice in and through schools, in both individual and communal patterns.

The first project occurred during the 1980s in the state of Victoria, Australia, and the second in the late 1980s and early 1990s in an urban area of the USA. The former, the School Improvement Plan, was a state-wide initiative aiming to redevelop the notion of 'school communities' by supporting partnerships among teachers, parents and students of a school engaging in ongoing school self-evaluation. The image of change central to this project was that of a community of enquirers, working together across their differences to address major issues of educational access and success (Brennan and Hoadley 1984). For the latter, the identification of an actual beginning date needs to take into account its origins, which lie in a local African-American community's struggle over the welfare of its children in the public school system. Such efforts rarely have a starting date, but emerge in the records of public meetings held after the informal gatherings which provided the impetus for change. The African and African-American Curriculum Project was a local initiative in which the aims, as they emerged in practice, outlined the tensions between anti-racist and multicultural agendas (Soudien 1996). The image of change embedded in this project was multiple, according to the various participants, and continued to emerge throughout the project. An 'each one, teach one' image for professional change and development often clashed with a perceived need for systemic mandates, including the use of testing, to achieve curriculum change. At the same time, there was a strong recognition that the formation of communities of struggle around issues of racial justice required a commitment to self-examination, especially in relation to cultural identity (Clark 1994; Noffke 1994; Palmeri-Santiago 1994; Sadler 1994; Shujaa 1994, 1995; Noffke, *et al.* 1996).

Both projects worked from our interest in action research as a commitment to particular, participatory ways of changing the world of schools, through ongoing cycles of action and reflection on at least two levels: the direct participants at the schools and the outside facilitator/co-research groups – the state school improvement office in the first project and university faculty, school administration and, later, teacher involvement in the second. Through examination of both of these projects, we hope to identify significant dynamics which can help in understanding the change process in schools, especially in terms of the tensions between local and state control so evident in contemporary reform efforts.

Much about work in schools is inimical to community: teachers' classroom work tends to be isolated and individualized, partly a material circumstance of separate classrooms and timetabling histories, and partly a reaction to external attempts to intervene in non-educational ways. The two sets of dynamics have operated to create a space which is both a site of resistance and a site of conservatism. Students, too, tend to be caught up in an ethos of individual competition for access to the distributive goods of education, made to appear as a function of 'natural' merit through the technologies of testing and reporting. While schools have played a role in the reproduction of inequality (Apple 1979), there is also a simultaneous history of schooling as creating community and as being a focus for local struggle (Reese 1986; Shujaa 1996). Perhaps the school community is even more important now, as the school is both the sole common institution in our society and a major means for definition of self and 'other'. Schooling is also one institution in which virtually all have participated, and it provides a continuing reason for investments in societal futures – both for continuity and for change. The projects reported here, then, become important organizing foci for attempts to create different kinds of community from those often held to be the norm. These projects were also constructed on long traditions, within and outside education, of community building and activism (Clark 1990; Horton and Freire 1990; Hinsdale *et al.* 1995). The simultaneity of new and old forms of individual and community, we argue, create both the substance and the means for social and educational change in this era of globalization.

Victoria's School Improvement Plan 1982–1990

The School Improvement Plan (SIP) was established as an effort to redirect state Education Department priorities in Victoria, Australia, during the 1980s. As the initial publicized initiative among a bank of other democratic reform-oriented policies following the election of a Labor government to replace a long conservative rule, SIP worked with and complemented a series of changes to structures that were to occur in curriculum goals and organization, restructurings of the bureaucracy along more representative and democratic lines at all levels and an expansion of funding to an education system which had been strangled for lack of funds. As a system-wide initiative, SIP explored the extent to which a state system of schooling could replace an inspectorial system of quality control in a centralized system with a programme of local participation in evaluation. Several hundred schools each year were able to volunteer to engage in school self-evaluation, requiring a mixed team of parents, teachers and students, who used an action research approach to identify and act upon major areas of improvement for that school community.

To the categories of evaluation – bureaucratic, autocratic and democratic – proposed by MacDonald (1973) was added a further category of 'participatory evaluation' (Brown 1982). MacDonald's work at that time emphasized the political dimensions of outside evaluations, and the consequences for truth and methodology arising from different positionings of the evaluator(s). By raising these political dimensions of truth and value among school communities quite explicitly, SIP aimed to develop new language with the new practice of widespread evaluation. SIP emphasized the development of ongoing capacities among diverse communities of interest and background to share and interrogate their values-in-use in the operations of the school. This entailed redefining who was counted as part of the school's 'community' and therefore a partner in the research-cum-evaluation activity used to regenerate the schooling system. Many of those involved in outside evaluation were sceptical of the possibility that ordinary school communities, now placed in a position of greater responsibility for meeting the curriculum and learning needs of their local students, would be able to engage in the development of informed judgement. The resolution of their own conflicts and the development of better quality education programmes were intended not only for the 'best schools' but, over a six to eight year cycle, were to extend to all two thousand plus schools in the state.

Schools were not left on their own, with a mandate from an official policy to 'implement'. Rather, schools were seen as co-producing the policy, and the experience from the first group of schools funded was used to develop the formal memorandum outlining evaluation and accountability interrelationships for the department. As part of the process, support and professional development were provided and networks across schools with similar interests were formed. Schools carried out documentation of their methodologies for community building around evaluation, related to learning outcomes and culminating in sharing of resources through a central office learning exchange.

It became clear that the understanding of participation as primarily oriented to membership of functional groups (e.g. teachers or parents or administrators) in decision making was a seriously limited concept, often working against the inclusion of some groups and refusing to acknowledge significant differences among parents and among teachers, not to mention student groups. But these reworkings of the concepts were not accomplished by outside forums in which such matters were debated and explored, and new action was formulated, with input from all those involved. Rather, officials and support staff, and outside critical friends, played an important role in raising issues which might have been too difficult to address without assistance, or which might have remained among the taken-for-granted operational shibboleths of a group immersed in its own practice.

The principles upon which SIP aimed to hold its overall operations up to scrutiny, internally and externally, were directed towards achieving a more democratic schooling system, in terms of student access and in terms of greater success in open and two-way connections between schools and their communities. The school was thus treated as a microcosm of the rest of society, and the school system as in a position to support systemic and rigorous changes. Basil Bernstein's discussion of democracy and pedagogic rights outlines three rights necessary to achieve conditions for democratic schooling: individual enhancement; social, intellectual, cultural and personal inclusion;

and (political) participation, not only in terms of discourse but in terms of outcomes (Bernstein 1996: 6–7). These form a useful summary for understanding the practical hopes which SIP embodied as a state-wide initiative that was only as good as its continued support in schools. SIP tried to create a context of confidence in which individuals and groups of students, teachers and parents would be able to question, explore, develop judgements and see outcomes for their evaluative work, i.e. schools worked to *enhance* the contribution of individuals. Differences among the school community were seen as a resource to be worked with, despite the many practical and time-based activities needed to achieve an outcome. By directing explicit attention to the underlying/embedded values in the practices of schooling under investigation, SIP assisted schools in addressing the fundamental norms by which they operated, opening up to change the ordering of the system as a whole.

As more schools were funded and shared their resources, a number of outcomes can be briefly noted. Schools developed new methods for action-oriented evaluation and community building. The networking activities across schools gave different groupings in schools the opportunity to mix with others as speakers and as audiences, providing important different access to what had previously been largely professional domains of information and professional development. The 'bureaucracy' became 'peopled' rather than an organizational chart – people who were met and interacted with at regular policy development and overview evaluation activities for the initiative as a whole. Rather than rampant localism, privileging only the specific community around one school, community became a matter of diverse interests, including other school groups from different parts of the country, as well as representatives of organizations such as teachers' unions or parent associations, or head office administrators.

The African and African-American Curriculum Project

This project, which continues to be invented in various forms, has no clear beginning date; nor will it have a clear ending date short of the resolution of major racial injustices in the US educational system and the social structures which support them. Its origins lie in African-American community efforts towards more African-centred curriculum content, fuelled by the disproportionately high rates of suspensions and of referrals for special education evaluations for African-American students, particularly males. In the domain of school district educational policy and practice, though, work began in 1986 with a task force whose final report recommended more course offerings in African and African-American civilization and history, across the curriculum at all grades for all students, as a means to address the problems. From 1987 to 1989, various versions of an advisory committee were established, an outside consultant was hired (who withdrew after a year, citing differences within the district administration regarding the approach to and pace of the project's implementation), in-service workshops were held and a curriculum guide was developed. The guide was organized by grade level and subject area and consisted mainly of a set of 'infusible facts', intended to be incorporated into the everyday planning of teachers, supplementing rather than altering the 'regular' curriculum.

By 1989, a new consultant from the local university was involved, resulting in the recommendation that teachers who had a longstanding commitment to African-centred content and who had successfully worked with other teachers be invited to participate in the project. As sound as that procedure may have been, because of several factors including teachers' union policies, the initial list was expanded. After a series of conflicts, the newly formed, district-wide Multicultural Education Instructional Support Team (MEIST) began work in 1992. For all the meetings of the project, MEIST members were paid at an extra daily rate. In addition, 80 building liaisons were chosen to represent the staff from each of the district schools and to work with the MEIST group on curriculum and staff development issues. As a part of the effort, MEIST members participated in data collection and the analysis of some liaison meetings, which were used to identify issues and to plan subsequent sessions. The idea of action research as a potentially useful means for furthering the aims of the project was introduced to the group late in 1992. In 1993, the securing of external funding resulted in the ability to expand the MEIST to include recruits chosen by group members from their buildings, rather than from the usual methods determined by union contract. The focus of the funded project was on the development of 'study and practice groups', who would engage in collaborative action research in their school settings, focusing on curriculum and pedagogical changes in the area of 'multicultural education'. Monthly Saturday morning sessions were held with MEIST members, with additional sessions scheduled for work with building liaisons.

Through the work of MEIST, a change was initiated in the overall structure of the curriculum being developed. Instead of 'infusible facts' being added in, new lessons were developed which centred on an inquiry orientation to teaching and learning. Study and practice groups did in some cases develop, resulting in projects which were shared at a meeting towards the end of the funded project. Yet it was what occurred at those monthly sessions that was perhaps most significant. Tensions emerged between the original focus on the need for reforms to address injustices towards African-American students and the more global focus on 'multicultural education'. For many participants, the multicultural focus was seen as a way to derail needed discussions on racism and schooling, and the attention to action research was potentially a diffusion of the energy required to address the needs of the children in their classrooms. Much time was allocated to discussion and development of 'statements of common purpose', which emphasized both the diversity of the group and the shared commitments 'to changing the educational system from one that has been traditionally racist . . . to one that is fair and equitable to all people' (MEIST notes, 16 June 1993). As a result, attendance shifted racially across the months, as some who perhaps found the discussions too difficult or too diverting did not always attend.

The outcomes of the project cannot be evaluated in any standard sense of the word. There was a distinct form of community attempted. It was both a new form of social solidarity across difference and one which centred on older forms, most particularly African-American traditions of resistance in education. The creation of such a form of community is still in need of much work. From the standpoint of educational change, there are several aspects to note. First, action research was imported, as a 'grassroots' methodology, but into a context which did not recognize or necessarily support such efforts. While classroom innovations were clearly taking place in the district, there was not enough attention to building from these. The longer history of top-down curriculum development and the overall context of testing were not taken into consideration, although they clearly were part of the reform strategies and everyday worklife of some of the participants. Second, there was a need to work with communities of resistance that existed prior to the reform effort, not only communities that were advocating change but also those whose efforts resisted new ideas. Finally, a major outcome of the project was the idea that those involved in the process, particularly but not exclusively the European-American participants, needed to examine their own personal identities as a precursory but also concomitant aspect to the engagement in collaborative struggle for social and educational change.

Change-oriented projects

Action research, other forms of innovatory work and democratic evaluation have sometimes been justified in primarily Enlightenment terms, bolstering a notion of the critical individual, rationally engaging in choice for progress. This individualistic approach tends to over-valorize dominant groups' understandings of rationality and choice, rather than to emphasize the relation of reflection, action and interaction. Collaborative work in action research has been given little publicity, since much of what is written tends to be done either by academics or by students requiring individual assessment for certification or grading. In these projects, we suggest that a different notion of interrogating and developing shared values comes to the fore, one attuned to the work of Iris Marion Young (1990), for whom difference is seen as a necessary resource for democratic organization. Young argues that the individual and the community are all too often set up as an 'exhaustive dichotomy', each side of which can deny difference in favour of presumed unity. The projects described above clearly demonstrate non-predictable lines of fracture and difference, within the 'local' as well as within and across sites and interest groups. Yet it is only when such difference is accepted and worked with that shared and worthwhile products are derived from the effort put into them.

The school community provides a convenient and pragmatic boundary at one level: it defines who ought to be involved, who counts as the school community. At another level, however, it also suggests that the boundary of the school is necessarily permeable and unstable. Schools are part of wider 'systems', connected to authorities and policies, funding and conditions which are much broader than any single school or district can hope to affect. Their communities are characterized by much more than the local school. In providing a different way to consider community as centred in joint action, the participants may have developed a sense of being able to affect their local setting, complex as it is.

In the two projects analysed, we can see tendencies to address old problems in new ways and also the limits of these, both for the direct participants and for state educational reform initiatives. The significant constraints of operations of school systems within the diminishing fiscal capacities of the Western capitalist state continue to loom as a spectre over any reform effort in the public sector. Perhaps such projects serve to bolster optimism of the will to counteract the pessimism of the intellect. Stories about such projects are woven into the oral traditions of school change, providing further opportunities to develop sophisticated reflection and implications for action. Specific individuals recognize how their own settings and activities are shaped by wider contexts, and further understand the mechanisms of that shaping as they press against the constraints. This version of the individual is thus an instance in which 'individual' is defined not only singly but in relation to both community and context. The social constructed, historical nature of schooling and school systems is already apparent at local school sites, partly through the operation of projects such as these.

References

Appadurai, A. (1990) Difference in the global cultural economy. *Theory, Culture, and Society*, 7, 295–310.

Apple, M. W. (1979) *Ideology and Curriculum*. New York: Routledge.

Bernstein, B. (1996) *Pedagogy, Symbolic Control and Identity: Theory, Research, Critique*. London: Taylor & Francis.

Brennan, M. (1996) Multiple professionalisms for Australian teachers in the information age? In H. Simola and T. Popkewitz (eds) *Professionalization and Education*. Department of Teacher Education: University of Helsinki Research Report, pp. 200–31.

Brennan, M. and Hoadley, R. (1984) *School Self Evaluation*. Melbourne: Victorian Government Printing Office.

Brown, L. (1982) *Participatory Evaluation*. PEP Ideas Group. Mimeo. School Improvement Plan. Melbourne: Education Department of Victoria.

Clark, B. G. (1994) Collaborative process of writing and sharing. Symposium paper presented at the Fifteenth Annual Ethnography in Education Research Forum, Philadelphia, February.

Clark, S. (1990) *Ready from Within: a First Person Narrative*. Trenton, NJ: Africa World Press.

Hinsdale, M. A., Lewis, H. M. and Waller, S. M. (1995) *It Comes from the People: Community Development and Local Theology*. Philadelphia: Temple University Press.

Horton, M. and Freire, P. (1990) *We Make the Road by Walking: Conversations on Education and Social Change*. Philadelphia: Temple University Press.

Luke, T. (1996) Identity, meaning and globalization: detraditionalization in post-modern space-time compression. In P. Heelas, S. Lash and P. Morris (eds) *Detraditionalization: Critical Reflections on Authority and Identity*. Oxford: Basil Blackwell.

MacDonald, B. (1973) Evaluation and the control of education. In D. A. Tawney (ed.) *Curriculum Evaluation Today: Trends and Implications*. Basingstoke: Schools Council Research Studies/Macmillan.

Noffke, S. E. (1994) Uncovering the incredible Whiteness of being. Symposium paper presented at the Fifteenth Annual Ethnography in Education Research Forum, Philadelphia, February.

Noffke, S. E. (1996) Personal, professional, and political dimensions of action research. In M. W. Apple (ed.) *Review of Research in Education, Volume 22*. Washington, DC: American Educational Research Association, pp. 305–43.

Noffke, S. E., Clark, B. G., Palmeri-Santiago, J., Sadler, J. and Shujaa, M. (1996) Conflict, learning, and change in a school/university partnership: different worlds of sharing. *Theory into Practice*, 35(3), 165–72.

Palmeri-Santiago, J. (1994) Diversion and subversion: A case study in progress. Symposium paper presented at the Fifteenth Annual Ethnography in Education Research Forum, Philadelphia, February.

Reese, W. J. (1986) *Power and the Promise of School Reform: Grassroots Movements during the Progressive Era*. New York: Routledge.

Sadler, J. (1994) Diversion and subversion: a case study in progress. Symposium paper presented at the Fifteenth Annual Ethnography in Education Research Forum, Philadelphia, February.

Shujaa, M. (1994) Issues of self-location in the implementation of an African and African American curriculum project. Symposium paper presented at the Fifteenth Annual Ethnography in Education Research Forum, Philadelphia, February.

Shujaa, M. (1995) Cultural self meets cultural other in the African American experience: teachers' responses to a curriculum content reform. *Theory into Practice*, 34(3), 194–201.

Shujaa, M. (ed.) (1996) *Beyond Desegregation*. Thousand Oaks, CA: Corwin Press.

Soudien, C. (1996) Race, culture and curriculum development in the USA: a study of the process of introducing a multicultural dimension into the curriculum. *Curriculum Studies*, 4(1), 43–65.

Young, I. M. (1990) *Justice and the Politics of Difference*. Princeton, NJ: Princeton University Press.

6

Social change, subject matter – and the teacher

J. MYRON ATKIN

Much of this book centres on the settings in which schools operate and the impact of these conditions on the ways in which they and the teachers within them do or do not change. Community expectations have a strong effect on what happens in classrooms. So do norms of professional teaching practice. So does the organization of the school itself. Outside influences like these are receiving increasing attention not only because they are potent but, at least as importantly, because they are the factors most readily accessible to those who set educational policy. Thus, the most available policy instruments seem to reside *outside* the individual teacher: conditions of work, status, authority, professional socialization, organizational arrangements.

This chapter adds two elements to the picture that are somewhat different. First, it introduces images of the subject matter itself and what they imply for educational change. Second, it raises issues about the teacher as a person: who she is, who she wants to become, what she values and how her personal goals influence her view of desirable changes in her own classroom and school. There is a connection between the two.

A central goal of virtually all educational change is to affect the beliefs, skills and general perspective of the individual teacher. But individual beliefs and preferences seem to present an indistinct, elusive and seemingly inefficient target for school reformers. It is difficult to detect 'progress' in one's underlying attitudes and values. Even over relatively long periods of time in policy terms (like five years), change in these dimensions, if it occurs at all, tends to be modest. Nevertheless, students are as powerfully affected by how teachers view the world as by any other aspect of the teacher's thought and action, regardless of how accessible those thoughts might be, how well articulated they are or how readily they yield to the hopes of reformers. A focus on subject matter and associated beliefs of the teacher does not minimize the saliency of more contextually driven approaches to change. Instead, it receives attention in this chapter to illustrate the kinds of factors that must receive thoughtful attention if significant change is to take root in schools, and if otherwise plausible (and sometimes expensive) strategies are to have some of their intended effect.

When one is trying to understand the teacher's eye view of educational reform, there are at least two potentially relevant starting points. One might examine psychological factors: motivation, a sense of personal efficacy and the ability to deal with ambiguity, for example. One might also try to understand the personal *philosophical* predispositions and goals of the individual teacher – and their links to the priorities of educational innovators, reformers and policy makers. This chapter pursues the latter, particularly as it relates to curriculum content. The underlying assumption of this chapter is that the impetus to become a better teacher is connected intimately to the impetus to be a better human being, and, in the case of a teacher, both these factors have a foundation in *what* the teacher chooses to teach. Thus it attempts to examine teachers' personal images of their field, where the images might come from, what those images imply for teachers' professional satisfactions – and how all this influences educational reform.

Images of subject matter

Science teaching is used for illustrative purposes here for two reasons. First, the author has greater knowledge of science education. Second, it might be assumed that science is more objective than many other school subjects, and so reform in science education is somewhat less dependent on the personal and philosophical orientations of the teachers. To demonstrate otherwise may strengthen the argument about the connection between subject matter and personal values.

Science teachers voice many different reasons for believing their subject is important for students, and consequently tend to employ a range of images when talking about their work. Some teach to maximize the chances for their students to enter the college or university of their choice; much of their effort is designed to help students meet the entrance requirements of higher education institutions. Often that includes attaining competitive scores on certain examinations. Others accord priority to preparing students for technically oriented jobs on graduation, whether or not the students are likely to pursue formal schooling. In these cases, knowledge of the subject matter is viewed, at least in part, as a stepping stone to some other desired goal.

Some believe that because technology and science are increasing in their influence on human society, everyone must have deeper knowledge of these subjects and how to use them. This conviction applies both to helping students to make personal decisions wherein science knowledge seems relevant (about diet, about smoking, about sexual behaviour, for example) and to helping people to make decisions about public policy that appear to have a significant scientific or technical basis. Should public money be invested in cleaning up toxic waste sites? How much? Should the public support science research? If so, to what extent and for what purposes? What about investing in road building compared with public transport? Or funding for disease prevention? Citizens must have an informed basis for influencing public policy if democracy is to reflect the collective will.

The list goes on, and the differing goals are not necessarily mutually exclusive. Most teachers have many goals. Virtually all science teachers believe that the rate at which new scientific information is accumulating makes it impossible to be anything but superficial if coverage is the priority. So choices must be made. But on what basis? In the National Science Education Standards in the United States released in 1996 by the National Academy of Sciences, *inquiry* is the central *content* standard. The framers of the Standards place knowledge of how science works, to be acquired by having students engage personally and directly in scientific investigations, as the core objective. Their assumption is that such knowledge makes one a more intelligent consumer of science, whether or not one plans to pursue a career in the subject.

For further illustration, some teachers emphasize what might be called an aesthetic image of their subject. Science and mathematics reflect and reveal patterns and regularities. The world is not capricious. While every event may be unique, there are universal and consistent conditions operating. Apples do not fall down in some places, and up or sideways in others. (Or, when they seem to, the scientist's challenge is to demonstrate either that fundamental principles can account for such observations or that the principles must be revised.) Such teachers tend to select content that reveals the regularities in natural events, and perhaps the underlying beauty of such patterns. Many of them emphasize, too, the evidence that humans have used to reach such conclusions. Without it, they believe, both the understanding of the principle and the appreciation of it may be superficial and inadequate. They have an image of science as investigation.

Changing images

Images of desirable science education not only coexist at any particular period of time, they change over the decades. In the early nineteenth century in the United States, science was used as a vehicle to teach children about the wonders wrought by the Deity and about the virtues of obeying one's parents. On a walk in the countryside in one book for children, curiosity is aroused when the youngsters hear an echo. Father explains the phenomenon and demonstrates. Then they see a flower. With the aid of a magnifier, father names the parts and some of their functions. But then he concludes the lesson by pointing out that the complexity and beauty of the flower surpasses the ingenuity of man, so the flower proves the existence of God. As the children continue their walk, one of them trips and skins his knee. This event accords father an opportunity to lecture for several pages about the matter of carelessness in untied shoestrings – and note that if the boy had listened to his mother that morning, he would not have bloodied his knee. Thus the image of science teaching was one of helping children to appreciate a wonderful and awesome world – towards the end of revealing a divine presence. Closely linked, apparently, were lessons about family virtues, like obedience to parental authority.

In the late nineteenth century, the goal of science teaching shifted to training of the mind. It was the height of faculty psychology: the mind is composed of various faculties that must be exercised to develop properly. Some of the 'lower' faculties, fit for younger children, were identified as observation and memorization. ('Higher' faculties, like generalization and reasoning, were thought to be developmentally appropriate for older students, and provided justification for teaching subjects like Latin and formal grammar.) In England, a science education movement called Object Teaching was invented, which spread aggressively to the United States. This approach to science education derived its name from the fact that various objects were brought to school to be examined carefully by the students. Children learned a range of adjectives to demonstrate their ability to observe carefully. The teachers' guide listed the adjectives to be learned by students between ages 10 and 12: vitrifiable, oleaginous, ductile and argillaceous, for example. Then they were to memorize the adjectives, to develop the faculty of memorization. Based on the precepts of faculty psychology, the teachers' guide carefully spelled out which observations were to come first and which later.

While it is still commonplace today to cite psychological theories and their associated images of mental activity (constructivism, multiple intelligences, recent neurological research on how the brain functions), teaching approaches derived from other social and behavioural science theories and images compete powerfully. It is unlikely that any widespread teaching movement of the past 200 years was based as strongly as Object Teaching on a particular theory of how the mind works, in this case a muscular image: the mind develops through exercise of the distinctive faculties of which it is capable. The major volume for teachers on the subject (Sheldon's *Lessons on Objects*) went through at least 62 editions and prevailed for students in England and the United States for several decades.

In the early twentieth century, the purpose of science teaching shifted to the study of nature. The reason? Urbanization was coming to be seen as a critical social issue. The muckrakers were turning their attention to every form of corruption. The cities are evil, dirty and sinful, in every sense. The countryside is pure and beautiful. How are we to keep the new generation on the farm? The response was to devise a new set of priorities for science education that came to be called Nature Study. The objective was to teach about plants and animals in the countryside in a way that would lead children to love nature. 'Love', in fact, was prominent in exhortations to teachers about the new subject, replacing the image of exercising mental faculties that characterized Object Teaching.

To achieve this goal, for the first time in science teaching, a strong anthropomorphic emphasis began to appear. The way children could be helped to love nature was to begin to see plant and animal life as similar to people. It was in the early 1900s that the birds began to talk with the trees, and mature flowers gave lectures to flower buds. Most of the conversation, however, was about their respective parts, so a large amount of technical botanical and zoological information presumably was conveyed. Thus the mature flower told the bud about the stamens, anthers, petals, pistils and ovaries it would have when it became an adult. Even the non-living world was portrayed differently: electrons, for example, sprouted legs in textbook illustrations and ran through wires to simulate current flow when voltage was applied.

With rapid technological progress in the second and third decades of the twentieth century, the purposes of teaching science shifted again. It was possible to enter a vehicle on the east coast of the United States and be on the west coast in little more than a day, much faster than even the railways. Electrically powered subterranean trains began to rumble under the biggest cities, and widespread distribution of electric power made gaslight obsolete everywhere. Central heating was introduced. It was no longer necessary for ice to be delivered frequently to prevent food from rotting. Vaccines were developed to eliminate previously dreaded childhood diseases like diphtheria. It seemed to be the dawn of a new scientific and technological age that would bring rich and lasting benefits. Human life was being transformed to eliminate drudgery and dramatically reduce the incidence of life-threatening diseases.

Science teaching began to change to reflect these influences. Since automobiles were becoming common, instruction was introduced about the four-stroke-cycle petrol-engine. Children were taught about the development of vaccines to prevent disease. Thirteen-year-olds made models of hot water home-heating systems. They were taught about Bernoulli's principle and aeroplane lift, about contour ploughing, about the principles of refrigeration. They wired model houses to demonstrate home electrification, including the characteristics of parallel and series circuits and how fuses work. The emphasis, in short, was on applications of science in daily life. Science was pursued to make life safer, more productive, and to relieve humans for other pursuits.

The Second World War, however, produced major changes. Scientific effort during the war produced awesome weapons that altered the course of the conflict. Furthermore, much of the science that underlay the most dramatic new weaponry, the atomic bomb, was the product of 'basic' research. That is, it flowed from an attempt to understand some fundamental principles of matter. Such an intellectual activity was seen before the war as a pursuit that engaged unworldly and impractical people. In August 1945, though, everyone learned how very consequential such thought could be. It turned out that the abstract $e = mc^2$ has awesome results.

Soon after the war, some of the very scientists responsible for developing the bomb (and radar, and jet aircraft, and rockets) turned their attention to the improvement of science education – and they turned sharply from the emphasis on applications that characterized the 1920s and 1930s. Students in school should learn about the kind of 'basic' science that captured the interest of the most accomplished of the nation's researchers. It was, after all, these pursuits that led to advances that not only shortened the war but perhaps made victory possible. With support from a new federal agency, the National Science Foundation (NSF), new courses were created for elementary and secondary schools, and the university-based scientists determined the content to be selected.

It may be interesting to students to learn about house wiring and the principles of refrigeration, but these are not the sorts of topics that engage the most advanced physicists, the public was told. Research scientists are interested in puzzling about such matters as the nature of light. In what ways does it behave like waves? In what ways like particles? With support from the NSF, a new physics course was developed that reflected the priorities of the most prestigious scientists in the academic community. There were similar developments in chemistry and biology. In mathematics, some outstanding researchers contributed to wartime developments by intellectual accomplishments like cracking enemy codes, and thereby saved thousands of lives. They turned to the curriculum of the elementary and secondary schools and introduced topics like set and number theory, to replace the study of topics like compound interest and consumer discount problems. They introduced the 'new maths'. As was the case for science, the new educational approaches were advanced by a group of highly recognized scholars who had gained credibility and legitimacy from their wartime accomplishments.

Beliefs about the social relevance of science – and the nature of science itself

Today, priorities in science education – images of the most desirable future for this subject in the lives of students – are more contested. Scientists are no longer the dominant group in determining the science content that is to be taught in elementary and secondary schools. For one thing, they no longer enjoy the unusually high esteem in which they were held in the decades immediately after the war. Their own priorities with respect to the science research agenda are scrutinized more closely by sceptical legislatures intent on reducing public expenditure; in a budget-cutting climate, basic research and the priorities of those that pursue it tend to lose out to scientific and technical initiatives that promise relatively quick and practical results. Even the NSF expanded its support of research in engineering dramatically in the 1980s.

But that is not the only reason why their influence in matters educational has declined. Teachers themselves have become more assertive, not only about their conditions of employment but about what they teach. Part of that assertiveness reflects a greater inclination to claim professional prerogatives. They argue, for example, that they must serve a more varied student population than was the case 30 years ago. A much higher proportion of the age cohort stays in school for the number of years required for graduation. Furthermore, a higher percentage speaks some language other than English, and fewer are academically oriented. To reach this more inclusive group, content must centre on topics of greater immediate relevance to the students, they say. There seems to be greater interest in the general public, as well, in more overtly practical aims. Environmental problems are seen as serious and requiring amelioration. So, too, with the maintenance of personal and community health. There is also a need to enhance employment prospects in a society that becomes ever more technical – as well as a perception that national economic competitiveness must be strengthened for the country to prosper. All of this exerts pressure for devising a curriculum that emphasizes the personal and social aspects of science.

A curriculum based on such concerns requires information that is highly contextualized. It prizes knowledge that relates to specific circumstances. There is often a premium on action. What must be done to reduce pollution in *this* stream? What diet makes sense in *my* family? Deliberations about such matters depend in considerable measure on local knowledge. Furthermore, the aim of science education moves towards a conception of schools as producers of knowledge, not solely as transmitters (see Kelley-Laine and Posch 1991).

In these matters, the teacher's perspective on the content of greatest relevance assumes greater saliency. Practical matters like arresting environmental deterioration call for a different view of the nature of science and science education from an emphasis on understanding the ways in which light is wavelike and the ways in which it seems to behave like a particle. Furthermore, practical issues – improving the dietary habits of a family, figuring out the best way to prevent heat loss from a private residence, deciding on whether or not a community should construct a new sewage treatment facility – are quite concrete. The aim is to act wisely and well, not solely to understand the general principle. In such deliberations, there is often no single best answer, as there typically is in science instruction aimed at helping students to comprehend scientific principles of broad applicability, which has been the typical goal of science instruction. Factors that must be considered include what is prudent, what is required (by law, for example) and what is moral. The emphasis shifts from the abstract to the concrete, from thought and reflection to action, from the timeless to the timely.

For some teachers, this image of science is deeply troubling. What happens if science education policy begins to move strongly towards the applications of their subject to social issues that face the community? If the students are expected to reach conclusions about actions that might be taken to ameliorate water pollution or its effects, the outcome is unlikely to be clear and unambiguous. Different interests in the community are inevitably at play in determining such policy, and the relevant considerations often turn towards risk, probabilities and values (see, for example, Posch 1993). To develop the knowledge necessary for an acceptable course of action, there must be a significant level of interaction between the people who develop a course of action and those who are affected by it.

In some cases, it is precisely these features of the issue that represent the territory that the teacher hoped to avoid when she chose to become a science teacher. Many teachers entered science because they had an image of an authoritative subject with a high degree of certainty and predictability. Many mathematics teachers were attracted to their discipline because of the precision they saw in the subject. To move into science instruction that seems more ambiguous and subject to social pressures, like deciding on the site of a sewage treatment facility, is to move to a subject that does not match the teacher's own view of herself and what she stands for.

Teachers are intimately connected not only to the general ethos of a service-oriented profession, then, they are also linked to the subjects they teach. More to the point of this chapter, they often identify personally with the image their subject projects. If science teaching – and science itself – is less about certainty and more about particular circumstance, there can be a sense of deep unease. And it is a very personal matter, not solely a question of shifting professional priorities. For many, the images they hold of their subject are a reflection of themselves. There is a sense, for many teachers, that they *are* their subject. To change the subject in a way that challenges some long-held assumptions is to call into question one's own personhood.[1]

Teachers' images of their subject and educational reform

Images of the subject count when one is devising strategies for educational change, and they can be deep. This point is often recognized and addressed only tangentially, if it is considered at all. Fortunately for those who seek changes in schools, focusing on core values is not entirely new territory. Modifying a school's organization or developing a new plan for student assessment can also touch people profoundly and personally. Many innovations in education affect deeply held beliefs of the teachers (and parents, too, which may be one reason why they are often controversial). When students work in small groups on different projects, some people see a weakening of the central role of the teacher. When students examine conflicting viewpoints about personal and social issues, some people believe the school risks the promotion of behaviour that may not comport with community norms. Almost any sort of change in school that affects either teaching or curriculum content can touch sensitively on core convictions.

The difference with regard to images of subject matter is that changes in curriculum can call into question the nature of knowledge itself.[2] This territory is less familiar in the literature of educational change, despite the fact that it has always been a powerful factor, as we have seen in the case of Object Teaching, Nature Study and the other curriculum movements in the history of science education. Questions about the nature of science and mathematics are not new. It is just that the mainstream group of today's educational reformers tends to focus most of its resources on other characteristics of schools and schooling: how schools track students, for example, or how they do or do not foster democratic values, or how they can accord equitable conditions for all students. To these kinds of important and controversial issues, it is claimed here, they must also add perspectives on changes in the subjects themselves. No less than serving an ever more varied student group or figuring out how to accord teachers the flexibility they need to respond to unpredictable circumstances, strategies need to be devised that recognize just how deeply projected changes in subject matter itself can challenge the images teachers have of *themselves* as the custodians and proponents of their disciplines. It is not an easy or simple matter.

Notes

1 For this formulation and much else in this chapter about the connection between subject matter and teacher identity, I am indebted to Jenifer Helms. See, particularly, Helms (1998).

2 Much of the conceptual analysis regarding the interactive development of knowledge in the formulation of policy was developed in the field of evaluation. See, for example, MacDonald (1977 and 1987).

References

Helms, J. V. (1998) Science – and Me: subject matter and identity in secondary school science teachers. *Journal of Research in Science Teaching*, 35(7), 811–34.

Kelly-Laine, K. and Posch, P. (1991) *Environment, Schools and Active Learning*. Paris: OECD.

MacDonald, B. (1977) Evaluation and the control of education. In D. Hamilton *et al.* (eds) *Beyond the Numbers Game*. Berkeley, CA: McCutchan.

MacDonald, B. (1987) *Research and Action in the Context of Policing*. Norwich: Centre for Applied Research in Education.

Posch, P. (1993) Research issues in environmental education. *Studies in Science Education*, 21, 21–48.

PART III

Conceptualizing school change processes

7

Changing school cultures

CHRISTINE FINNAN AND HENRY M. LEVIN

Introduction

Through the important work of educational change researchers, exemplified by Barry MacDonald (1986), Peter Posch (1996) and others (e.g. Cuban 1984; Evans 1996; Fullan and Hargreaves 1996), the 'black box' of what happens in schools when innovations are implemented and school change occurs (or doesn't occur) has been opened. One of the discoveries within this 'black box' is that schools have a culture. In this chapter we attempt to explain how different conceptualizations of school culture influence our understanding of how and why schools change. We suggest that action research as well as other deep processes of inquiry by members of school communities lead to systematic reflection and understanding of school practices and serve as an impetus to change. Action research processes make participants more aware of the fact that their school has a culture, and give them the tools to change the culture to improve student learning.

What is school culture?

School culture describes both the sameness and the uniqueness of each school. When one enters almost any school one is struck by how familiar it is. There is something about the place that just says 'school' – a place to provide a site for teaching and learning – that is palpable. Most schools share a similar design for classrooms and common areas, organize the day in predictable ways and develop recognizable patterns for relationships among the students and adults. Despite these similarities, it is easy to recognize the differences and uniqueness of each school. Even the casual observer will recognize that each school feels, looks, sounds and smells different from any other school. It is the culture of schooling and the culture of each school that account for the common and the unique.

The concept of culture, whether used to describe schools or larger societies, is not easy to define. It is something that surrounds us, gives meaning to our world and is constantly being constructed both through our interactions with others and through our reflections on life and our world. Culture is so implicit in what we do that it dulls our knowledge that it is there. Margaret Mead is credited with saying of culture that it is like fish and water – fish will be the last creatures to discover water. It surrounds and nurtures us, even when we can't see it.

Two features of culture are important to delineate for the purpose of this chapter. First, culture exists at societal, localized and personal levels. At a societal level, culture provides meaning and a web of understanding to otherwise diverse groups of people. Culture at a societal level can be as large a concept as Western or Eastern culture, the culture of childhood or, as in this case, the culture of schooling. Culture at a societal level serves essentially as an umbrella of agreement among otherwise diverse people. Because of a culture of childhood, for example, children from different parts of the world can play together even when they lack a common language.

Culture also exists at a more localized or discrete level. At this level, people with a shared geography, religion, ethnicity, occupation or workplace (such as a school) share a culture. It is this level of culture that is usually the focus of study by anthropologists or sociologists. Ethnographic studies of schools, such as those by Wolcott (1967; 1973), Peshkin (1978) and McQuillan (1997), provide in-depth pictures of the culture of an individual school.

Culture resides both within and between people (Brunner 1996; Evans 1996). At this personal level, culture provides a frame for making sense of the world while it shapes our interactions with people within it (Spindler and Spindler 1982). It is through individual action and perceptions, at this personal level, that we see culture manifested.

The second feature of culture that is critical to a discussion of change is the seemingly contradictory fact that culture is both conservative and ever changing. On the one hand, culture is essentially conservative, protecting people from the unknown, providing answers to what would otherwise be unanswerable (Shein 1992; Evans 1996: 44). By providing these answers, it also restricts our objectivity; it shapes our judgements of what is good, beautiful, valuable etc. (Spindler and Spindler 1982; McDermott and Varenne 1995; McQuillan 1997). On the other hand, culture is also ever changing (Wax 1993: 109). It adapts to influences from other cultures and from changes in the physical, social and political environment. In the following discussion of school culture change, we explain that culture's resistance and responsiveness to change rest in part on whether we are talking about culture at the societal or localized level and if we are discussing the surface manifestations of culture or the basic beliefs and assumptions that underlie it.

At the societal level, school culture is more appropriately termed the culture of schooling. It is at this level that culture appears to be most conservative and resistant to change, because it exists primarily at an abstract, generalized level. The culture of schooling creates and perpetuates the image members of our society call forth when they think of education, schools and schooling. Since one cannot see or know all schools, it is comforting to hold a belief that schools in general remain the same, even as changes occur in individual schools. The effect of the culture of schooling is visible in such concrete aspects of schooling as the design of schools and the organization of classrooms. Because of a shared culture of schooling, we can visit nearly any school in the United States (and in most corners of the world) and know that we are in a place called a school or that we are seeing something called 'education' taking place. The shared culture of schooling is responsible for the stability in the size and design of classrooms (Tyack and Tobin 1994), in the persistence of school activities and practices that have characterized schooling since the beginning of the twentieth century (Cuban 1984) and in the egg crate structure vividly described by Lortie (1975). The culture of schooling perpetuates a view of schooling in which teachers are responsible for the transmission of knowledge and culture and for shaping the minds of children (Spindler 1987; Spindler and Spindler 1990). For this reason, the public is most comfortable when the teaching/learning process is dominated by a teacher and textbooks. Many people assume that learning can occur only when the teacher orchestrates it from the front of the class.

The culture of schooling perpetuates a set of basic beliefs and assumptions that include: what schools should teach; how children should learn; who should learn what; who should be teaching; how schools should be run and organized; how students should be sorted; and schools' role in addressing broader social issues. That these basic beliefs and assumptions exist in the United States and in other countries does not mean that we agree on how every minute detail should be played out in individual schools (e.g. we can still disagree about the importance of desegregation and about the role of prayer in schools). These basic beliefs within our culture of schooling lead to interesting dichotomies. For example, one common assumption shared by most of the US population is that there is a crisis in public education (Mathews 1996; Sarason 1996), even though most people are satisfied with their own children's school (Berliner and Biddle 1995).

Change and constancy

We use the term 'school culture' to describe the unique culture of each school; this is culture at the local level. A school's culture accounts for why it feels, looks, sounds and smells different from any other school. Specific school cultures are moulded by the unique and shared experiences of participants, which are influenced by their class, race and neighbourhood as well as the school's history and its leadership. Unlike the culture of schooling, school culture is constantly changing. It accommodates a continuous influx of new people (administrators, faculty, students, parents), new directives from the district and from state and federal agencies, and new directions recommended by professional organizations, institutions of higher education and unions. To say that school cultures resist change is to discount the mini-changes that happen daily in every school around the world and the larger ones that take place over time. For example, a new school principal may shift the school from one in which teachers participate in decision making to one in which the principal makes all decisions and evaluates the responsiveness of personnel to his dictates. School cultures may not change in the ways external change agents want, but they do change.

Studies of change have found that most changes are at a somewhat superficial level. Sarason (1996) describes these as type B changes. They occur when teachers choose to post student work in the halls, when they change seating arrangements to allow for more group work, when the school sets up a computer lab and when parents are named to site councils. Changes at a slightly deeper level occur when teachers change their way of delivering instruction and when schools allow for more shared decision making. Real, sustained change, however, does not occur unless basic beliefs and assumptions also change. For example, if expectations about the role of adults in the school do not change, school site councils and shared decision making will be no more than what Fullan and Hargreaves (1996) describe as 'contrived colleagiality'. The following text details five critical components of the basic beliefs and assumptions that shape school culture. If school culture is to be truly changed, these basic beliefs and assumptions must be addressed.

The first is the school's expectations for children. The basic beliefs and assumptions of a school's culture undergird a tacit acceptance that the students, as a whole, are capable of performing at a certain level academically, physically and emotionally. No school explicitly states that it has low expectations for children, but studies comparing schools serving students in at-risk situations and those serving middle-class and upper middle-class students point to markedly different expectations of students of similar ability levels at the different schools (Wilcox 1982; Oakes 1985; Page 1987; Hanson 1990). The signs of different expectations are subtle but evident, even at the elementary school level. Schools serving lower-income students often stress following directions, while the middle-class students learn to think more critically (Wilcox 1982). Teachers of low-income students often place more emphasis on discipline, and children's experiences are circumscribed because of concerns that they will not behave appropriately if given challenging or enriching experiences or provided with too much independence.

A second feature of a school culture's basic beliefs and assumptions includes children's expectations for their own school experience. Student expectations for their own school experience are shaped both by the explicit and subtle messages that they receive from adult members of the school community and by the trust placed in education by their community. Examinations of the chronic school failure of indigenous ethnic and racial minority students point to the development of an oppositional culture among such students (Fordham and Ogbu 1986; Solomon 1992). This theory holds that minority students, usually high school students, believe that the notion of achieving economic success through school success is a cruel hoax. They see in their community the results of years of inequity, and they develop an opposition to all avenues to mainstream success. Other minorities – those arriving in the United States as immigrants – often succeed in school, largely because they live in communities that brought with them a belief in education as a route to success, and they do not have a history of subordination in the United States (Ogbu 1987; Suarez-Orozco 1989).

A third set of basic beliefs and assumptions includes expectations for adults. The expectations for adult members of the school community depend largely on the characteristics of the students. Expectations for teachers are shaped by the students they teach (Metz 1978), and expectations for parents draw largely from the characteristics of their children. Teachers and administrators working in schools serving at-risk children often feel inferior to their colleagues in more affluent schools. Typically the staff and administrative turnover at schools serving at-risk students is great, and there is a feeling that only the poorest teachers and administrators remain in such schools (even though some very good teachers and administrators choose to teach in schools serving at-risk children). The lower expectations for children feed the lower expectations the staff have for themselves. The staff members are often reluctant to try new ideas because they are afraid that the ideas will not work with 'our children'. As staff members withdraw from challenging themselves with new ideas, they lose confidence in themselves.

Differences in expectations for parents are also evident. Schools with high expectations for all students treat parents as partners in the education of the children. Parental opinion is valued, and involvement in their children's education is taken for granted. Where expectations for children are low, however, expectations for parents are also low. Instead of having their opinion valued, parents of children in these schools are seen as a problem and a hindrance to their child's development (Lightfoot 1978; Fine 1991).

Opinions about acceptable educational practices form a fourth set of basic beliefs and assumptions. A school's culture also provides support for the educational practices used in the school. The nature of these practices is related to expectations for students and adults and to the mission of the school. Where expectations for students and teachers are low, beliefs about appropriate educational practices lead to an emphasis on rote memorization and basic skills. School cultures fostering high expectations for students and teachers emphasize active learning and challenging curriculum. Schools that base their mission on an identifiable philosophy of education (e.g. Montessori schools, bilingual schools, back to basics or open classroom schools) can assume that opinions on acceptable educational practice are shared by all members of the school community, and this philosophy shapes all school practices. In many schools, the culture allows for considerable variation among teachers on how and what to teach. This does not usually arise from a respect for diverse teaching strategies but from limited discourse among teachers and a lack of communication with parents on effective teaching.

Basic beliefs and assumptions about the desirability of change also shape school culture. In the USA most public school decisions are made at the district or state level, creating a sense of powerlessness among personnel at the school site. Teachers and administrators often actively and passively resist externally imposed change (Shein 1992) because the proposed changes do not fit their school culture, are not well designed or are not presented in an understandable way. There are schools, however, that encourage and foster change and continuous improvement, especially if the changes build on the strengths of the existing school culture (Deal 1990).

Origins and consequences of school culture

The preceding discussion focuses on school culture as it currently shapes and is shaped by the school, but an important determinant of school culture is the history of the school – both real and perceived. Most schools have a history that moulds both the structure and culture of the school (Schlechty 1991). The origins of the school, the population it has served, its unique claims and accomplishments all constitute this background. From this history come heroes and villains, ceremonies, rituals, legends and stories. These are very important links to the community and can give children the feeling that they are attending school in an important place, and that by being a part of this school, they too will 'make history'. Alternatively, as in many inner cities, it can also create the impression that the school is for losers, affecting teaching and learning roles and expectations negatively. It is impossible to understand the organization of a school without examining what preceded the current organization.

We have referred primarily to the collective nature of school culture, encompassing beliefs, practices, operations and expectations of the school community. But individuals who join the school as staff, parents and students also have personal histories which reinforce school culture through self-selection. The involvement of participants in a school is hardly a random event. Students from fairly homogeneous neighbourhoods attend schools that reflect community values, aspirations and expectations. Even when choosing public schools outside their neighbourhoods and private schools, families select school environments that reinforce their beliefs about what schools should do. School staff tend to choose the environment and practices that they feel most attracted to and comfortable with. At the same time, new participants are socialized into the culture of the school and its practices and role expectations. Over time those who feel themselves to be sufficiently in conflict with the dominant culture of the school and who are unable to adapt will leave. For these reasons, the culture of a school can show great stability over time, even as new participants join it and others depart.

It is important to acknowledge school culture explicitly because it has consequences for both stability and change. We have emphasized the stability and conserving nature of school culture, in that it is like a vast web of intricate and interlocking ideas, values, beliefs and practices that protect the school from change. Both societally and locally it protects participants from external pressures for change because of its comprehensive and ubiquitous nature. Pressures for change tend to be piecemeal and can only pierce a small part of this protective web, while the vast remainder remains intact. In this respect school culture serves as a barrier to change and effectively fends off attempts to transform the school (Cuban 1984).

But one can use school culture as a vehicle for effecting and sustaining change, rather than trying to undermine it directly or get around it surreptitiously. It is unfortunate that school culture is viewed only as a conserving force and not one that might be used for transformation. We have found that when schools are provided with both pressures for change and the tools to transform their culture, remarkable changes in school culture can take place (Finnan 1992, 1996). Our own experience shows that this can take place locally when members of the school community recognize a pressing need to change and are provided with a shared process in which they can address the most fundamental aspects of their functioning. Such a process must establish a shared language, a process for ongoing communication, research and professional interactions, a highly participatory governance structure that incorporates all members and the involvement of significant other parts of the educational system to support the process of change (MacDonald 1986; Evans 1996; Fullan and Hargreaves 1996; Posch 1996).

The Accelerated Schools Project and school culture change

The Accelerated Schools Project (Hopfenberg *et al.* 1993; Finnan *et al.* 1996; Levin 1996) is a notable example of an educational reform movement that recognizes the importance of working within the context of each school's existing culture. The project began in 1986 with just two pilot schools and a collaborative philosophy to accelerate the learning of all students, especially those at risk of failure, to bring all students into the academic mainstream. This represented a major cultural shift for these schools. Instead of imposing particular changes in curriculum or instructional strategies on schools, the project introduces a process by which the school takes over its own destiny and that of its students. This process includes fundamental explorations of all dimensions of the school, the construction of a living vision and goals, a setting of priorities, a governance system in which all participate, a systematic approach to action research and problem-solving, and an overall pedagogy, called powerful learning, that enlists the entire school to develop constructivist solutions to learning challenges.

Since 1986, the Accelerated Schools Project has spread to about 1,000 elementary and middle schools in 40 states, with 12 regional centres to provide support and about 300 trained coaches who follow up schools. The project's philosophy and process address each of the five components of school culture listed above, which helps school communities to reflect on their existing culture and make changes, resulting in a culture that supports increased learning for all children.

In relation to expectations for children, the Accelerated Schools Project is based on the belief that all children respond favourably to the enriched learning environment usually reserved for students identified as gifted and talented. The project recognizes that many low income, minority students come to school with experiences, beliefs and expectations that differ from those of middle-class white and Asian students. When these differences are seen as strengths rather than weaknesses, and are not used as excuses to lower expectations of children, student achievement and behaviour improve.

When adults begin to hold higher expectations for children, the children begin to raise their expectations for their own school experience. In accelerated schools, the curriculum, instruction and course sequences become increasingly challenging. Rather than being alienated or overwhelmed, most students rise to the challenge and exhibit increased pride in themselves and in their school, and increased achievement (National Center for the Accelerated Schools Project 1997).

The democratic decision-making process and governance structure of the Accelerated Schools Project encourages higher expectations for adults associated with the school. Teachers and parents are given the tools to work collaboratively to bring about research-based change. Parents and teachers form cadres devoted to the systematic investigation of challenges and solutions to problems. Even when parents are unable to meet regularly with the cadres (owing to work and family obligations), they become more engaged in the school through outreach by the cadres and through their child's enthusiasm for learning. Through taking responsibility for change, teachers and parents develop more confidence in their ability to work productively with children and in their role in making a difference in their school.

The Accelerated Schools Project is explicit about acceptable educational practice. The project is built upon a concept of 'powerful learning' – learning that is authentic, interactive, learner-centred, inclusive and continuous (Keller and Heubner 1997). Many schools join the Accelerated Schools Project because their school community members want to move away from the emphasis on drill and practice that characterizes many schools serving students in at-risk situations. Through the development of a shared vision, accelerated school communities work towards a common goal of providing powerful learning experiences to all children. Teachers share their excitement over new ways to promote student learning with colleagues, and they increasingly work together to build on each other's strengths.

By joining the Accelerated Schools Project, schools demonstrate a desire for change. Schools engage in an extended investigation of the project (Chenoweth and Kushman 1996) prior to joining, and at least 90 per cent of the full-time teaching staff must vote to join the Accelerated Schools Project. Everyone knows that the project will bring about change, but the change will be of their design, not the design of the district office, the state or a local university. The Accelerated Schools Project creates an environment where change is seen as natural and desirable. This is not to say that change is always easy or that all members of the school community embrace personal change, but the structure exists within the school to effect change at both the surface level and the level of basic beliefs and assumptions.

It is noteworthy to report that even with success in transforming school culture within individual school sites and school communities, changing societal culture is more problematic. The reasons are fairly obvious. At the local site the participants interact with each other on a regular basis and are able to put their ideas into practice, to test them for their consequences. But at a societal level there are not the close interactions or participation that allow for such intensive scrutiny and testing. Instead, the culture of schooling is carried around in the form of a more abstract set of beliefs, values, habits and expectations that cannot be scrutinized through direct evaluation and practice. For this reason, it would seem that it is only when there is a large enough mass of transformed institutions that the societal culture of schooling is challenged and transformed. Far from discouraging attempts at changing school culture at individual sites, this should encourage it along a more ambitious scale to get to the point where the societal culture of schooling is challenged (Carnoy and Levin 1985).

Summary

In this chapter we have attempted to define and discuss school culture in its societal, localized and personal dimensions. We have also shown how the culture of schooling shapes processes that take place in schools and thus can limit or promote educational goals held by policy makers. In turn, we suggested a number of salient dimensions of school culture and why they are central to defining a school. We identified both school history and personal history of school participants as moulding and reinforcing school culture. Finally, we examined the consequences of school culture for stability and change, setting out some dimensions for internal transformation of schools. We concluded with an illustration from the Accelerated Schools Project which has applied these dimensions successfully to the internal transformation of school culture.

References

Berliner, D. and Biddle, B. (1995) *The Manufactured Crisis: Myths, Fraud, and the Attack on America's Public Schools*. New York: Addison-Wesley.

Brunner, J. (1996) *The Culture of Education*. Cambridge, MA: Harvard University Press.

Carnoy, M. and Levin, H. M. (1985) *Schooling and Work in the Democratic State*. Stanford, CA: Stanford University Press.

Chenoweth, T and Kushman, J. (1996) Building shared meaning and commitment during the courtship phase. In C. Finnan *et al.* (eds) *Accelerated Schools in Action.: Lessons from the Field*. Thousand Oaks, CA: Corwin Press, pp. 82–103.

Cuban, L. (1984) *How Teachers Taught*. New York: Longman.

Deal, T. (1990) Reframing reform. *Educational Leadership*, 47(8), 6–12.

Evans, R. (1996) *The Human Side of School Change: Reform, Resistance, and the Real-life Problems of Innovation*. San Francisco: Jossey-Bass.

Fine, M. (1991) *Framing Dropouts*. Albany: State University of New York Press.

Finnan, C. (1992) Becoming an accelerated middle school: initiating school culture change. Report prepared for the National Center for the Accelerated Schools Project, Stanford University, Stanford, CA.

Finnan, C. (1996) Making change our friend. In C. Finnan *et al.* (eds) *Accelerated Schools in Action: Lessons from the Field*. Thousand Oaks, CA: Corwin Press, pp. 104–23.

Finnan,C., St John, E., McCarthy, J. and Slovacek, S. (eds) (1996) *Accelerated Schools in Action: Lessons from the Field*. Thousand Oaks, CA: Corwin Press.

Fordham, S. and Ogbu, J. (1986) Black students' school success: coping with the 'burden of acting white'. *The Urban Review*, 18(3), 176–206.

Fullan, M. and Hargreaves, A. (1996) *What's Worth Fighting for in Your School?* New York: Teachers College Press.

Hanson, S. (1990) The college-preparatory curriculum across schools: access to similar learning opportunities? In R. Page and L. Valli (eds) *Curriculum Differentiation*. Albany: State University of New York Press.

Hopfenberg, W., Levin, H. M. *et al.* (1993) *The Accelerated Schools Resource Guide*. San Francisco: Jossey-Bass.

Keller, B. and Huebner, T. (1997) Powerful learning in accelerated schools: researching the opportunities for implementation as well as impediments of developing powerful learning school-wide. Paper presented at the annual meeting of the American Educational Research Association, Chicago, 24–28 March.

Levin, H. M. (1996) Accelerated schools after eight years. In L. Schauble and R. Glaser (eds) *Innovations in Learning*. Mahwah, NJ: Lawrence Ehrlbaum Associates, pp. 329–52.

Lightfoot, S. L. (1978) *Worlds Apart: Relationships between Families and Schools*. New York: Basic Books.

Lortie, D. (1975) *Schoolteacher*. Chicago: University of Chicago Press.

McDermott, R. and Varenne, H. (1995) Culture as disability. *Anthropology and Education Quarterly*, 26(3), 324–48.

MacDonald, B. (ed.) (1986) Coming to Terms with Research. Norwich: Centre for Applied Research in Education, University of East Anglia.

McQuillan, P. (1997) *Educational Opportunity in an Urban American High School*. Albany: State University of New York Press.

Mathews, D. (1996) *Is There a Public for Public Schools?* Dayton, OH: Kettering Foundation Press.

Metz, M. H. (1978) *Classrooms and Corridors: The Crisis of Authority in Desegregated Secondary Schools*. Berkeley: University of California Press.

Metz, M. (1986) *Different by Design: Politics, Purpose and Practice in Three Magnet Schools*. New York: Routledge & Kegan Paul.

National Center for the Accelerated Schools Project (1997) *Accomplishments of Accelerated Schools*. Stanford, CA: School of Education, Stanford University.

Oakes, J. (1985) *Keeping Track: How Schools Structure Inequality*. New Haven, CT: Yale University Press.

Ogbu, J. (1987) Variability in minority school performance: a problem in search of explanation. *Anthropology and Education Quarterly*, 18(4), 312–34.

Page, R. (1987) Teachers' perceptions of students: a link between classrooms, school cultures, and the social order. *Anthropology and Education Quarterly*, 18(2), 77–99.

Peshkin, A. (1978) *Growing up American: Schooling and the Survival of Community*. Chicago: University of Chicago Press.

Posch, P. (1996) Changing the culture of teaching and learning: Implications for action research. In Christine O'Hanlon (ed.) *Professional Development through Action Research*. London: Falmer Press, pp. 61–9.

Sarason, S. (1982) *The Culture of the School and the Problem of Change*, 2nd edn. Boston: Allyn & Bacon.

Sarason, S. (1996) *Revisiting 'The Culture of the School and the Problem of Change'*. New York: Teachers College Press.

Schlechty, P. (1991) *Schools for the Twenty First Century: Leadership Imperatives for Educational Reform*. San Francisco: Jossey-Bass.

Shein, E. (1992) *Organizational Culture and Leadership*, 2nd edn. San Francisco: Jossey-Bass.

Solomon, R. P. (1992) *Black Resistance in High School*. Albany: State University of New York Press.

Spindler, G. (1987) The transmission of culture. In G. Spindler (ed.) *Education and Cultural Process: Anthropological Approaches*. Prospect Heights, IL: Waveland, pp. 303–34.

Spindler, G. and Spindler, L. (1982) Roger Harker and Schonhausen: from the familiar to the strange and back again. In G. Spindler (ed.) *Doing the Ethnography of Schooling*. New York: Holt, Rinehart & Winston, pp. 21–47.

Spindler, G. and Spindler, L. (1990) *American Cultural Dialogue and Its Transmission*. New York: Falmer.

Suarez-Orozco, M. (1989) Psychological aspects of achievement motivation among recent Hispanic immigrants. In H. Trueba, G. Spindler and L. Spindler (eds) *What Do Anthropologists Have to Say about Dropouts?* New York: Falmer Press.

Tyack, D. and Cuban, L. (1995) *Tinkering toward Utopia: a Century of Public School Reform*. Cambridge, MA: Harvard University Press.

Tyack, D. and Tobin, W. (1994) The 'grammar' of schooling: why has it been so hard to change? *American Educational Research Journal*, 31(3), 453–80.

Wax, M. (1993) How culture misdirects multiculturalism. *Anthropology and Education Quarterly*, 24(2), 99–115.

Wilcox, K. (1982) Differential socialization in the classroom: implications for equal opportunity. In G. Spindler (ed.) *Doing the Ethnography of Schooling*. New York: Holt, Rinehart & Winston.

Wolcott, H. (1967) *A Kwakiutl Village and School*. New York: Holt, Rinehart & Winston.

Wolcott, H. (1973) *The Man in the Principal's Office: an Ethnography*. New York: Holt, Rinehart & Winston.

8

Some elements of a micro-political theory of school development

HERBERT ALTRICHTER AND STEFAN SALZGEBER

During the past decade there have been massive changes in the governance of educational systems in many countries. Somewhat surprisingly, these reforms have sailed under the same flags of 'school autonomy', 'decentralization' and 'devolution' in both formerly 'centralized systems' (such as those of Austria and other mainland European countries) and formerly 'decentralized systems' (such as England and Wales). Despite the different histories of different systems, almost everywhere these changes have been accompanied by a common rhetoric which appears to give schools more leeway in developing their profiles, their internal organization and their daily operation according to their own aims and understanding (see Posch and Altrichter 1993).

In Austria, in the wake of legal and administrational changes, a number of development activities have emerged (see Bachmann *et al.* 1996). Teachers have developed in-school curricula and organizational patterns intended to give their school a distinctive profile suited to the specific needs of their clientele or the specific potential of their staff. Consultants have offered services designed to support organizational and curricular development. Some observers have been astounded by the sheer number of activities; others have considered some of the results to be 'irrational'; some have been irritated that 'school development' has appeared to cause conflict among staff; and in some cases schools have become locked in outright polarization.

We suggest that such outcomes stem from different (and often vague) conceptualizations of 'development in organizations' which were employed or implied by the various actors and spectators. If we can identify these points of difference, then perhaps we can realize a concept of organizations which accounts for the various outcomes we have observed occurring in school development processes, when they are viewed across different systems.

The chapter begins with a short illustration of the traditional rational contingency approach to organizations, and the counter-movement of a micro-political approach. While the rational contingency approach reifies organizational structures, the micro-political perspective usually finds it difficult to account for the obvious stability of many aspects of organizations other than by recourse to explanations framed in terms of deception, defeat or submission. To cope with these problems, some elements of a theory of interactive constitution of organizations are outlined, taking a lead from Elliott (1993).[1]

Organizations as objective structures or as fields of power struggles

According to predominant 'theories of *rational-contingent structuration*, organizations are goal-oriented, rationally planned systems with a lasting objective structure' (Türk 1989: 23). These structures are contingent in the sense that they are dependent on, but not strictly determined by, different 'context variables'. Thus, organizational structures are seen to be relatively autonomous. The 'rationality' of these structures is seen as a major cause of efficiency within an organization. Furthermore, *organizational development* is, according to this view, effected by 'rationally calculating constructors of organisations' (Türk 1989: 51). These specialists analyse the situation and design new sets of goals and organizational structures possessing the knowledge and the skills to implement this blueprint against resistance from organization members. In these terms, organizational development is considered successful if the reality comes close to the blueprint and if relatively little energy had to be spent to overcome the frictions of the implementation process.

However, experience tells us that conflicts are endemic in organizational life (Ortmann *et al.* 1990; Neuberger 1992). Different stakeholders – teachers, headteacher, pupils and parents – pursue their own interests, which are not necessarily identical with the goals which have been formulated in the mission statement of the school. Coalitions are formed, meetings are boycotted, external actors are exploited by particular interests and very often in this process formal structures are ignored. As such phenomena frequently occur in organizations, they need to be considered as normal, not as exceptional. It makes no sense to exclude them from organizational theorizing, as suggested by rational-contingent theories. We have to look for concepts which promise to cope with this 'dark side of organisational life' (Hoyle 1982: 87). Micro-political approaches to organization theory consider 'power struggles' and other 'irrational phenomena' as crucial for the understanding of organizations.

Although this perspective was originally developed for profit-making organizations, it has recently been used for analysing educational organizations (Ball 1987; Blase 1991; Kelchtermans and Vandenberghe 1995). In our school development projects we have also noticed that teachers used political vocabulary to describe processes which had occurred in the course of educational innovations, such as 'formation of alliances', 'shift of power', 'putsch', 'opposition', 'battle for influence' and 'declaration of independence' (see Ball 1987: 226–7; Rauch 1993: 45). This suggests that the notion of schools as rationally planned organizations glosses over very different perceptions by those who work within them.

In times of change, micro-politics may take on considerable significance, involving 'those activities taken within organisations to acquire, develop, and use power and other resources to obtain one's preferred outcomes in a situation in which there is uncertainty or dissent' (Pfeffer 1981: 7). It must suffice here to characterize this approach through three central elements (see Altrichter and Salzgeber 1996: 99–104). Summarizing an extensive literature, we can say that micro-political approaches involve:

1 A certain image of *organizations* as containing diverse goals and unclear areas of influence.
2 A certain image of *action and actors* as pursuing their own interests as they try to put their own values into practice.
3 Special attention to interaction processes in organizations, which are interpreted as *strategic and conflictual struggle* over the definition and structure of the organization.

Theoretical problems of the 'micro-political perspective' and options for further development

What are the counter-arguments to a micro-political view of schools?

- The micro-political approach is right to criticize the taken for granted presupposition of consensus (e.g. in the sense of 'organizational goals' or shared meanings and values) and to put the spotlight on power, control and conflictual negotiation processes. On the other hand, it is unsatisfactory to interpret any consensus as a form of domination, elimination, pre-emption or covering up of conflict (see Ball 1987: 278).
- The micro-political approach is right to criticize the taken for granted presupposition of stability of organizations and to put the spotlight on the potential instability of organizational processes. On the other hand, the question arises as to how the relative stability and durability of organizations, which we can observe day by day in many organizations, might be conceptualized.
- The micro-political approach is right to criticize the image of an organization determined by its environment and to draw attention to the inner life of organizations. In this, however, the external relationships of the organization are sometimes dissolved into the interactions between individual actors, the boundaries between the organization and the environment are blurred and external contingencies are almost totally faded out.
- The micro-political approach is right to focus on political processes of

> negotiation in organizations. However, its understanding of politics is quite unsatisfactory, not to say unpolitical. Politics is mostly seen as the opposite to truth and reason; it is associated with treason, conspiracies and the accumulation of influence. The word 'democracy' does not exist. Like populist politicians, micro-political theorists speak disparagingly of politics, but still they deal with it.

To sum up, the strength of the micro-politic approach is also its weakness. However, some of these weaknesses may be overcome by reference to Giddens's (1984) theory of structuration and to Ortmann *et al.*'s (1990) studies of power in organizations. We will try to prove this point – at least with respect to the first two of our four criticisms – in the following passages, but let us start our argument with some case material.

The integration of a new teacher into the staff of a primary school

As part of a study of 'good schools' (Altrichter *et al.* 1994), we interviewed staff, pupils and parents of a suburban primary school with 157 pupils. The school shared the building with two other – administratively independent – primary schools. Among the characteristics of the school in question was a special 'free method of teaching first grade pupils how to read and write'. The headteacher and some staff considered this method to be a major reason for the school's excellent reputation, which attracted a substantial number of parents to enrol their children in this school (but not in the other two schools under the same roof). The staff room was characterized by intensive communication between teachers and a high degree of coherence with respect to educational ideas and methods. The assessment of the inspectorate and the parents corresponded to that of the teachers.

How do newcomers feel when they enter such a homogeneous culture? A teacher who – after ten years of professional experience at other schools and well protected by a tenured position – was in her first year in this school said:

> *A*: I was advised to teach according to a different teaching method in grade 1, as this has been the established practice in this school for a couple of years. Since I have taught first grade pupils many times before, I said to myself: 'Should I really do that?' I had no experience of the method, and had to rely upon information in papers and books, which I studied during the four days before the new school year started.
>
> *Q*: You said that you were 'advised'. How did that happen? You got some literature?
>
> *A*: Yes. Three or four days before the beginning of the new school year I did not know which grade I would teach. I talked to the headteacher about this new method. She told me that I would manage it because I had taught grade 1 many times before. I have also received a heap of material from a teacher who had already taught this

> method for six or seven years, and I have worked that through. I arranged to meet the other grade 1 teacher every week to compare what we are doing and talk about how we are doing it.[2]

The teacher had been 'advised' to teach according to this new method, 'because the parents expected it . . . I could have refused to teach that method, but then they would have given me grade 3 instead.'

> *Q*: Had the other grade 1 teacher been using this method for quite a while?
>
> *A*: She had used it once in a grade 1 before but she had learned this method from this other teacher who taught it for some time already . . . Now we work together and it really works out well. We have a lot of teaching materials and we exchange them between the two of us. It is a relief for both of us. It really works well. Every Thursday we talk about the week ahead of us and what new words we are going to teach. . . . On the whole, collaboration with my colleagues in this school is very positive, quite a good understanding. When I first got here, one of the fellow teachers took me aside and said to me: 'Don't worry – together we will manage.' I have to admit that I was a little desperate in the beginning. I was supposed to know everything within four days. How could you do that? I was supposed to explain the new teaching method at the parents' meeting during the first week. If they asked me anything – I didn't have any experience. I felt like a novice teacher again.
>
> *Q*: You did have a lot of experience with other methods . . . Sounds like an unreasonable demand to ask you to learn a new method within four days.
>
> *A*: Well, it grows slowly. I read the papers and materials in four days. Step by step, after two weeks, I did understand how it works. In the beginning, I could not imagine how children would remember words and spell them correctly only after 'tracing' them many times. The new method is certainly better for recalling and repeating words with only a few mistakes. With the help of my fellow teacher it really worked out well.

Collaboration with her colleague and the exchange of teaching materials and ideas were thought of very positively and considered to make work much easier. This collaboration was embedded in understanding and emotional support by fellow staff, which helped to overcome initial feelings of desperation and doubt. Several 'offers' made by the interviewers to interpret this situation as a 'conflict' were ignored by the teacher. She did not complain about the obligation or about workload. Even the quite strong invitation 'Sounds like an unreasonable demand to ask you to learn a new method within four days' was no reason for her to mention any difficulties she had confronted with the 'system'.

Conflict and consensus

What would a conflict-oriented micro-political theorist make of such an example? Stephen Ball provides a starting point, reminding us:

> First, I have tried to indicate the conflictual basis of the school as an organization. Second, and concomitantly, I have attempted to indicate that the control of school organizations, focused in particular on the position and role of the head teacher, is significantly concerned with domination (the elimination or pre-emption of conflict). Thus domination is intended to achieve and maintain particular definitions of the school over and against alternative, assertive definitions. The process which links these two basic facets of organisational life – conflict and domination – is micro-politics.
>
> (Ball 1987: 278)

If conflict is the basic element of organizations, our case example must be interpreted as a very skilful form of domination, elimination, covering up or pre-emption of conflict in a public arena.

It is not too difficult to interpret the new teacher's acceptance of a new teaching method as resulting from subtle coercion. As a matter of fact, the new teacher was under considerable pressure: a very late assignment to the new school; a situation of having to decide between two alternatives (either teaching her preferred grade 1, but then having to use a new method, or getting grade 3 instead); strong consensus between the rest of the staff; and parents expecting that this new method would be taught at this school. One interpretation could be that the teacher internalizes potential conflicts which surface as desperation ('I have to admit that I was a little desperate') or scepticism ('I could not imagine how children would remember words'), instead of being externalized as conflictual interaction. However, these 'internal conflicts' do not appear to be 'suppressed' to the extent one might expect when it comes to 'dominated or pre-empted conflicts': the teacher herself believes that she has overcome her 'scepticism' ('The new method is certainly better for recalling and repeating words with only a few mistakes'). At the end of the study the teacher – who had told us before that she missed the close and friendly atmosphere of her former school – spontaneously said: 'My year of mourning is over.' Her initial desperation had been actively dealt with through emotional and practical support by the head and some staff – which also means that 'initial desperation in the face of new challenges' was defined as 'institutionally permitted' and as something which would be eventually overcome.

When the teacher praised staff support and the advantages of the new method after six months, a purely conflictual perspective would consider this as a case of perfect domination or submission. This interpretation is possible, but its price is to neglect the frame of perception and interpretation of the persons involved or to dismiss it as an expression of 'false consciousness'. Such an interpretation may be sensible in some cases, but is laden with a special burden of proof in all cases where the analyst's interpretation differs so profoundly from that of the actor. In this specific case, however, we have not found any indication that would support a predominantly conflict-oriented interpretation.

From a power strategic perspective, the concept of consensus is, in the end, disintegrated: areas of consensus become reinterpreted as 'coalitions' limited by time and locality which have only been formed for pushing through partial interests. Instead of such a 'disintegrated image of consensus' we could turn to a 'strong concept of consensus' (as Habermas did): a consensus based on reasonable negotiation in which actors of equal rights reach agreement in a free and open discourse without any reference to means of power. This discourse might start with a conflict, but that will be eliminated by the 'forceless force' of better argument.

While the concept of consensus is disintegrated in a conflict-oriented perspective, it is separated from the concept of power by Habermas.[3] We argue for a third option: determine the actual relationship between power and consensus in specific empirical cases instead of theoretically presupposing it for all empirical cases. Such an understanding of consensus is based on the assumption of a 'pact of productivity and sociality' (Malsch and Seltz 1987: 29), i.e. a partly implicit agreement on the validity of certain principles and norms which is conscious of the mutual dependence of those agreeing. This 'agreement', however, usually has a power-penetrated core: 'Power is not [only] a counter-concept of consensus . . . Consensus creates power, and power creates consensus – however, a sad consensus that cannot deny the stigma of its origin' (Ortmann 1992: 241). Such a concept describes a weak and fragile consensus. It does not exist prior to or independently of the organization, but is produced by the actors in their actions of organizing. 'Compromise' describes an important facet of the term 'consensus': it involves mutual compliance as well as mutual agreement, and will only come into being when it is (explicitly or implicitly) negotiated.

Such a 'weak concept of consensus' allows a plausible interpretation of our case example: Certainly, the new teacher did not agree to teach the new method because she reached some inner conviction about its quality after intensive free and open discussion with the head, colleagues and parents. Nevertheless, she agreed, even though she had an alternative of teaching grade 3 instead. Her decision is embedded in support measures by the head and some fellow teachers, and even these reflect the interwovenness of power and consensus. Support offers the opportunity for increased control and influence by the supporters. Thus, the new teacher's refusal to ask the head to attend the parents' meeting (who had offered to do so) can be interpreted as rejecting external control and asserting the independent professional self. What the interpretation proposed here stresses is that there *is* presently a consensus about the advantages of the method among the most parties involved (new teacher, head, parents, most staff).

Organizations can hardly be conceived as just a conglomerate of power games, 'force and fraud'. To understand their stability it is necessary to include the partial production of consensus in the argument. The production of consensus does not only take place in explicit negotiations, but also has sources in the *Lebenswelt*. It is rooted in more or less vague, more or less scrutinized or traditional, more or less stable convictions, norms and images of the world which actors refer to in strategic or communicative actions. The *Lebenswelt* may be understood as a more or less diffuse, historical consensus of earlier generations which is reproduced through present actions.[4]

During the integration process of the new teacher, ideas about the legitimacy of hierarchies and the headteacher's power, the parents' role, the importance of 'child-centred teaching' during primary education etc. are not explicitly discussed, but are likely to play a role as elements of a presupposed *Lebenswelt* of teachers. All these factors led a quite experienced and tenured teacher to accept a new method instead of insisting on the alternative norm of *Methodenfreiheit* (i.e. the professional right of teachers to use appropriate teaching methods of their own choice).

Agency and structure

Until now, our analysis has stressed the level of action and actors. We have referred to situational conditions only as a context of action. The term 'organization' has remained a vaguely defined 'political arena' which could be used – depending on the skills of the actors – in very different ways. The rules of the organizational game seemed to be partly unclear: they could be partly neglected, reinterpreted, perverted or ignored. Additionally, these rules seemed to be objects and products of 'organizational games' themselves.

Crozier and Friedberg (1993) have introduced the concept 'game' in their essay on 'power and organization' in order to conceptualize the relationship between an action-oriented and a systemic-structural perspective on organizations. The term has been used frequently in micro-political texts but mostly in a vague and metaphoric way. 'Games' are associated with 'risk', 'winning', 'cheating' etc. Crozier and Friedberg, however, have used the term to point to modes of integration and building relationships in social situations.

Some micro-political analyses tend to describe the relationship of action and structural conditions as *contingent*. In contrast to this, we argue for a *constitutive* relationship of action and structure (see Joas 1992: 235). We assume a *duality of structure* (see Giddens 1984), which implies that structure is both a means and a result of actions. On the one hand, actors necessarily refer to enabling and limiting structures in their action. On the other hand, structure only exists in action, as it were, having no stability in space and time other than through their reproduction in action.

We try to explain this idea more clearly by discussing the significance of 'parents' meetings' in our case example. 'Intensive collaboration with parents' and, in particular, 'well-prepared parents' meetings' are central elements of the primary school's image, both in their self-concept and in their perception by the parents, inspectorate etc. (see Altrichter *et al.* 1994: 60). The head-teacher takes it for granted that the new teacher will stick to this tradition: we assume that the parents expected likewise. A situation like this means 'pressure' for the new teacher. The head and a fellow teacher offer their support in order to alleviate this situation of pressure, but also to pass on their specific tradition of school organization. The new teacher turns down the head's offer to join her in the parents' meeting and instead does it all by herself. And – in the parents' and head's judgement – it is a success. By holding this parents' evening she uses, reproduces and reinforces existing characteristics of the school. At the same time, she uses these traditional forms to demonstrate her competence and knowledge of the structures which constitute this school. Thereby, the parents' and the head's confidence in her is increased and her room for manoeuvre widens.

The reproduction of structures results from intentional actions, but structures do not necessarily represent the result of intentional designs. More often, the structuration of an organization happens as a by-product of the pursuit of the various actors' own interests. Thus, unintended consequences of actions are the building blocks of further actions.

The new teacher reproduces a certain social practice (i.e. the method of early reading and writing) which is widely considered an essential component of the school's definition. Her initial intentions were to teach at grade 1 and, perhaps, to get on reasonably well with the headteacher, fellow staff and possibly the parents. One can be sure that she did not intend to collaborate in order to stabilize the new method. But this was exactly the effect of what she was doing.

How is relative stability of structures achieved, if they have to be reproduced through action again and again? Ortmann *et al.* (1990: 464ff) distinguishes between routine games and innovation games in organizations. *Routine games* are usually collaborative games from which participants draw gains which have been formally promised or have informally evolved. Routine games are unspectacular and therefore rarely the subject of micro-political case studies.

For example, Doyle and Ponder (1976) interpreted the difficulties which arose in primary schools when more complex learning tasks were introduced as 'negotiation processes'. The introduction of more complex and educationally demanding tasks increased insecurity for the pupils. They threatened to withdraw their implicit consent to existing discipline and, thus, implicitly offered a 'deal' to the teacher: security for students (by giving easier tasks) in return for security for the teachers (by being disciplined in the classroom).

The 'teaching' routine itself is further divided in sub-routines (e.g. with respect to examinations or holding discipline) and it is linked to a range of other 'games' which are routinely played in schools: the grade conference, time-tabling, the school bazaar etc. Organizational stability derives partly from the fact that typical 'games' are closely interwoven and hierarchically interlinked (see also Crozier and Friedberg 1993: 172): 'Subtle game structures and modes of playing developed a micro-political web which is made of fine-spun threads. The very subtlety provides for the elasticity which is necessary so that it will not be torn up by the rawer winds of the organization' (Ortmann *et al.* 1990: 465).

Summary

To sum up the argument, we have pointed out the constructed and changing character of organizations, their diverse goals and diffuse borders. In the second section we tried to specify the relationship between the structure of the organization and its members' actions. We discussed structure as an outcome of and a resource for social actions which enables and restricts actions, but never fully determines them. Organizations, in our understanding, are webs woven from concrete interactions of (self-) interested actors (see Türk 1989: 122). They acquire some spatio-temporal extension (i.e. some geographical situatedness and some temporal permanence which only give an interactive phenomenon a social place) through the actors' use and reproduction of 'games' or 'social practices'. The 'game' is the point of conceptual intersection at which the analytically divided elements of 'agency and structure', of 'individual and organization', meet. It is the point of social intersection in which a multitude of (self-) interested actors come into a specific relationship.

The interlocked character of the games and the large number of routine elements in social practices (which means that they are largely based on a 'practical' and not on a discursively articulated consciousness) are major reasons for the relative stability of organizations. The actors' autonomy is relative, too. All actors have, in principle, power, because they can choose between options.[5] They are subjected to a 'dialectic of control' (Giddens) as they can only change structures by relating to these very structures.

The game works as an 'indirect integration mechanism which relates the diverging and/or contradictory action of relatively autonomous actors' (Crozier and Friedberg 1993: 4). In order to take action and to pursue their own interests, the members of organizations must use, at least partly, structural resources of the organization, i.e. they are forced to play, at least partly, within the organizational rules, and in this way, they reproduce these resources and rules. Therefore, the functioning of an organization may be explained 'as a result of a series of games articulated among themselves, whose formal and informal rules indirectly integrate the organization members' contradictory power strategies' (Ortmann *et al.* 1990: 56).

Notes

1 A more extensive elaboration of this argument based on additional case material has been presented in Altrichter and Salzgeber 1996.
2 Translations from the case material (see Altrichter *et al.* 1994: 43).
3 This criticism is not new and Habermas has reacted to it. He argues that the critics improperly mix in an inadmissible way the formal-pragmatic and the sociological analysis of forms of life (see Habermas 1986: 381). Strictly speaking, we have to talk about consensus and dissent and cooperation and conflict. On the one hand, consensus turns into a conflict phenomenon, as soon as the person concerned does not view the consensus any longer in a performative attitude as a successful understanding, but uses it in a strategic way. On the other hand, a strategic use of dissent can produce cooperation.
4 Unlike Habermas (1981: 182), we do not associate the concept of Lebenswelt only with communicative actions. Furthermore, we would think of a specific Lebenswelt of organizations (Türk 1989: 109; Volmerg *et al.* 1989).
5 The choice can be very limited, indeed, so that pointing to the existence of 'choice' can be very cynical, e.g. in the case of 'money or life'.

References

Altrichter, H. (1994) Eben ein bisserl mehr für die Kinder. In H. Altrichter, E. Radnitzky and W. Specht (eds) *Innenansichten guter Schulen*. Vienna: BMUK, pp. 43–109.
Altrichter, H. and Posch, P. (1996) *Mikropolitik der Schulentwicklung*. Innsbruck: Studien Verlag.
Altrichter, H., Radnitzky, E. and Specht, W. (eds) (1994) *Innenansichten guter Schulen*. Vienna: BMUK.
Altrichter, H. and Salzgeber, S. (1996) Zur Mikropolitik schulischer Innovation. In H. Altrichter and P. Posch (eds) *Mikropolitik der Schulentwicklung*. Innsbruck: Studien Verlag, pp. 96–169.
Bachmann, H., Iby, M., Kern, A., Osinger, D., Radnitzky, E. and Specht, W. (1996) *Auf dem Weg zu einer besseren Schule*. Innsbruck: Studien Verlag.
Ball, S. J. (1987) *The Micro-politics of the School*. London: Routledge.
Blase, J. (ed.) (1991) *The Politics of Life in Schools*. Newbury Park, CA: Sage.
Crozier, M. and Friedberg, E. (1993) *Die Zwänge kollektiven Handelns*. Frankfurt am Main: Hain.
Doyle, W. and Ponder, G. A. (1976) *The Practicality Ethic in Teacher Decision Making*. Denton: North Texas State University.
Elliott, J. (1993) What have we learned from action research in school-based evaluation? *Educational Action Research*, 1(1), 175–86.
Giddens, A. (1984) *The Constitution of Society*. Cambridge: Polity Press.
Habermas, J. (1981) *Theorie des kommunikativen Handelns, Volume II*. Frankfurt am Main: Suhrkamp.
Habermas, J. (1986) Entgegnungen, in A. Honneth and H. Joas (eds) *Kommunikatives Handeln*. Frankfurt am Main: Suhrkamp.
Hoyle, E. (1982) Micropolitics of educational organizations. *Educational Management and Administration*, 10, 87–98.

Joas, H. (1992) *Die Kreativität des Handelns*. Frankfurt am Main: Suhrkamp.
Kelchtermans, G. and Vandenberghe, R. (1995) Vulnerability and power: the political domension in teachers' professional development. Paper presented at the conference of the International Study Association on Teacher Thinking, St Catherines.
Malsch, T. and Seltz, R. (1987) *Die neuen Produktionskonzepte auf dem Prüfstand*. Berlin: Ed. Sigma Bohn.
Neuberger, O. (1992) Spiele in Organisationen, Organisationen als Spiele. In W. Küpper and G. Ortmann (eds) *Mikropolitik*. Opladen: Westdeutscher Verlag, pp. 53–86.
Neuberger, O. (1993) Mikropolitik. In L. von Rosenstiel, E. Regnet and M. Dmosch (eds) *Führung von Mitarbeitern*. Stuttgart: Schaeffer-Poeschel, pp. 39–47.
Ortmann, G. (1992) Macht, Spiel, Konsens. In W. Küpper and G. Ortmann (eds) *Mikropolitik*. Opladen: Westdeutscher Verlag, pp. 13–26.
Ortmann, G., Windeler, A., Becker, A. and Schulz, H.-J. (1990) *Computer und Macht in Organisationen*. Opladen: Westdeutscher Verlag.
Pfeffer, J. (1981) *Power in Organizations*. Boston: Pitman.
Posch, P. and Altrichter, H. (1993) *Schulautonomie in Österreich*. Vienna: Ministry for Education and the Arts.
Rauch, F. (1993) Die 'Plakataktion'. Unpublished manuscript, Innovationsprojekt, Graz.
Türk, K. (1989) *Neuere Entwicklungen in der Organisationsforschung*. Stuttgart: Enke.
Volmerg, B., Senghaas-Knobloch, E. and Leithäuser, T. (1989) *Betriebliche Lebenswelt*. Opladen: Westdeutscher Verlag.

9

Changing conceptions of action research

BRIDGET SOMEKH

'Will you walk a little faster?' said a whiting to a snail,
'There's a porpoise close behind us, and he's treading on my tail.
See how eagerly the lobsters and the turtles all advance!
They are waiting on the shingle – will you come and join the dance?
Will you, wo'n't you, will you, wo'n't you, will you join the dance?
Will you, wo'n't you, will you, wo'n't you, wo'n't you join the dance?

'You can really have no notion how delightful it will be
When they take us up and throw us, with the lobsters, out to sea!'
But the snail replied 'Too far, too far!' and gave a look askance –
Said he thanked the whiting kindly, but he would not join the dance.
Would not, could not, would not, could not, would not join the dance.
Would not, could not, would not, could not, could not join the dance.

'What matters it how far we go?' his scaly friend replied.
'There is another shore, you know, upon the other side.
The further off from England the nearer is to France –
Then turn not pale, beloved snail, but come and join the dance.
Will you, wo'n't you, will you, wo'n't you, will you join the dance?
Will you, wo'n't you, will you, wo'n't you, wo'n't you join the dance?
(Lewis Carroll, 'The Lobster-Quadrille', 1865)

Experiencing change

I became a teacher in a girls' grammar school (for the more able) in England in 1971, two years before ROSLA (raising of the school leaving age to 16) and three years before the Cambridgeshire education system was reorganized to replace a two-tier selective system with open-entry comprehensive schools. Impington Village College, where I moved to work in 1973, was well known nationally as an innovative school under the leadership of an exceptional headteacher, John Brackenbury. It was an 11–18 mixed-sex, bilateral school (i.e. its pupils were separated into those who had passed or not passed the 11+ exam) which became comprehensive in 1974. Its educational values gave priority to serving 'the young' and according them respect and dignity as individuals. Within a year of reorganization Impington unstreamed all classes and adopted 'mixed ability' teaching. There were staff development days and the opportunity for considerable discussion beforehand, but in the end John Brackenbury said, 'I'm an old man and I'm in a hurry', and the decision was made to teach all subjects in mixed ability groups for the first three years. Thus, by the time I was introduced to action research in 1978, I had been immersed in the process of change for five years.

Action research provided me with a mechanism for managing change in my own classroom. It put me in control. It enabled me to use my intellect to understand the process of teaching and my own role in students' learning. And it focused my attention on psychological aspects of teaching and learning such as the 'hidden curriculum' of enacted values and the 'unintended outcomes' of teachers' behaviours (Elliott 1993: 69). My initial fascination with action research lay primarily in understanding how the mismatch of assumptions between teachers and their students, and their differential power, could have a detrimental effect on students' ability to learn. For example, when a physics teacher follows up a 17-year-old student's answer with the question 'Why?', he may mean to provoke scholarly debate but he may be interpreted as trying to 'show the student up' for giving the wrong answer (Somekh 1983). Rather as in psychoanalysis, in which I had, and have, considerable interest, I believed that teachers could have greater control over the effectiveness of their teaching if they better understood the impact on students of their own behaviours.

Lewis Carroll's poem, 'The Lobster-Quadrille' illustrates a very different model of change: one with which I was to become very familiar over the next twenty years. The whiting, an ordinary sort of fish, but rather bigger than a snail, is anxious to plunge into some innovatory practice which is being portrayed as jazzy and fun ('the dance'). He is anxious to persuade the snail to join in too, not because it is likely to be in the snail's own interests (it will involve being 'thrown out to sea'), but because the snail is blocking his path and there is a threat hanging over him (a porpoise is 'treading on my tail'). Pressure is being placed on the snail by a bigger fish to act against his own intelligence. He is being pushed to take part in the dance because it will suit the talents of others, like whitings and lobsters, who will be in their element in the sea. The 'dance' is in fact a trap – which is being sold to the snail for its inherent value (dancing/educational good) when in reality it will result in a dangerous evil (being thrown to your death/the subjugation of one group in society to serve the interests of another). This is a model of change in which teachers are expected to take part in something because they are told it is good. They are not enabled, or even expected, to understand it; instead they are under considerable pressure from heads of department or subject co-ordinators, as part of a rat race in which everyone is looking over his or her shoulder afraid of pressure from someone more powerful. Like the snail, their only intelligent response is resistance, but they are small and vulnerable.

Action research had provided me with a model of change which embodied principles of ownership and teacher professionalism, and was grounded in theories of individual and group behaviour derived from research (e.g. Lewin 1952; Schön 1983). At Impington in the 1970s this model of change was in harmony with the educational values of John Brackenbury and broadly supported by principles of social justice which had underpinned government policy in the UK since the 1944 Education Act, whatever the party in power. During the 1980s and 1990s there was a radical shift in political ideology under the Thatcher and Major governments. The concept of social justice was replaced by the competitive imperatives of the market place. The model of change embedded in educational policy making was based on principles of centralized control (specified subject contents and the testing of learning outcomes in the National Curriculum), individualism and competition (assisted places in private schools, city technology colleges, opted out schools, league tables). Concepts of empowerment and teacher professionalism were replaced by 'weeding out poor teachers', denigrating the knowledge gained from educational research as 'barmy theory' and allowing market forces and competition to create failing schools whose teachers and students were *de facto* punished for their failure to compete effectively. In this context, it was more difficult to get funding to carry out action research, and although it remained powerful as a means of supporting teachers engaged in change, the focus and purpose of enquiry was increasingly constrained by centralized control over educational policy and practice.

Throughout the 1980s and 1990s, I have been continuously engaged in action research in a range of roles: teacher-researcher, facilitator, project coordinator and academic supervisor. Each project or role has had its own focus, but the central theme of my work has been an investigation of the way in which different approaches to action research can support the process of change. Reading has been an integral part of this investigation, providing ideas that I have been able to try out through action research. In the next two sections I want to discuss a small number of key theories from reading that underpin my changing conceptions of action research.

Action research and the double task

Thatcherism was pre-eminently radical. As Barry MacDonald used to say, when I first went to work at the Centre for Applied Research in Education (CARE) in 1987, this gave evaluators and researchers of change a rich field of investigation. Thatcher had ambitions to change British society fundamentally. With this aim, the professions, as guardians of traditional standards and values, were systematically attacked. Writers such as Winter (1989) have noted the impetus towards dualism inherent in Western thought and culture. As a student of English literature in the 1960s, I was strongly influenced by the writing of the Irish poet W. B. Yeats. It was in an attempt to overcome the fracture within himself between man of action and man of imagination and reflection that Yeats adopted the mystic image of human identity as the dark and bright phases of the moon, always changing and always balancing one another in harmony – an image of the Yin and the Yan of Eastern thought (Ellmann 1961). Action research provided me with a mechanism with which to strive for unity of being. However, Thatcher's oppositional stance had the effect of increasing the dualism already inherent in all Western societies: capitalism versus socialism, rich versus poor, individualism versus society (Thatcher famously said, 'There is no such thing as society').

My early conception of action research assumed a model of change in which the relationship between cause and effect was relatively unproblematic. It was essentially a problem-solving approach that sought out answers to questions and strategies for improving practice. The process of change was complex because of the varied and unpredictable motivations of the human psyche multiplied many times by the interactions of individuals in a social situation; but fundamentally it was about overcoming differences and finding solutions through negotiation. Over time my conception of action research has changed as a result of focusing less upon problem-solving and more upon dialogue and interaction as means of identifying and respecting difference rather than reaching resolution. An important influence on my thinking has been Giddens, for example:

> Dialogic democracy stands in opposition to fundamentalisms of all types . . . It doesn't imply that all divisions or conflicts can be overcome through dialogue – far from it. Nor does it mean that, in any system or relationship, dialogue has to be continuous. Dialogue should be understood as the capability to create active trust through an appreciation of the integrity of the other. Trust is a means of ordering social relations across time and space. It sustains that 'necessary silence' which allows individuals or groups to get on with their lives while still existing in a social relation with another or others.
>
> (Giddens 1994: 115–16)

Another important influence on my thinking has been the work of Peter Posch, with whom I collaborated closely during 1990–2 on the English edition of the book he and Herbert Altrichter wrote originally in German (Altrichter and Posch 1990; Altrichter, Posch and Somekh 1993). Posch (1996) identifies the need for changes in the organization and culture of schools in response to the changes in twentieth-century society, which have reduced the 'proportion of human routine activities', increased the need for 'mutual dependence between hierarchical levels' in organizations and increased 'the heterogeneity of demands on the individual employee' (Posch 1996: 62). In another article, Posch develops a concept of 'dynamic networking' which illustrates how Giddens's 'dialogic democracy' can be encouraged to develop through an inter-institutional and international action research project. Posch shows how schools in the Environment and School Initiatives Project (ENSI), of which he was the international coordinator, were able to become active participants in raising the awareness of their local communities, influence the thinking of ministers engaged in international policy making on the environment, and even become active themselves in developing environmental awareness at an international level (Posch 1997: 269).

Francis (1996), in an article that draws attention to the common origins of action research and psychodynamic therapy in the work of Lewin in the USA and Bion and Trist at the Tavistock Institute in London, identifies 'the double task' as 'a recurring theme for action research'. Like Francis, I take the double task to be the ability to reject oppositional thinking and instead explore and build upon relationships between: 'theory and practice; conceptual knowledge and perceptual knowledge; valuing objectivity and subjectivity; individual and group issues; the personal and the professional; conscious and unconscious processes' (Francis 1996: 430). She suggests that the lack of 'a coherent rationale' in action research, identified by Carr (1994), is due to failure 'to attend to the dynamics of the double task'. She points out that Giddens's description of 'dialogic democracy' as 'relationships ordered through dialogue rather than through embedded power' (Giddens 1994) 'resonates with the aspirations of action researchers' (Francis 1996: 430). It seems to me that there is an inherent tension between the dialogic imperative of action research and the inherent dualism in Western thinking, and that this tension was exacerbated in the UK by the oppositional nature of Thatcherite education policy.

To be effective in supporting change regardless of the political context, action researchers have to live with tensions and dare to cross discourse boundaries, fearlessly (for a classic description of the nature of discourse, see Foucault 1972: 131). At the simplest level there is a need to accept that conceptions of action research must and should change. Instead there has sometimes been a tendency to defend orthodoxies; for example, there is a relentless suspicion of management-led, whole-school action research projects, which tend to be condemned under the label 'institutionalized action research' no matter what steps have been taken to guard against this by managers experienced in action research. The term 'institutionalized action research' was used by John Elliott at the Classroom Action Research Network (CARN) conference, held in Norwich in 1989, to condemn the co-option of action research by managers as a mechanism to make teachers comply with imposed change. While there is no doubt that there is a danger of teachers being co-opted to carry out research which is low level and encourages conformity rather than critical engagement, this is not the automatic result of large-scale school-wide action research projects. At the 1997 *Educational Action Research Journal* conference in Birmingham, Non Worrall and Mary James gave an account in an invited lecture of a whole-school, management-led action research project attempting to integrate staff development with school improvement. Although it was clear from the presentation that considerable care had been taken to give teachers autonomy in their practice and control over their research, questioning from some conference participants was unremittingly suspicious and hostile in tone. They were confronted by a controlling orthodoxy.

In describing the phenomenon of discourses as 'regimes of truth' constructed by groups of like-minded people, Foucault foresaw the inevitability that all systems, however intentionally empowering of others, would develop orthodoxies and mechanisms for enforcing them, and wrote of the need to use the ideas in his books 'as tools . . . to smash systems of power, including eventually those from which my books have emerged' (Foucault 1975: 115). In the case of action research it has, indeed, been postmodernist writers, building upon the ideas of Foucault, who have provided the kind of radical critique necessary to promote the crossing of discourse boundaries (Couture 1994; Maclure 1995: 111).

Straddling discourse boundaries

In another article, Maclure (1996) analyses the autobiographical narratives of ten individuals who have been influential in developing and promoting teacher action research. Her focus is specifically the 'boundary phenomenon' in these 'stories of transition – from teacher, to action researcher, to academic.' She notes 'the appeal to practice in all versions of action research' and identifies 'guilt' as a characteristic of the narratives: 'The exit is an occasion of both regret and celebration – guilt transmuting almost imperceptibly in the telling into exhilaration.' As one of those interviewed, I can confirm her insight. The guilt arises from an unnatural perpetuation of the moment of transition. If action research is the province of the practitioner, the ex-practitioner who continues to work as an action researcher must attempt to live at the boundary. These interview narratives are constructed within a strong frame of expectation that the interviewees, chosen for their prominence in action research, will demonstrate their credibility as the upholders of its values ('regime of truth'). Action research is premised on the concept of practitioners as researchers. Practitioner knowledge is celebrated for its unique and essential contribution to the understanding of classrooms. Yet all the interviewees have to tell a story of abandoning their primary practitioner role as classroom teachers. It is hardly surprising that the narratives consistently reveal guilt. The interviewees may have sought a modernist 'resolution' for their stories in the context of an interview that necessitated it, but from day to day these are individuals who must continue to live 'at the hyphen', in the phrase that Maclure quotes from Fine (1994). They struggle to reconcile their role as 'double task agents' with their formal situation within an education system that enforces separation between dualities.

The action researcher is, in practice, always straddling boundaries, and this gives rise to considerable problems in reporting action research. The practical and case-specific discursive narratives of the classroom are quite different from the analytical textual style of research reports that claim to present knowledge and understanding that is generalizable to a wide range of contexts. The two discourses are quite distinct, so much so that academics gain little credit towards career advancement for writing in 'professional' journals, and teachers seldom read articles in 'academic' journals, frequently saying that they find them 'boring' and their language impenetrable ('jargon-ridden').

Looking back, it seems certain that this is the reason why I have frequently used images to transmit meanings about my research. I have used them consciously to convey an emotion and an attitude as well as a concept, drawing in amateur fashion upon the power that writers like Shakespeare convey through the use of imagery. In poetry, T. S. Eliot calls these images 'objective correlatives' because they present an idea embodied in a representation. Sometimes I have chosen acronyms for projects, which convey an image, such as PALM for a living, growing tree. Sometimes I have used these images as the titles of papers or reports; for example, 'Take a balloon and a piece of string' was intended to convey playfulness and 'connectedness', since the idea was of two balloons spanning the Atlantic, carrying the electronic link between children (Somekh and Groundwater-Smith 1988). Of course, these images then have to be put forward in a written context: they never convey meaning uncontaminated by spoken or written discourse. Barthes's essay 'The photographic message' (Barthes 1983) contains the following passage, which I think sheds light on this process:

> The photographic paradox can then be seen as the co-existence of two messages, the one without a code (the photographic analogue), the other with a code (the 'art,' or the treatment, or the 'writing,' or the rhetoric, of the photograph) . . . The paradox is . . . that the connoted (or coded) message develops on the basis of a message *without a code*.
>
> (Barthes 1983: 198–9)

I have found it interesting to reflect upon two of the images I have used in this way. In both cases they have a dual role: first, to communicate a meaning without any 'code' or discourse-specific meaning; second, as an analytical tool to explore the relationship between teachers and the project team in a collaborative action research project of which I was the coordinator. The project in question was Pupil Autonomy in Learning with Microcomputers (PALM), in which around 100 teachers in 24 schools in Norfolk, Cambridgeshire and Essex carried out action research into the role of computers in learning, supported by the project team of myself, three project officers and a secretary.

The Russian doll

During the first year of our work, I used the image of a Russian doll as the subtitle of a paper describing the action research methodology and project management of PALM (Somekh 1989). The sequence of nesting dolls, contained one within another, with the largest encapsulating all the rest, seemed at first to convey the mirroring effect that we noted in the different 'layers' of PALM. Our own role in the project team was to support the teachers in carrying out action research into their use of computers in teaching, and by this means to empower them to use computers in ways that transformed their pedagogy. The teachers' role in the classroom was to support their pupils in using computers in their learning and to empower them to take greater responsibility for their own learning. As project coordinator, I had the further role of supporting the three project officers in carrying out action research into their role as facilitators of the teachers' research and empowering them to develop their own particular style for the project in their own local education authorities.

I later retitled the paper and discarded the image because it made me aware of a tension in the design of the project. Put simply, the fact that the dolls decreased in size suggested that they were decreasingly powerful; but the aim and rhetoric of the project was to give equality of power and status to all participants. Indeed, we strove so hard to give the teachers control over their own research that at one stage we came close to reducing our own roles to those of administrators only. The problem was that the design assumed an inequality of power, status and prior knowledge between the project officers and the teachers which did not, in fact, exist. PALM was essentially a very grassroots project, since I had been a teacher myself until only three years previously and the three project officers came straight from the classroom with no prior experience of action research. The original design of the project, with its classic separation of first-order and second-order action research (Elliott 1988: 165), was not appropriate, and during the second year of the project's life we gradually evolved roles that helped to blur the distinctions between teacher-researcher and outsider-facilitator. Not only was the design inappropriate to the prior experience of the team members, it was also inherently patronizing of the teacher-researchers. Thus, the image of the Russian doll was helpful as a tool of analysis that showed us that the project design had unintended outcomes.

Inhabiting each other's castles

In a paper written after the project was finished, I used the metaphor of inhabiting each other's castles in a retrospective analysis of the relationship between teachers and members of the university-based project team in PALM (Somekh 1994). It is intended to convey the mutual respect and equal status of two quite different discourse groups. It derives from Bruner's insight that knowledge is constructed by each individual in the light of experience and context and 'it is far more important . . . to understand the ways human beings construct their worlds (and their castles) than it is to establish the ontological status of the products of these processes.' The image of two castles gives the sense of 'otherness' and separation between the two groups (teachers and academics) who in a very real sense inhabit different worlds. In using the image I am assuming that researchers 'bring to the process of enquiry their own prior knowledge, values and beliefs, and that these, as much as any research data, construct their research outcomes.' I am assuming, too, that each castle is equally complex and interesting to explore – and 'that the castle of the school . . . substantiates its own important questions about the nature of education and the human condition'. The discourses of the two castles are fundamentally different and each determines 'what "counts" as knowledge, and how we decide that knowledge is sufficiently trustworthy for us to act on it' (Somekh 1994: 358, 378). The image is theoretically grounded, having originated in my reading rather than arising serendipitously from my experience of action research. It carries coded meanings that are only partly drawn from Bruner: for example, that teachers and academics have different but equally interesting and valid ways of theorizing from action; and that they can enter each other's way of looking at the world, learn to understand it and even live there for a while, without losing the security and status of having their own castles to which they can return. The uncoded messages of the image lie in teachers' and team members' common knowledge and experience. Castles invite exploration and have a solidity that stands the test of time – they cannot be brushed aside. They are also fun places to visit, and in the present day have generally, but not totally, lost their connotations as sites of conflict.

Learning through change

In an analysis of British government and European Union policy for building a learning society, Coffield (1996: 3) identifies a 'heavy concentration on the role of individuals' as 'the weakest aspect of both British and European policies on education, training and employment.' Much the same can be said of the action research model of change that I found so empowering myself as a teacher in 1978. Although my approach to action research has always involved working with others, prior to 1990 it was essentially individualistic. Normally the practitioner-researcher worked full-time as a teacher and carried out action research as an additional work load. I myself, when I worked in the TIQL project with John Elliott in 1981–2, and the teachers who worked with me in the PALM project in 1988–90, identified our research foci, collected data, analysed and interpreted them, and wrote our research reports, all as an addition to the full-time job of a teacher. Ultimately, this emphasis upon the individual is a weakness, for two reasons: first, it means that action research has limited value as a model of change in the education system because it is suited only to a few 'super-persons' (workaholics); second, it can focus upon only a small field of study, such as a single classroom, because that is the domain of the individual concerned.

I have come to believe that action research is more powerful as a means of enabling and supporting change if the model is interpreted more flexibly, with a focus on group endeavour rather than individual endeavour. In the Initial

Teacher Education and New Technology Project (INTENT), we carried out multi-level action research in which a senior manager worked in partnership with a staff development officer (a specialist information technology (IT) tutor) to promote IT development, and both carried out action research into their own roles in doing this effectively (Somekh *et al.* 1992). The model of change developed by INTENT extends action research principles to allow an effective purchase on the problems of organizational change (Somekh *et al.* 1997). Rather than reinforcing the negative effects of the power differential between the two partners, the approach allows the two to work together and use their different positions in the formal hierarchy to gain more effective leverage on both the formal and micro-political power structures of the organization.

In 1994–6 I coordinated the Management for Organisational and Human Development project (MOHD), funded by the EU Human Capital and Mobility Fund, which involved six research centres in four European countries (Austria, Spain, Italy and the UK). The central question for MOHD was whether involvement in participatory action research could enable individuals, regardless of their formal position in the hierarchy, to understand their own power and make a conscious contribution to organizational development (Somekh and Thaler 1997). The model of change that emerged from MOHD is premised on a concept of power derived from the work of Foucault and Giddens, in which individuals in organizations are constrained by the discourse of the organization (what can and cannot be said and done), but always have power which they often do not recognize and therefore use mainly negatively through resistance. Building on the work of Mead (1934: 155), Goffman (1959) and Krappmann (quoted in Hanft 1991: 169), we developed a model of change in which the phenomenon of the multiple self enables individuals to position themselves strategically and politically to further the process of change (Somekh and Thaler 1997). Participatory action research becomes the framework methodology for a collaborative endeavour in which as many members of the organization as possible are drawn into the process of change management. The emphasis is upon openness: control over the direction of change shifts away from managers towards the participant-researchers as an outcome of the action research process (Whyte 1991). In this model, individual learning and development are an intentional outcome of involvement in managing change: if the strategy is effective, participatory action research becomes the means of turning the vision of the learning organization into a reality. The focus upon issues of organizational structure and micro-politics makes this form of action research particularly effective in enabling individuals to develop Aristotle's fourth kind of knowledge, 'intelligence or intuition' (*nous*), which ensures that decision making is informed by a habit of self-critical reflection rather than being based on the unprocessed assumptions and habitual behaviours built up through experience (Aristotle 1955; Somekh 1993; Somekh and Thaler 1997). This is the model of change that informed my own management practice as a dean at the time of writing the first draft of this paper.

References

Altrichter, H. and Posch, P. (1990) *Lehrer erforschen ihren Unterricht.* Klinkhardt: Bad Heilbrunn/OBB.

Altrichter, H., Posch, P. and Somekh, B. (1993) *Teachers Investigate Their Work: an Introduction to the Methods of Action Research.* London: Routledge.

Aristotle (1955) *Ethics,* trans. J. A. K. Thomson. London: Penguin.

Barthes, R. (1983) The photographic message. In S. Sontag (ed.) *Barthes: Selected Writings.* London: Fontana, pp. 194–210.

Carr, W. (1994) Whatever happened to action research? *Educational Action Research,* 2, 427–36.

Carroll, L. (1865) *Alice's Adventures in Wonderland.* London: Macmillan.

Coffield, F. (1996) A tale of three little pigs: building the learning society with straw. Paper presented at the conference of the European Educational Research Association, Seville, Spain, 28 September.

Couture, J. C. (1994) Dracula as action researcher. *Educational Action Research,* 2, 127–32.

Elliott, J. (1988) Educational research and outsider–insider relations. *Qualitative Studies in Education,* 1(2), 155–66.

Elliott, J. (1993) Professional education and the idea of a practical educational science. In J. Elliott (ed.) *Reconstructing Teacher Education.* London: Falmer Press.

Ellmann, R. (1961) *Yeats: the Man and the Masks.* London: Faber.

Fine, M. (1994) Working the hyphens: reinventing self and other in qualitative research. In B. R. Denzin and Y. S. Lincoln (eds) *Handbook of Qualitative Research.* New York: Sage.

Foucault, M. (1972) *Power/Knowledge: Selected Interviews and Other Writings 1972–77.* Bury St Edmunds: Harvester Press.

Foucault, M. (1975) Interview with Roger-Pol Droit, *La Monde.* In M. Morris and P. Patton (eds) *Michel Foucault: Power, Truth, Strategy.* Sydney: Feral Publications, pp. 109–47.

Francis, E. (1996) The discursive project and the psychodynamic voice. *Educational Action Research,* 4(3), 429–34.

Giddens, A. (1994) *Beyond Left and Right.* Cambridge: Polity Press.

Goffman, E. (1959) *The Presentation of Self in Everyday Life.* London: Penguin.

Hanft, A. (1991) *Identifikation als Einstellung zur Organisation. Eine kritische Analyse aus interaktionistischer Perspektive.* Munich: Rainer Hampp Verlag.

Lewin, K. (1952) Group decision and social change. In G. W. Swanson, T. M. Newcomb and E. L. Hartley (eds) *Readings in Social Psychology.* New York: Henry Holt and Co.

Maclure, M. (1995) Postmodernism – a postscript. *Educational Action Research,* 3(1), 105–16.

Maclure, M. (1996) Telling transitions: boundary work in narratives of becoming an action researcher. *British Educational Research Journal,* 22(3), 273–86.

Mead, G. H. (1934) *The Works of George Herbert Mead, Volume 1. Mind, Self and Society.* Chicago: University of Chicago Press.

Posch, P. (1996) Changing the culture of teaching and learning: implications for action research. In C. O'Hanlon (ed.) *Professional Development through Action Research in Educational Settings.* London: Falmer Press, pp. 61–70.

Posch, P. (1997) Dynamic networking and community collaboration: the cultural scope

of educational action research. In S. Hollingsworth (ed.) *International Action Research: a Casebook for Educational Reform*. London: Falmer Press, pp. 261–74.
Schön, D. (1983) *The Reflective Practitioner*. London: Temple Smith.
Somekh, B. (1983) Triangulation methods in action: a practical example. *Cambridge Journal of Education*, 13(2), 31–7.
Somekh, B. (1989) Teachers becoming researchers or the Russian doll. Paper presented at the National Educational Computer Conference, Boston. Revised (1991) as: Teachers becoming researchers: an exploration in dynamic collaboration. *Qualitative Educational Research Studies: Methodologies in Transition, RUCCUS Occasional Papers*, 2, 97–144.
Somekh, B. (1993) Quality in education research – the contribution of classroom teachers. In J. Edge and K. Richards (eds) *Teachers Develop Teachers Research*. London: Heinemann.
Somekh, B. (1994) Inhabiting each other's castles: towards knowledge and mutual growth through collaboration. *Educational Action Research*, 2(3), 357–82.
Somekh, B., Blackmore, M., Blythe, C. *et al.* (1992) A research approach to IT development in initial teacher education. *Journal of Information Technology in Teacher Education*, 1(1).
Somekh, B. and Groundwater-Smith, S. (1988) Take a balloon and a piece of string. In D. Smith (ed.) *New Technologies and Professional Communications in Education*. London: National Council for Educational Technology, pp. 125–45.
Somekh, B. and Thaler, M. (1997) Contradictions of management theory, organisational cultures and the self. *Educational Action Research*, 5(1), 141–60.
Somekh, B., Whitty, G. and Coveney, R (1997) IT and the politics of institutional change. In B. Somekh and N. Davis (eds) *Using IT Effectively in Teaching and Learning: Studies in Pre-service and In-service Teacher Education*. London: Routledge.
Whyte, W. F. (1991) *Participatory Action Research*. Newbury Park, CA: Sage.
Winter, R. (1989) *Learning from Experience*. London: Falmer.

PART IV

Preparing teachers for creative engagement with educational change

10

Reflective education and school culture: the socialization of student teachers

ANGEL PÉREZ GÓMEZ

Professional socialization factors during practical training

There is little doubt that the complex and indeterminate interactions between theory and practice represent one of the more substantial problems in education. The true objective of all educational activity is to help to construct a sound framework of practical thinking that will help teachers to interpret reality clearly in a way which will enable them to cope with it. Since Schön pointed out the importance of practical thinking for teaching professionals, faced with complexities of teaching in a rapidly changing society, no one has doubted that to teach practical thinking requires much more than the sterile contents of an academic syllabus. There is now a great deal of evidence that mere rote learning of facts and theory is not enough. Even when facts have been thoroughly learned, they are soon forgotten and, more seriously, they do not necessarily help the student teacher to develop practical understanding (Feiman-Nemser and Buckmann 1989; Morine-Dershimer 1989; Segall 1997).

How do we prepare teachers to be 'reflective practitioners' so as to be able to cope with the problems of educating their students in a rapidly changing society? It is often assumed that the answer lies in creating stronger, more interactive links between higher education-based and school-based learning experiences. Yet, as this chapter demonstrates, changing the teacher training system into a form which sustains these links and a more interactive relation between theory and practice is beset with problems.

This chapter summarizes the conclusions of case studies of the *practicum* of eight student teachers in eight different universities in Andalusia (Spain), aiming to identify and understand the development of their practical pedagogical knowledge and behaviour and the factors affecting their socialization processes. Every case study lasted for four months, as long as the *practicum* lasted at the end of the three-year teacher training programme. It involved observation and interviews with the student teacher, the tutor teacher and the university supervisor.

Across the range of cases, there were many different factors which significantly affected the socialization of students in the professional teaching culture. However, while it should be noted that their effects tend to differ from case to case, with respect to 'intensity' and 'importance', some factors emerge as the most influential and persistent in all cases:

- The pressure of the school and classroom culture to which trainees have to adapt if they wish to survive with a certain degree of success during this period of training.
- The evaluation aspect of academic and professional acquisitions made during the period of practice within the teachers' training curriculum.
- Personal insecurity with regard to the mastery of a complex, alien medium and the fear that trainees will not be respected as teachers or that they may be perceived as students.
- The lack of diversified theoretical/practical references and alternatives by which to judge what they observe and experience.
- The socializing function of the tutor and the bureaucratic function of the supervisor in most of the teacher training programmes.

It would appear that the whole of the structure built up around the period of practical training induces the reproduction of dominant forms of teaching behaviour and styles in each particular scenario. I now take a more detailed look at each of the factors which inhibit alteration of the teacher preparation process in the direction of a more reflective professional learning process.

School culture

When they enter a class, trainee teachers do so as new elements within a microculture whose rules and climate are already set. If they wish to be accepted, they have to adapt to the normal rules of the game already approved by tradition, to the various relationships, to the teaching rhythm and dynamics of the classroom and to the teaching style of the teacher in charge, so as to make sure that their admission does not give rise to conflict or to any interruption in the normal rhythm. The effect of all these pressures for accommodation is to reinforce the tendency towards an imitation and reproduction of the status quo, as a means of preserving the delicate balance which the institution has achieved throughout its existence (Posch 1996).

> On entering the third-year elementary school classroom the tutor teacher indicates to the student-teacher the task to be carried out and she does nothing more than imitate the classroom activities of the tutor so that the student carries out exactly the same task.
>
> (Researcher in Jaen)

The pressure exerted by the school environment and by the institutional culture, as basically transmitted by the tutoring staff, is so strong that some trainee teachers even react defensively against any attempts at analysis or critical observation by a supervisor or researcher. Similarly, it is worth noting that even some of the researchers who were involved in activities in the course of these case studies were aware of succumbing to unwanted pressures arising from this scenario.

> On the other hand, we understood the ease with which the students' teacher, and even the researcher, adapted to classroom routines. At times I surprised myself adopting certain attitudes and behaviour that were closer to the dynamics and subculture of the classroom than my own beliefs and ideas.
>
> (Supervisor in Almería)

A further aspect to be considered regarding the socializing pressures brought to bear by the school's cultural and professional environment is the acceptance of forms of pedagogic behaviour which are considered legitimate within the establishment as a whole. These routine forms of behaviour are usually propagated to the exclusion of any alternatives, especially of an innovative kind, since these would threaten the reproductive equilibrium and be doomed to failure on the grounds that they are sterile, pernicious or lacking in the necessary realism.

Finally, I should emphasize that the satisfactory personal and social relations that student-teachers established with the children they worked with served merely to reinforce the prevailing school culture. The pleasure the students derived from pupils' affection made them defer the possibility of asking more demanding questions about the quality of their teaching.

Dependence and insecurity

Another decisive factor in the socialization of future teachers during their *practicum* which appeared in the case studies is the dependent, provisional nature of their position within a complex environment of social exchanges. This environment shapes the conduct of all those involved, especially the trainee teacher, whose situation is so uncertain and unstable.

> During the *practicum* I felt myself to be only an assistant to the tutor or a substitute, a part-timer without overall responsibility for the process in which I was involved.
>
> (Student-teacher in Málaga)

The tutor's attitude and the insecurity felt by the trainee when faced with a group of students combine and reinforce an attitude of submission and dependence. We observed this in most of the trainee teachers who featured in the case studies. Most of the time, a student-teacher's way out of this situation of personal insecurity and extreme dependence on the tutor consists of imitating and reproducing the behaviours he or she observes in the tutor's teaching style. Such a strategy was successful in achieving acceptance within the complex human scenario of social and academic interrelationships. Attempts to direct the life of the classroom from a clear position of institutional and professional inferiority logically encourage styles of behaviour which overcompensate in terms of authority.

One curious exception to this pattern of dependence and subordination in relation to the tutor, induced and practically demanded both by the school culture and by the students' own feeling of insecurity, occurred in Seville. Luis, the selected trainee teacher, was a specialist in physical education, and as such appeared to be better equipped in terms of theoretical knowledge and practical skills than his tutor. Physical education is a relatively new area in the Spanish education system, so that a trainee teacher's training tends to be more thorough than that of the tutor, which makes it difficult to establish the usual relations of powerful dependence and hierarchy.

Lack of theoretical or practical alternatives

The influence of the immediate school environment proves to be much more decisive when no theoretical or practical alternatives that could be used on such occasions have ever been offered or accommodated in the school environment or in previous academic training. It is easy to prove that the trainees imitate the teacher, not only because of the pressure on them to adapt, but also because they lack other more appropriate teaching methods and ways of doing things.

The theory inculcated at university in previous years turns out to be generally too far removed, in terms of time and interest, to be used as a helpful reference, a store of useful knowledge and experience with which to understand current reality and to guide on-the-spot decisions. The absence of any interesting, reflectively appropriated, alternatives then becomes a powerful factor in socialization, abandoning the trainees to obvious tendencies that encourage the reproduction of the conventional standards established in the school environment.

> Even at the beginning of his practical work the student is sceptical about the ideas and concepts taught in the university teacher-training programme. His first contacts with the reality of the school, after hearing the opinions of his tutor-teachers, lead him to think of them as useless.
>
> (Researcher in Granada)

Furthermore, the tutors in general not only act as the guardians of continuity in the professional and institutional culture of the school, defining what is right in practice, but also frequently pour scorn, in the presence of trainees, on other pedagogic alternatives and the validity of 'theoretical' university studies. As a result, the 'horizon' for the generation of knowledge, habits and attitudes closes in on itself within the shrunken scenario of repetitive experience.

Evaluation

The assessment character of this training period appeared in every case study to be one of the factors which most influenced the socialization of future teachers. If the school environment, with its institutional and professional culture and the tutor's mediating thoughts and actions, exerts so much influence on the trainee teacher's ways of feeling, thinking and acting, this is to some extent because it controls and censors judgements of success in the learning process (MacDonald 1976, 1983). As we had occasion to note, future teachers set a high priority on establishing a close working relationship with their tutor, on accepting the classroom and school dynamic and on avoiding confrontations or threatening the status quo, because in this way they hope successfully to pass the test of their *practicum* in the academic curriculum.

> She is aware of her imitative behaviour and tries to eliminate it, but the tendency to adopt routine is now firmly established and she fears making mistakes. She must do things that she thinks are inappropriate or risk the disapproval of the tutor, and this is more imperative than her wish to innovate.
>
> (Researcher in Almería)

The socializing function of the tutor and the bureaucratic function of the supervisor

In the light of evidence from the case studies we have to confirm that the relationship between the tutor and the trainee teacher does not focus on educational content. It has a significant, powerful socializing influence in mediating the school culture to which the tutor belongs, but none of the case studies reflects the existence of an educational relationship, where the tutor systematically develops and performs a role of reflective mediation, stimulating student-teachers to analyse and compare the influences and tendencies to which they are exposed, and which shape their teaching activity.

It may be that, in the theoretical design of the *practicum* and in the meaning and function of the part played in it by the different agents involved, the role of the university supervisor should be to fulfil this task of achieving a critical detachment and reflective mediation; hence serving to offset and compensate the powerful socializing influence of the school environment. In fact, in the case studies investigated, such a function failed to emerge at all clearly. Neither the theory assimilated in the course of previously or simultaneously studied disciplines, nor the direct and systematic intervention of the supervisor, was able to offer any opportunities or conceptual instruments for analysing the educational value of practical work, or for personal or shared reflection on practices to offset the inertia of the institutional environment. In most cases, the intervention of the supervisor was restricted merely to recording and checking the fulfilment of the bureaucratic requirements of the practical programme for the purposes of final assessment. Whether on account of disenchantment resulting from earlier experience, a poor appreciation of the educational value of this period or habits acquired at university, where this period of training tends to be looked down upon academically, the fact is that the supervisor's influence is unable to offset the powerful socializing effect of the trainees' experience. The supervisor's attitude in general tends to be either indifferent or bureaucratic, or supportive of the socializing experience of practical work.

> The supervisor played no active role during Luis's practice period. Luis knew his name, but had no contact with him either during or after his practice. The teacher-training school considered his contribution to be very negative because his task was simply to indicate the type of report he wanted and to grade it. 'He came for five minutes, arrived and said that he might go and do something in the first class. Five minutes, that was all. Better not come at all. It would have been better not to come than to come out of obligation. Let's not kid ourselves, his work was nil.'
> (Researcher in Seville)

> For Mar and the three students-in-practice in human sciences, who were doing their *practicum* in the same primary school, their supervisor organized a meeting every two weeks, because she was obliged to do so, but really she had little interest. 'She was totally uninterested in the practice period she was supervising by obligation.' The supervisor asked if they had had any problems, and as they had not had any, she explained history to them. This is the general way many supervisors act.
> (Researcher in Granada)

A reflective appraisal of practice requires investigating the effects the training is having on the trainees' thoughts, feelings and behaviour, by: (a) encouraging them in the course of individual or group tutorials to express what they have experienced in their period of practical work, to comment on differences and to analyse their implications; and (b) facilitating contact with alternative pedagogical practices which are different from those experienced in the actual establishments where their training is taking place. The function normally served by seminars in terms of debate, communication, analysis of problems, stimulation of queries and a consideration of alternatives, which should be the main responsibility of the university supervisor, does not appear as such in any of the cases investigated.

The meaning of *practicum* in teacher training

It is interesting to note the marked discrepancy between the opinions of trainee teachers and those of researchers about the actual meaning of the practicum. As far as the majority of trainees are concerned, and this was true for all our case studies, the period of the *practicum* is considered, with greater or lesser enthusiasm, as the most important part of their training curriculum. It is seen as the real part of the curriculum, where they have the opportunity not only to come to grips with the true nature of their profession, its possibilities and limitations, but also to develop the knowledge, techniques, attitudes and behaviours which they can use in their future jobs. But, perhaps most importantly, it is the period when they have a chance to find out whether they themselves are really suited to the profession, and whether the profession is really suited to them.

> The practicum has been the most attractive phase of my training . . . in which one can apply the knowledge and ideas learned during the three previous courses and dedicate oneself to a career as a primary school teacher.
>
> 'I learned a lot, it helped me a lot.
>
> As I learned in the practice period.
>
> Now I have learned something.
>
> Theory is useful, but . . . practice is something else.
>
> Now I know that I can be a good teacher.
>
> You start with fear, well, you don't know how you will manage, if you will be capable of dealing with all the situations that might occur, or, something more important, if you are really suitable for the profession of school teacher that you chose.'
>
> (Student-teacher in Almería)
>
> For Lucía, the most important part of her training process in the university teacher-training school was the practicum, the rest was 'theory'.
>
> (Researcher in Córdoba)

This perception of the practicum as the key component of their professional training does not, generally speaking, entail a rejection of the theoretical training they received at university, but more a reaffirmation of a technical conception of the relation between theory and practice. Classroom work is appreciated as an opportunity to check the validity of theoretical principles in practice, to complete previously acquired knowledge, to fill in the gaps and to select or reject aspects of theoretical training which appear unconnected and sterile when the time comes to understand and solve everyday problems. In the end, practice is the seal and crucible of theory.

> The first impression, or the misconception, that students-in-practice have is that all that was imparted in the teacher-training school is of no use at all. This leads to their feeling that they have been deceived because, well, the practicum is left to the last part of the teaching course and you must wait until the third year to discover – according to what

> they tell me – 'what being a teacher is all about', and then doubt their choice of career.
>
> (Researcher in Cádiz)

This perception of the greater importance which should be attached to the practical as compared with the theoretical component of the professional training of future teachers does tend, however, to become mitigated as the *practicum* continues and the students become better acquainted with the routines, the repetition and the sheer boredom of practice where there is little room for innovation. The traditional, routine nature of most of the teaching styles met with by students in their *practicum*, combined with the often bureaucratic, administrative, evaluative character of this practical component of some teacher training programmes, leads inevitably to discouragement and fatigue when practical work goes on without any innovations. Thus, as we found in the case studies, future teachers, once they have overcome their initial surprise and the illusion of entering into contact with professional practice, begin to experience fatigue and disappointment caused by the monotony of the way of working in school, which is boring for both students and teachers.

> 'I was bored, always the same thing, the same methods . . . a pain in the neck . . . The routine. Too much time and always repeating the same thing, you get tired. You don't know what to observe. You say, "Well, OK. We'll do it the same old way".'
>
> (Student-teacher in Córdoba)

Logically, in a situation where practical work is seen purely in opposition to theory, or as the imitative acquisition of traditional habits, techniques and routines used successfully by experienced teachers to govern the life of the classroom, the trainees' experience of practice in this period will be no more or less interesting than that of their 'experienced' colleagues. But let us enquire a little further: what was really learned during the period of *practicum* in the case studies considered?

All the evidence we were able to gather appears to show that practical training serves to enable acquisition of the practical knowledge, techniques and strategies, together with the attitudes and behaviours, required by the dominant school culture. The student-teacher learns to relate to other teachers and to pupils, learns to master the classroom dynamic, learns to become a professional with the right attitudes and responsibilities for the task as defined in practice by the majority of teachers and learns the language of the profession. In other words, he or she assimilates and assumes the predominant teaching role in the school culture. That is also to say that beginning teachers recover the memory of the school culture they experienced as a pupil – from the other side. This is why this training period appears so easy and so effective, because in fact the trainees are socialized into the same culture as they themselves experienced for at least 15 years of their lives.

The great weakness of practical training becomes evident when this period is expected to provide a fundamental component of the reflective training of teachers as intellectuals who investigate the prevailing conditions in the situations where they have to act; or when trainee teachers are expected to develop strategies adapted to the reality they are experiencing, evaluating and reformulating them in the light of analysis and ongoing exchanges with the others involved; or when the future professional is supposed to be able to investigate the meaning of education in the modern world and to test the significance of his or her practical work for future generations (Posch *et al.* 1993).

One may even go as far as to assert, in the light of these arguments, that in this sense practical training in Andalusía becomes more of an obstacle to than a tool for changing the education of future generations of teachers. Considering that neither the schools nor the tutors are selected for the quality of their practical work, trainees are generally socialized according to a pedagogic culture dominated by reproduction, which induces, stimulates and sometimes imposes the imitation of traditions as a legitimate form of professional learning. The effect of imitation is to inhibit and remove reflection from the field of thought and action in our future teachers. The status quo is accepted, while innovations are rejected and denigrated as potential threats to the precarious balance achieved by the school tradition. For this reason, when the trainees were asked if they were satisfied with what they had learned in the course of their practical training, and whether they had learned anything new compared with their previous experience as students in the different levels of the education system or as university students already studying education, they were unable to give any answer.

Thus, even on the assumption that the theoretical and practical training of teachers must take place in the school, in the actual situation where pedagogic values and procedures are generated and transformed, this case study research agrees with the work of MacDonald (1984), Pérez Gómez (1987), Beyer (1988), Munro (1989), Hoy and Woolfolk (1990), Elliott (1991a,b), Pérez Gómez and Gimeno Sacristan (1992), Smith (1992), Staton and Hunt (1992) and Zeichner (1992). It recalls what is at stake in succumbing to the powerful socializing influences exerted by the prevailing culture of schooling. As the above authors have shown, the indiscriminate and ill-prepared development of practical training, merely as a way of introducing future teachers to the school environment and culture, has all too often led to a rapid and premature socialization linked with undesirable and outdated methods of working and conceptualizing educational activity. This tends to occur as a result of the inertia of schools, which reproduce and perpetuate teaching strategies that are consistent with their own social, professional and institutional expectations, in combination with the reasonable desire of student-teachers and new teachers to develop successfully and to become socially accepted by their colleagues. In this context practical work encourages an understandable tendency to imitate and reproduce the type of social and professional behaviour which is believed to be that of the apparently successful majority within the social environment of the classroom and school. Change must take place not only in the direction of being within the scenario but in promoting critical and continuous reflection about the educational meaning of teaching activities in their institutional and curriculum contexts. The dissociation between theory and practice can only be overcome through the development of professional learning, which focuses on the reconstruction of pedagogical knowledge through active and collaborative reflection on practical situations and the teaching strategies employed in them. This will involve an interactive process linking reflection on the personal theories that underpin teachers' everyday interpretations and actions to relevant theoretical knowledge in the public domain.

Note

This chapter is derived from the multi-case study research programme financed by CYCIT, Project no. 90-0813 Report no. 8. The following investigators participated in the case study work: Carmen Rodríguez Martínez, Juan Pérez Rios, M. Dolores Díaz Noguera, M. Dolores González, M. Luisa Fernández Serrat, Marina Fuentes-Guerra Soldevilla, Pilar Sepulveda, Rocío Anguita.

References

Beyer, L. E. (1988) *Knowing and Acting: Inquiry, Ideology and Educational Studies*. London: Falmer Press.

Beyer, L. E. (1992) Educational studies, critical teacher preparation and the liberal arts: a view from the USA. *Journal of Education for Teaching*, 18(2), 130–48.

Elliott, J. (1991a) The relationship between 'understanding' and 'developing' teachers' thinking. In J. Elliott (ed.) *Reconstructing Teacher Education*. London: Falmer Press.

Elliott, J. (1991b) Three perspectives on coherence and continuity in teacher education. In J. Elliott (ed.) *Reconstructing Teacher Education*. London: Falmer Press.

Feiman-Nemser, S. and Buckmann, M. (1989) Describing teacher education: a framework and illustrative findings from a longitudinal study of six students. *Elementary School Journal*, 89, 365–77.

Hoy, W. K. and Woolfolk, A. E. (1990) Socialization of student teachers. *American Educational Research Journal*, 27(2), 279–300.

MacDonald, B. (1976) Who's afraid of evaluation? *Education*, 4(2), 3–13.

MacDonald, B. (1983) La evaluación y el control de la educación. In J. Gimeno Sacristan and A. Pérez Gómez (eds) *La enseñanza: su teoría y su práctica*. Madrid: Akal.

MacDonald, B. (1984) Teacher education and curriculum reform: some English errors. Presentation to the symposium Theory and Practice of Teacher Education, Madrid, Ministry of Education, February.

Morine-Dershimer, G. (1989) Preservice teachers' conceptions of content and pedagogy: measuring growth in refletive pedagogical decision-making. *Journal of Teacher Education*, 40, 46–52.

Munro, R. (1989) A case study of school-based innovation in secondary teacher education. Unpublished doctoral thesis, University of Auckland, New Zealand.

Pérez Gómez, A. I. (1987) El pensamiento práctico del profesor/a. Implicaciones en la formación del profesorado. Presentation to II Congreso Mundial Vasco, Bilbao, October.

Pérez Gómez, A. I. and Gimeno Sacristan, J.(1992) El pensamiento pedagógico de los profesores: un estudio empírico sobre la incidencia de los cursos de aptitud pedagógica (CAP) y de la experiencia profesional en el pensamiento de los profesores. *Investigación en la Escuela,* October (17), 52–73.

Posch, P. (1996) Changing the culture of teaching and learning: implications for action research. In C. O'Hanlon (ed.) *Professional Development through Action Research.* London: Falmer Press, pp. 61–9.

Posch, P., Altrichter, H. and Somekh, B. (1993) *Teachers Investigate Their Work.* London: Routledge.

Segall, A. (1997) Practising what we preach: bridging the theory–practice and practice–theory dicothomy in teacher education. Paper presented at the Annual Meeting of the American Education Research Association, Chicago.

Smith, S. (1992) Teacher's work and the politics of reflection. *American Educational Research Journal,* 29(2), 267–300.

Staton, A. and Hunt, S. (1992) Teacher socialization: review and conceptualization. *Communication Education,* 41, 1–35.

Zeichner, K. (1990) Contradictions and tensions in the professionalization of teaching and the democratizacion of schools. Paper presented at the Annual Meeting of American Educational Research Association, Boston, April.

Zeichner, K. (1992) Conceptions of reflective practice in teaching and teacher education. In J. Harvard and P. Hopkinson (eds) *Action and Reflection in teacher education* . Norwood, NJ: Ablex.

11

Case study and case records: a conversation about the Hathaway Project

SUSAN GROUNDWATER SMITH AND ROB WALKER

'Hathaway' Primary School exemplifies the complexities of change. Located in a migrant neighbourhood in Sydney and designed to be 'open' in classroom organization and in relation to the community, the school daily copes with policy changes from above and social change at the door. The 'Hathaway Project' was initiated by Susan Groundwater Smith more than a decade ago in an attempt to create a case record of the school to be used in teacher education programmes. In its latest version this record is in the form of a CD-ROM which Rob Walker and Ron Lewis have developed for use in a distance education programme (Deakin University 1999). Our concern with 'images of change' is therefore both metaphorical and literal, since the case record includes visual, audio and print material. Further, our aim is not to create images of change, but to provide teachers, and others, with the resources to create and explore their own images.

The conjunction of 'educational change' and 'case study methods' is not accidental. In education, case study methods were developed in parallel with projects which attempted to implement curriculum and organizational change. The notion of 'case study' is central to contemporary developments in action research, evaluation, curriculum development and policy studies. In the methodological literature, it is often taken to be a pantechnicon term, of the same order as 'qualitative research', and loosely associated with an array of cognate terms: 'illuminative' and 'responsive' evaluation, 'participant research', 'educational ethnography', 'naturalistic research' and so on. But to use these terms interchangeably is to misread significant subtleties to be found in shifts and shades of meaning. Our purpose in this chapter is not to be definitive but to explore issues that have been masked by construing differences in meaning in global terms (between quantitative and qualitative methods or between interpretive and emancipatory paradigms, for instance).

We have chosen to adopt a conversational mode for our discussion. The conversation is one which has continued between us for more than a decade. We have chosen this medium as a way of interrupting the conventional academic discourse, with its caveats and footnotes, its quotes and citations, because we wish to uncover the kind of knowledge which builds between academic friends as they grow together in understanding an unfolding phenomenon. One of the dangers of this form is that it may become inward looking and self-referential. We have tried to avoid this but apologize in advance for lapses.

Rob: One of the important things to say about Hathaway case study is that it has multiple uses; it is a resource, not a course. It becomes educational only in the context of its use. So to talk about it as an object apart from its context of use is misleading – just as it is misleading to look at a set of curriculum materials and not to consider the form of their enactment within teaching.

The way we've been using it currently is to prompt teachers to think about the classroom in new ways. We have set them tasks to do, in which we try to shake them out of the idea of seeing the classroom only as a teacher sees it. The box contains an example (slightly edited).

Task 31

You are acting as an adviser to a video producer who is planning a series of films in primary schools in countries with very different cultures and conditions. The initial plan is to include an edited half-hour film from each of six countries: Korea, Canada, Japan, Norway, Indonesia and Australia.

During the development of the project, the producer shows you three classroom extracts from Hathaway and asks you to write a commentary that sets them in context for an international audience. 'I want to know', she says, 'what this tells us about Australia and what we expect of our primary schools. How can these extracts make sense to audiences which might have quite different ideas and expectations of their primary schools? We need to explain what we think are the educationally important aspects of the activities shown in the film.'

'Don't forget', she adds, with a wry smile, 'film-makers hate words!'

You recall that this is a reference to an earlier conversation in which she had said that the trouble with working with academics (and teachers) on projects of this kind is that they always want to write too much. The secret, she explained, is not to explain everything but to use commentary to effect, to complement the visual image, not to make it redundant.

Susan: By setting that task you are asking teachers to develop a coherence in relation to the materials, drawing on their resources as classroom teachers. I find that is developmentally very interesting, because it has gone a long way from what I was thinking of. What I had at the start was four cardboard boxes. Each box contained the records from a different school. In the boxes were observations about teaching, photographs, work samples, interview transcripts from discussions with the teachers conducted after the observations and a wide range of planning and policy documents. The teachers were asked why they had decided to teach in the way that they had, how that particular curriculum area had been developed within the school and how it fitted with the larger purposes of the school.

What students were being asked to do was to become researchers of these case records and develop a portrayal of curriculum in action. I wanted them to see that curriculum is a far more complex construct than they had originally thought. They tended to believe that curriculum was just the specified syllabus to be taught in classrooms: they came to see that curriculum is the interactions between all the players and the media used. We talked about that as the curriculum *text*, they were made to see this in a curriculum *context*, from the local school through to New South Wales state policy, and then we intersected that with curriculum *pretexts*, the reasonings which lay behind why people made choices given that they were in a particular context.

This created an opportunity for a form of curriculum theorizing that I didn't think was possible without those kinds of resources.

Rob: The continuity lies in that what we are both asking is that the reader takes an active role in making the case record yield meaning.

Susan: Putting the students together to work on the case records of the individual schools meant they had to produce questions for themselves. To start with they had to think about where their own ideas about schooling came from. I had built into the process a means where they had to share autobiographical fragments about their experiences and publicly take these apart for others to challenge and question, so that they understood that they already had a mind set, if you like, with which they were approaching these materials.

The other thing I wanted them to do was to ask questions of the ways in which the materials had been collected. They needed to see that these were not neutral materials, that as a researcher going into the schools, collecting these observations and conducting these interviews, I already had a theoretical stance, and that they had a right to challenge that in their analysis. So they weren't just bringing these materials together to develop a portrayal, they were also bringing them together to develop a critique of the material with which they were presented.

Rob: When we first presented students with the edited version of the printed material some of them would say, 'Not knowing Susan I need to know why she asked these questions in this way.' Some of the interviews didn't seem to fit together. They thought you talked differently to the principal and to the staff. We learnt that you can't just present the transcript and say 'this is depersonalized data'.

Susan: As the researcher, I was seen by some of the teachers as fairly remote from their experience – I was 'out there' so to speak. So I tried to soften that image in the interactions and adopted a more conversational style, whereas with the principal there was a greater reciprocity in the status relations and the questioning could be more robust.

Sometimes people ask why I did not require students to collect the data if I was so keen to embed the notion of research in this process. My argument was that they would need to engage in so much barrier breaking first, so much negotiation, that they would find it difficult to get to the actual questions.

Rob: That explains why you can't just put together descriptions as though the researcher didn't exist. People need to know what lies behind the questions, why this question was asked and not that one.

Susan: And I think that idea of silences in the text is really important; we need to be able to speculate on why that question wasn't asked; was it just oversight or was the area too sensitive? Even though students might not be able to produce the answers, the very fact that they ask the question is important. Nothing is ever complete, nothing is ever totally comprehensive.

I came as a visiting scholar to the Centre for Applied Research in Education, University of East Anglia (CARE) in 1983. Many of us who were associated with educational research and evaluation in Australia at that time saw CARE as a site where important debates regarding teacher participation in forms of research whose purpose was the improvement of school practices were being conducted. I was particularly interested in the ways in which case study might be used by teachers as evaluators and the ways in which the resultant cases might support teacher education.

When I arrived CARE was grieving the death of Lawrence Stenhouse, whose contribution to our thinking about teacher professionalism and evaluation was immeasurable. His work was greatly admired and respected in Australia, particularly by those who were interested in broad band equity programmes. It seemed to us that he wished to give both teachers and learners insight into the validity of that which they had learned. He also seemed to me to challenge the conventional wisdom of the day, which suggested that case studies were too singular to be of assistance in developing widespread understanding about school practices. My understandings of Lawrence's work were developed through his in-house memoranda, as well as through the many conversations I had while at CARE.

My six months at CARE emphasized for me the legitimacy of Lawrence's arguments, particularly in relation to the nexus between the case record and the case study (Stenhouse 1993). He saw the case record as a lightly edited primary source: the assembly and organization of the case data by the field worker prior to its interpretation and discussion. During his last year Lawrence had developed a project for the British Library which explored independent study by students using libraries in the academic sixth form. Field workers had amassed a large number of case records from a variety of schools across England and Wales, principally in the form of interview transcripts. However, this 'archive' had not been transformed into a case study. Under the guidance of Jean Rudduck and working alongside David Hopkins, I explored these case records and begun to construct a case study of the English curriculum.

I found myself deeply engaged with the archive. I was intrigued, among other things, with the silences in the texts. Why was it that so few of the interviews made any reference to the intrinsic value of studying literature? Why were the responses so instrumental? The case records led me to retheorize my understanding of curriculum as a phenomenon, as well as ask myself about the methodology.

As a teacher educator, I could see the potential in case records as the basis for students beginning to construct their own theories of curriculum. As I've said, Rob, it's such a hard thing for them to do. They need to synthesize their understandings of the classroom as text, they need to appreciate the context (from micro to macro) and they need to perceive the pretexts for the many decisions which are being taken. It occurred to me that assembling case records of schools which served very different communities, and presenting these to students as material to be mined for meaning, would be a challenge indeed. The joy, the intellectual joy, is in the construction of the case and the creative act of constructing the case.

Rob: As the researcher, it's so easy to become the person who has all the fun! Some years ago, one of our students felt that a marked silence in the case record was the lack of an interview with the architect who designed Hathaway. As it was not there, she wrote her own. She made me realize that a problem with a lot of case studies in the literature is that they don't really invite people to make a creative response. This is becoming a key methodological issue in contemporary case study research, hence the interest in more actively engaging approaches, like those of case methods (Shulman 1966) and scenario planning (Schwarz 1991).

Susan: Yes, I've had similar experiences. The students would need now and again to pause and demonstrate to the other students what they had learned from delving into the archive. They undertook to make a number of different kinds of presentations which brought up issues from their school. I remember a group working their way through a simulated staff meeting. They each took the role of someone in the school, so somebody became Adnan, the Arabic teacher, someone else was the teacher librarian, or the ESL teacher, somebody took on the role of the principal. They worked really hard to stay inside those roles. They found it challenging to get inside both the head and the position of the person they were portraying.

Rob: I think there's a quality of learning in a situation like that that you don't get, if you are *just* the reader. The appeal of case studies for me is in doing them. You get to enter places and conversations that normally would be closed to you. But I came to see that it was not enough just to report what I found to an armchair reader. What was needed was an approach which allowed me to take the reader with me.

I often return in my thinking to a favourite line that Bev Labbett uses. In a discussion, he will ask, 'But what is the question to which this is the answer?' When we first started putting a CD together I was asked to make a presentation to the library staff at Deakin University, and somebody asked me 'What is the objective?' And I said one of the assumptions that we make in distance education, or when we're developing curriculum materials, is that our responsibility is to simplify things, and here we're trying to do the opposite. We want students to understand that things that first sound simple, are often in fact complicated. Success for us is if students start to look at the case record and say 'I'm confused.'

I could tell that saying this created a level of confusion. So I went on: 'What we're trying to do is confuse people because it is one of the essential features of schools that they are overwhelmingly complex.' We are trying to help people to come to terms with working in a complex environment. We don't usually do that in education courses, we simplify and simplify and then present teachers with something that's appealingly simple but which won't work. I read recently that the UNESCO prize for education this year had gone to a Danish management institute that aimed to train people as 'chaos pilots'. This is what we are aiming to do. Helping people learn ways of navigating through chaos rather than standing back and admiring its patterns from afar.

Susan: I would have probably used the word 'unsettle'. In a pre-service context the students tend to see the most important moment of contact in the school as when they try to teach in the classroom. It's also the experience which produces the greatest anxiety for them. It's the one that they are most conscious of when they walk into a school. So they don't see all this other stuff around them. And the other thing is that while there's a huge literature on curriculum theorizing, unless you've got something to hold on to it remains just that, a set of detached theories. So the students started to identify, but not yet name, some issues such as 'the hidden curriculum'. They started to ask questions like 'what's being learned here, besides the substance of the lesson?' They started to raise issues with respect to ethnicity, culture, social class and so on, and how these things influenced what was happening.

Rob: As I understand it that's very close to what Barry MacDonald had in mind when he first developed school case studies at Jordanhill in the 1960s. Barry's aim was to construct accounts of schools which could be used to simulate teaching. Using film and video, interview transcripts and documentary materials, he intended to create case studies as contexts for developing practical action.

It was on the basis of this work that Lawrence Stenhouse invited Barry to evaluate the Humanities Curriculum Project (HCP). I think he did so because he saw the need to assess the effects of the project in the complex circumstances of a whole school, rather than only as a shift on an aggregated student performance measure.

Making the transfer of case study from teacher training to evaluation proved more problematic than it might seem in retrospect. What emerged eventually from the HCP evaluation project were school case studies that consisted almost entirely of transcripted interviews (with teachers and students). These were edited almost as a film might be edited, using juxtaposition to establish a narrative line, to suggest motivations and to pose dilemmas, and in which the success of the project was often incidental to other issues and concerns.

Creating these case studies proved to be a demanding and difficult task, and as a result a growing individualism emerged. And as the genre spread, others found new forms of presentation, tended to emphasize different themes and took the form of the case study in different directions. In this context, Lawrence Stenhouse's 'invention' of the case record was (as he saw it) an attempt to 'democratize' case study, to pull it back from literary pretension and to make it accessible and ordinary; a part of the vernacular of teaching. He was (at least in some conversations) less concerned to establish the legitimacy of case study as research, and saw as much more important the need to build it into the professional practice of teachers.

My impression was that Lawrence began talking about the 'case record'/'case study' distinction after the second Nuffield Cambridge Evaluation Conference in 1974 (reported in Adelman *et al.* 1976). Following the conference, what seemed to goad Lawrence was a growing elitism he detected in this meeting, and in retrospect it was a meeting characterized by a fair amount of male rivalry and bonding.

Susan: Well all that is pretty hard to detect from the other side of the world. I do remember reading the documentation of that conference at the British Council, here in Sydney. I was still teaching in a primary school, but had been asked to work on evaluation guidelines for teachers who were funded under the Disadvantaged Schools Programme. There was an expectation that they would evaluate their projects, not only for accountability reasons, but to build up a professional knowledge base about equity interventions.

It was so refreshing to get away from the dominant evaluation literature of the time, which came mainly from the United States and was highly technical and pervaded by positivist traditions. Coming into contact with the qualitative ideas and Barry McDonald's emphasis upon democratic processes was liberating.

Rob: Barry's concern at Jordanhill was that once young teachers were in the schools, they were very rapidly socialized by the conservative culture of schooling. So his idea of case study was to give them a sense of alternatives.

Perhaps paradoxically he saw case studies less as documentary realism and more as emancipatory.

Susan: Almost thirty years on, that kind of interruption that Barry was interested in doing has been appropriated. Having looked at recent publications which purport to be cases from which students can start to develop theories of teaching, learning and curriculum, to me they're so sanitized and decontextualized, their brevity is such that the readers can't grasp that enormous complexity that you speak about. In fact I don't think that they would necessarily unsettle anybody. Whereas I think that what we were trying to do, and what Barry was aiming at, was to provide something that was far fuller and richer.

Rob: Hence what I was saying before about complexity and confusion.

Susan: I was reading an EdD study recently where the metaphor of a kaleidoscope was used. You've got all these little fragments, you shake them up, and that's the unsettling and then they fall together into a pattern. But you can shake them again and find new patterns. So you start to see things afresh again. So when you go to the CD-ROM you can look for a set of references, perhaps to ethnicity, you shake all that up, then you find a pattern; then you search for something else and find another pattern. Then you start to ask yourself how these patterns start to interact with each other. I think it's really serious intellectual work, and I think that's something that's missing in a lot of teacher education.

Rob: The kaleidoscope image is a good one. The aim is for teachers to be able to create their own narratives within the discipline of the case.

Susan: Being authors works in two ways. Well it probably works in a number of ways, but fundamentally there's authoring in the sense of producing some sort of coherence for oneself, in making the transition from the case record to the case study, but there's also co-authorship, if you like, with the researcher. It comes back to those issues that you are concerned about with regard to case records of an ethnographic kind. Can we just turn to that for a moment, because I think it's an important evolution from the earlier concerns about the use of case records.

Rob: In the late 1970s Lawrence Stenhouse obtained a grant from the ESRC (then the SSRC) to develop the case study notion. His plan was to compare and contrast interview ('oral history') and observation ('ethnographic') approaches. As part of this project he set up a number of meetings in which I was involved, as were Jean Rudduck, who planned to conduct interview-based studies as part of the work that later was to form her PhD, and Stephen Ball, who was then just completing the Beachside Comprehensive study. As I recall it, Lawrence and Jean were to produce interview-based case records and Stephen and I, ethnographic case records.

The interview studies were technically relatively straightforward as the case record came to mean transcripts of audio-taped interviews with a fairly standard format. Lawrence saw the equivalent in ethnography lying in the ethnographer's notebooks, but Stephen and I both struggled with this, both of us seeing (as I recall) the notebooks as providing exploratory drafts of later writing rather than low inference data. Further, we voiced some suspicions about the character of the interview data, seeing these in similar terms and always wanting to look as much at the questions asked by the researcher as at the answers given by the interviewee. Stephen was, at the time, intensively reading Alfred Schutz, and kept coming back to the notion of the interview as a social construction, not amenable to treatment as decontextualized data.

This issue was amplified by Lawrence's intention to create 'archives' of data which a community of researchers might contribute to and use as a source of analysis. The problem both Stephen and I had with this at the time was in disentangling the ethnographer from the ethnography. By degrees we both withdrew from the project because of the difficulty we saw in creating a database of ethnographic material which could be treated as objective data without reference to its context of realization. Though neither of us said so at the time, we found ourselves unable to give up the notion of authorship in relation to ethnographic writing.

Now I would say that case studies are always provisional. There are always multiple case studies which can be written; and any one is provisional and open to criticism.

Susan: I agree. I think it's provisional in two ways. In that you never have the complete case record, that's one of the things that is absolutely fascinating about Hathaway. You've now got a critical mass of material, spanning ten years, and you're still adding to it. There are more stories to be told. There will always be more stories, historically, because the school is evolving and changing, the community is evolving and changing, the teachers are moving on and moving in; and laterally as well, because even if you only took a day in the life of the school you couldn't capture everything which had happened and been experienced.

Rob: We had this wonderful zen-like moment when we were putting the CD-ROM together. We kept seeing more and more links, and then we thought you could link everything to everything, and at some point everything is relevant to everything else. Even the various commentaries become part of the record. The case record is infinite!

Susan: I certainly know that this was the situation for me: I would continue to be surprised by what students who were new to the case records came up with.

The other thing which I think is important is to find ways for students to be able to challenge each other's accounts. Is there a validity in the ways in which they have constructed their case studies from the case records, what Lawrence talked of as *intersubjective verifiability*? Because there is a community of students working on the material and the fact that they have to make their accounts public and be prepared to defend them is absolutely fundamental to the process.

Rob: One of the concerns we have always had, and it's come up more than once, is how to handle a racist interpretation of the material. If you open the door to interpretation, what responsibility do you have in the face of responses that are consistent with the material but promote biased views? (Again the history of the HCP is relevant here.)

Susan: I guess it's who has the authority. And I think that is our responsibility. All views do not have equal status. We need to agree as a community of scholars that we use this material to adhere to ethical principles. But we also have sufficient regard for each other that we can ask how someone comes to hold that position, what the argument being made here is.

Rob: Also, people often want to make judgements. They come to the study wanting to measure the performance of people against an external standard.

Susan: I think that's something that one can counter by saying that what we are trying to do is understand what is happening, rather than make some kind of judgement about it. Trying to imagine how it was that things were as they were.

Rob: I think that goes back to Barry's original ideas about case study, that the purpose was to defer judgement in order to create space, because if you rush to judgement too quickly, you close off ways of understanding which can lead to other ways of acting.

So there we have it: a continuing conversation about teacher education. A conversation about research questions. A conversation about ways of knowing. It is a conversation that was only possible because we have that shared grounding from CARE and the challenges which have been set before us by its people and its processes.

References

Adelman, C., Jenkins, D. and Kemmis, S. (1976) Rethinking case study: notes from the second Cambridge conference. *Cambridge Journal of Education*, 6(3), 139–50.

Deakin University (1999) *Hathaway Primary School: A Multimedia Case Study*, 2nd edn, CDROM. Geelong, Australia.

Schwarz, P. (1991) *The Art of the Long View: Planning for the Future in an Uncertain World*. New York: Doubleday/Currency.

Shulman, J. (1966) Tender feelings, hidden thoughts: confronting bias, innocence and racism through case discussions. In J. Colbert, K. Trimble and P. Desberg (eds) *The Case for Education: Contemporary Approaches for Using Case Methods*. Needham Heights, Mass: Allyn & Bacon.

Stenhouse, L. (1993) *A Perspective on Educational Case Study. A Collection of Papers by Lawrence Stenhouse*. Coventry: University of Warwick/CEDAR.

12

Experts of the future?

CHRISTINE O'HANLON

This chapter addresses 'images of change' concerned with the practices of universities in relation to the professional development of teachers. There have been profound changes in global politics, academic knowledge and the moral focus of education and commerce in recent decades. Western society in Europe and the USA since the 1970s has experienced decline in economic growth, political empire and legitimated cultural currency. This loss of national confidence in the 'West' and the USA elicited a reaction which created space within academia for reflective and critical discourses, such as critical theory, phenomenology, ethnomethodology, Marxism, existentialism and postmodernism. These themes in academic focus are unified through the perspective of social constructivism, deconstructionism and postmodernism. Within the postmodern perspective society is viewed as a text, and accepted scientific and academic texts are themselves viewed as rhetorical acts with no logical or empirical legitimacy. In such a view, fact and fiction become blurred because they are seen as the products and resources for communicative action – they are representations of a constructed reality representing different ideologies, groups and interests.

What are the implications of this change for teacher education in universities? Ultimately the courses constructed in universities to legitimate teachers' professional practice are facing the tensions which arise from ideological and post-empiricist critique. Traditionally, their development has been based upon academic scholarship and intellectual ability, whereas the practical knowledge and experience gained in teachers' careers have been treated as incidental to this focus, and have even at times been dismissed as 'subjective' or anecdotal when used as evidence in written assignments and dissertations.

The focus of this chapter is on the inevitable changes that are occurring in university departments of education (UDEs) in the UK through an example of the author's own academic responses to ideological tensions in educational practice. These tensions are related to the long-term development of the teaching profession, and in particular the form that this process will develop through its investment in 'experts of the future'.

Do we really believe that a three- or four-year initial training period for teachers provides a sufficient foundation for a life-long career and continual educational support for all school students? The UK has yet to establish a life-long career plan for teachers who wish to remain in the profession for their employable lives, unlike other European countries, which use a contractable pattern of career development for teachers, e.g. where practising teachers are put under contract to attend in-service courses for continued professional development (CPD) at regular periods throughout their professional lives. Until recently the UK has left this development to the *ad hoc* annual diversities of government priorities, school priorities and the motivation of individuals who wish to find career advancement, or professional development in specific subjects or areas. As a result, we have a teaching profession that is 'educated' in a differential and variable degree to meet the needs of the new society in the twenty-first century.

I use the word 'educated' deliberately to distinguish 'education' from 'teaching', which is the actual practice of teaching in educational contexts within schools, colleges and educational institutions. The pedagogy of teaching in schools is related to ways of improving student learning and organizing classrooms and school for instruction. The pedagogy of teaching in UDEs is focused upon the improvement of professional practice through scholarship, research, reading and reflection about the ideas and conceptual structures which inform and shape their decisions and judgements in their professional lives and in the wider socio-political frameworks of society.

The pedagogical traditions in schools and in UDEs require the translation of complex socio-political issues in society into educational action. For example, the technical implementation of a National Curriculum, the testing of all children at 7, 11, 14 and 16 years, requires a technology of testing that maintains technical and ideological struggles within it. An awareness in both contexts must be created that recognizes pedagogy and curriculum knowledge as problematic, open to scrutiny and in need of critical appraisal and revision. The professional development of teachers becomes teacher education when a critical theory of the teaching situation allows professionals to explain and understand the ways in which teaching is controlled by factors outside the classroom in its societal and political context. Educational professionals need to recognize that pedagogy and curriculum knowledge is always problematic, and thus open to scrutiny, critical appraisal and revision. The development of teachers 'subject' knowledge often overlooks the wider political and national issues that frame it.

Debate about pedagogy in largely subject-specific areas may overlook the overall shape of the 'curriculum' at all levels, and fail to site it in broader, complex socio-cultural factors which relate to economic, political and strategic concerns in Western society. It is essential to create dialogue to challenge existing ideologies and raise issues for debate on current educational concerns. However, in 1992 the DfEE stated that principles supporting the National Curriculum (NC) were no longer the subject for debate;

> Debate is no longer about the principle of the National Curriculum, but about the detail . . . it is about how the subjects should be developed within the National Curriculum and about the crucial testing arrangements associated with them; it is not about whether subjects should form part of the National Curriculum.
>
> (DfEE 1992: 3)

The NC principle, or whether subjects should be included in the NC, is beyond debate according to the DfEE, but we are permitted to debate 'the detail'. However, it is crucial to the professional 'education' of teachers that they engage in a thorough critique of values inherent in the evolution and direction of national educational policies.

In the UK the Teacher Training Agency (TTA) is the government-sponsored body responsible for teacher training and the continuing professional development of teachers. It has recently been given the responsibility to ensure the quality of initial teacher training (ITT) and the CPD of the teaching profession through the use of £25 million a year funding to:

- be used for the long-term development of the teaching profession, and in particular, to form an investment in the *experts of the future*;
- fund provision which has a beneficial and has a demonstrable impact on practice in schools in order to raise the level of pupils' achievement (TTA 1997).

The TTA wishes to ensure that the future development of teachers is securely linked to school needs, that it develops teachers' knowledge, understanding, skills and effectiveness in the raising of the standards and achievements of their pupils. The agency proposes that any professional development should have a demonstrable effect on practice in schools and should provide a long-term strategy for professional improvement and career development (TTA 1997).

Like so many other proposals from government sources, it is left to the educational profession to interpret them best and find strategies for their development. Regardless of our personal views of these proposals, academics in UDEs are now required to interpret and critique them and put them into practice in the CPD of the teaching profession. In this context, I propose a means of implementing the principles inherent in the text above.

How do we prepare the experts of the future?

With a recent emphasis on the practice of teaching in initial teacher education and the importance of learning from practice in the professional lives of teachers, it is also important to find a means to allow teachers to learn and improve from their experiences in a way that will advance their careers and confer quality on their resulting efforts for students. But for teachers to understand the underlying influences in the general culture and practice of their profession, they must step beyond the everyday milieu of the school and into a space deliberately organized to provide them with the opportunity to practise critical reasoning about what they are doing, why they are doing it and how they can successfully achieve their educational aims. This is not to imply that they need to contemplate abstractions and ideas in a purely theoretical manner; instead it implies a rhetorical situation where ideas, theories, the practice of professional duties and responsibilities are examined in the contexts in which they occur. Teacher education concerns the education of teachers into a culture which increases their professional autonomy through the growth of a critical theory of teaching. The practice of teaching becomes educative when professionals have the opportunity to validate critical theories of teaching in their own school-based enquiry, e.g. achieved through various investigatory processes often referred to as reflective enquiry, investigatory practice or action research. The school-based enquiry requires a fostering of educational contexts where teachers can engage in critical reasoning. This process is based on a common-sense understanding of professional practice which develops into an argument for its defence or transformation. Any specific topic of relevance may be developed in a critical enquiring framework as long as it can be identified as democratic education, i.e. education that actively aims to work towards social equality and justice. Critical reasoning about the professionals' practice does not favour a specific or current view of practice, e.g. a correct view; instead it invites professionals to see the educational issues that arise in the argument as issues related to values in culture and judgement which require reappraisal, understanding and critical review.

Traditionally practitioners acquire their practice by submitting to 'an authority' built upon practical experience. It is only then that teachers obtain the practical knowledge and standards of excellence by which their own practical competence can be assessed/evaluated. This is what they first experience through the ITT courses and the professional award of Qualified Teacher Status (QTS), which is predominately based on practice and learning from more experienced professionals. However, the authoritative nature of tradition does not necessarily imply that practitioners should be compliant and accepting of all they receive. It is also important to find a means to allow teachers to learn from their own experiences in teaching and to improve their practice in the general advancement of their careers. It requires the fostering of contexts that enable teachers to engage in critical reasoning, like teacher education courses based on critical enquiry or action research. Teachers need space to engage in critical reasoning. This process is based upon arguments on any topic of relevance to the aims of democratic education.

However, mature teachers are experienced teachers, they have extensive practical experience in schools and are engaged in committed and morally informed action directed towards specific aims. Their expertise has been built upon a tradition of practical knowledge that has not been simply technically reproduced throughout the history of education, but has been constantly reconstructed through revisions resulting from raising questions related to 'What is the good/benefit of education and how can it be pursued?' The emphasis on values within the question has altered textually in past decades. In a tradition of critical review, the educational culture is transforming and changing constantly. To practise within the teaching tradition implies that because traditions are actively recreated, the process is always open to criticism. It is in this active and critical reconstruction that a tradition evolves and changes rather than stays constant and inert. It is only when the active criticism of a traditional practice is subverted or otherwise silenced that the practical knowledge will tend to be used in unproductive and/or unethical ways. This happens because the practice becomes formalized or routinized as traditionally 'good', without consideration of new and recent changes in society which may now demand more original professional skills.

Both Aristotle and Habermas have developed the notions of critical reasoning, but Habermas situates the basic ideas of Aristotle in a critique of the nature and functions of social science related to the action of professionals who attempt to work in the interests of rationality, justice and freedom – which he refers to as an emancipatory interest. Through participation in forms of democratic action, it is expected that a critical professional perspective will emerge within the context of argument and debate supported through the aims of valuing justice and freedom. In order to support the emergence of a more truthful perspective, professional action must be developed on evidence which is based on a rational critique, and a free dialogue. It is achieved through:

- a critique of ideological aspects of the production and reproduction of the culture;
- the organization of 'enlightenment' in social groups;
- collective/collegiate social action (see Habermas 1984, 1987).

On this basis I attempt to organize collaborative social action in the CPD of teachers, where educational theory and practice is concerned with the production and reproduction of the 'school' or educational culture. Teachers gather evidence from their practice which supports their educational argument and then deconstruct the evidence in dialogue with colleagues to find the contradictions and disparities which inevitably arise. In this process they learn to reveal the concealed factors which reproduce the educational culture. The process of deconstruction occurs with the input of peers, i.e. teaching professionals who recognize that encouraging their thoughts and actions in a public process helps to achieve renewed social and educational practice.

Teachers need to be trained to become critical intellectuals, which is an aspect of their professionalism which needs to be fostered. They have their own personal theories about education and about what works best in different teaching contexts. They ideally want to develop their teaching theories and improve their practices but may need help from colleagues and others to 'see' and understand exactly what is happening in the classroom and school. Such a process I want to explain further.

Group organization

When teachers join CPD courses in higher education they ideally need a collegial structure to support their textual deconstruction. The deconstruction of the academic and scientific texts may be primarily from specialist journals, review articles and books – the research literature. There is also the writing and interpretation of evidence that the teachers themselves prepare for the group dialogue. The recasting of the data gleaned from these texts into a dialogue of a Socratic form demands considerable effort and discipline. Teachers in the group are encouraged to develop their own individual means to express their research concerns and issues. They struggle to define the difference between fact and fiction in what they read and what is expressed. Often this may lead to the teacher taking an adversarial stance in the questioning of colleagues. However, it is essential to fill in the context and background on complex issues that are controversial, as, for example, did MacDonald and Stake (1974) in a government-sponsored curriculum evaluation. They developed an adversarial form of dialogue in reporting to a government committee on the issues inherent in curriculum development in computer-assisted learning. The dialogic form itself invited the reader's participation and left the issues open to interpretation, rather than the text being imprinted by the researchers' authoritative judgement. The reader's textual deconstruction was necessary for the truth to be revealed. Textual deconstruction is important to enable teachers to challenge the messages within the texts they read, whether overt or covert. They also need to challenge the text and their understanding of it, in their written evidence and the narrative context that they use in their research-based enquiry. The texts, in the group process, are deconstructed through:

- interrogating the data;
- laying them open to scrutiny;
- allowing peers to play a role in the process;
- attempting to understand and explain the conflicts in the process;
- reassessing their argument for the support of evidence and reflection on specific aspects of professional practice.

In this process teachers also need the opportunity to:

- articulate their values and ideas;
- have them critically deconstructed through dialogue.

This may happen in 'collegial' or 'research' groups, which I have developed through my own professional practice. However, the process of dialogue through critical reasoning needs some direction. Group members initially have to learn how to act as colleagues in a process of cultural critique. They learn how to ask fundamental questions about their colleagues' educational role and aims. Group members bring their research evidence, their analysis of data, their reflections and issues to the group, whose other members question them about their understanding of the evidence and its implications. They begin, as an introduction to the group, to relate their educational role and aims and to explain the reasons for their specific research-based enquiry. Techniques are used to test that group members are listening 'for' the other members and thinking 'for' them in their choice of questions which are aimed to help 'speakers' to perceive contradictions or incongruity in their argument or to develop their ideas further. Contradictions, once identified, enable the teacher to understand their problematic nature in the reflective and critical context of the group dialogue. This process is later supported by a diary/journal and note-taking during the group sessions. The group of teacher colleagues referred to as the 'research group' supports the process of critique by presenting and debating issues which arise in the evidence and reflective notes, ensuring an interactive and dialogic encounter essential to the process of critical reasoning.

In my experience, the group is usually a group of fellow teachers and educational professionals following the same course at the university, e.g. MPhil, MA, MEd or PhD. The group members may have similar interests because they are researching a similar subject or interest area in education. The group normally consists of 10–20 students who meet regularly, e.g. once a month for three or four hours outside formal timetabled course time.

New group members introduce themselves when they first attend the group, in terms of their professional history, career and research interests. In the initial set-up of the group certain steps need to be taken to form collegial structures for professional development in a manner that reflects democratic values and strategies, as follows:

- involving participants in negotiation of the form and organization of the collegial group;
- setting out basic agreed rules of procedure for meetings – which are constantly open to renegotiation or change;
- making sure that the rules adhere to equal time strategies for participants and strategies for dealing with difficult and sensitive issues;
- fostering an understanding about frank dialogue based on trust – necessitating a code of confidentiality within the group;
- negotiating access to the group by new members;
- agreeing a means of recording and reproducing ideas and materials created through group meetings;
- submitting every group member's contributions to the critical process, including the chairperson's voice.

The chairperson's role is to model a form of non-threatening, but not neutral, questioning, which is based upon:

- careful listening;
- sensitive raising of controversial or political issues;
- partially supporting but overtly challenging biased or prejudiced language and perspectives;
- probing beyond the basic presentation of ideas for the arguments and sources of experiences influencing possible biased perspectives;
- accepting the person but not necessarily his or her ideas or arguments without critical challenge.

Although I often act as the chairperson, the group may have a rotating chair and elect its own chairperson for specific group sessions, or even change chairperson during the meeting. When acting in the role of chairperson I am aware of the dialogue moving between multiple layers of personal explanation, abstraction, commentary and argument. I may at different times lead the discussion or chair the discourse taking place among the group members. I may deliberately play devil's advocate, provoking alternative viewpoints to those presented in the discussion.

I may pause to question the philosophical or conceptual basis of certain ideas or phrases used in the argument. I often use Socratic questioning techniques. I encourage reflection on what is being said and what is happening at other levels in the discourse. I encourage the multi-recording of the discussion and the minuting of members' personal reflections that arise during its development. I desist from presenting my personal viewpoint to the group during group sessions so that I do not bias the discussion through the imposition of my perspective, which may carry special weight because of my status and university role. However, this is not always an issue because with research students I act as their 'supervisor', supporting them through the process of their research. I am not ultimately responsible for the assessment of their work, which is undertaken by formal university procedures. I would encourage dialectical tensions in arguments and challenge group members to confront the tensions themselves, which means remaining silent, only listening for long periods in the group meetings.

All group members follow simple agreed procedures of strategy related to:

- listening attentively to 'speakers' in the group;
- questioning 'speakers' in relation to their presentation, for the purposes of clarification or deeper understanding;
- challenging assumptions underlying the expression of values and motives;
- identifying contradictions and tensions inherent in the presentation.

The group chairperson or facilitator provides feedback on 'how' ideas have been presented and also controls the time for group members to contribute. She or he vetoes the seeking of information for personal gain etc., or self-directed questions and comments, if it is not the person's time to contribute. Mostly, 'I' as the course tutor act as the group chairperson, but as the group rules are devised and agreed by the group members, this role can be undertaken by any experienced group member.

The group is run on agreed, democratic, negotiated principles which allow group members:

- to present their research ideas, problems, issues and developments to the group at agreed meetings and time allocations;
- to present problems and issues to others as closely and as truthfully to the context in which they arise;
- to use group members to extend their thinking by validating their investigations, challenging their research practice and conclusions, explaining their understanding of their investigation, analysis of evidence and conclusions.

In this way, group members learn to know each other and to develop reciprocal trust in meetings. They develop confidence through their questioning and commentary, which can be mutually beneficial to both speaker and listener, as major issues often relate to everyone's experience. Occasional commentary is allowable when the context is appropriate, e.g. when another group member has information or an understanding which will illuminate the speaker's dilemma or problem. What is avoided assiduously at meetings is 'hogging' of the agenda by dominant members, digression, irrelevant questioning and 'something similar happened to me' stories activated by the dialogue. The agenda for meetings is planned ahead each year. New members are given priority for presentation at their first meeting. Later, when members make progress with their research, they are given increasingly more 'group time' for the presentation of their investigatory issues. In addition to the dialogue which occurs in meetings, members write about what is discussed, its challenges and its implications for their research. These reflective records may eventually be included in their research theses to illustrate the learning process undertaken through the group, and its constraining or liberating effects on their education.

In the group, the research thesis or project is treated as a narrative whose guiding interests must be uncovered and critically interrogated. The group process provides active collegiality in the educational culture. The consolidation of ideas and critical challenge created by educational professionals at all levels, including higher education, forms a basis for educational fusion for political action and change. The collegial dialogue and debate generated in such groups encourages higher education tutors as professional educators to develop a critical voice in university courses, and in social situations that develop dialogue between teachers. It allows them to appreciate the nature of difference as a basis for democratic action. The dialogue creates a fundamental condition for critical reasoning, trust, sharing and a commitment to improving the quality of teaching and learning in schools and other institutional contexts.

Teacher educators also need to find a means for teachers to critique and experiment with different languages or forms of discourse as they are presented in papers, journals and other course materials. In this way teachers have the opportunity to analyse critically the ethical and political values that different voices represent in education. All educators, teachers and university tutors, need to recognize how knowledge is used to reproduce dominant hierarchies, how it is used to distort reality, how it influences their own lives, both personal and professional, in their perceptions about the world, particularly the world of education. Most relevant, however, is that in this engagement in the critique of educational contexts through research, teachers are better prepared for making choices about taking action that results in morally different consequences.

Critical thinking and reasoning is the basis from which to become reconstructive actors. Courses that support collegial dialogue through critical reasoning allow teachers to develop the vision and courage necessary to take risks in their practice. It allows them to encourage their own students' freedom to learn and to develop their practice on the basis of ethical principles that legitimate its own basis for criticism in a democratic, collegial and professional manner.

Self-knowledge and understanding

The group process, through its interaction, encourages teachers to identify individual differences in themselves which define their unique professional identities. There is a professional reluctance in the culture of teaching, which includes higher education, to define the self in a professional role and to develop professional knowledge on a basis of self-knowledge. Abstraction of knowledge in the form of theory is viewed as being academically valuable, whereas practical knowledge is often translated into 'description and commentary' of practice, which has little academic value without critique. Rarely are personal expectations in the role, assumptions about the curriculum, evaluation of the professional role and its development in practice critiqued within the practical context. My contention is that this critique can only take place away from the everyday relationships, practice and tensions which arise in the school context or sites of action. A reflective space is necessary for any rigorous thinking or planning for action. In another context, which is less threatening away from the school, collegial roles can be identified individually and personal values freely articulated. Constraints to the progress of practice and the ideal of realizing educational theory can be 'abstracted' and tested through the review of school-based evidence and its interpretation. Professional and personal limitations on the improvement of practice can be realized in a public process and thus acted upon. However, the extent of action is very much contingent upon the context in which the teacher works.

Because of the way the 'ethos' is built up within schools – forms of practice which are traditional in specific contexts – its grip on aims and practice is often obscure to the practitioner. However, in another context, i.e. in the group process, the questioning or critique of the school culture becomes possible within a 'new' perspective supported by critical reasoning and collegial feedback, which makes public the nature of the process. This 'new' perspective is largely initiated by other professionals and peers, who listen and respond to teachers' own understanding and justification of their priorities and values in educational practice. Although most of the teachers in the group are concerned with UK school policy, it is possible to distinguish multiple layers of value priorities in their articulation and translation of educational policies. Group members tease out different educational priorities between the individuals and schools which are represented and question the basis on which they rest.

Higher education tutors

The lack of understanding so many teachers and tutors have of themselves and their own agency results in a lack of academic writing on the lived experiences of working in higher educational contexts. Although academics are supporting teacher colleagues from schools, there is little opportunity for them to support fellow colleagues in higher education and develop theories about their own teaching practices. At all levels in educational practice there should be developing examples of democratic collegial groups formed for the purpose of critical thinking and action, and ultimately for the improvement of practice. In a consideration of what possibilities exist for new forms of teaching and learning, there needs to be a link to self and social empowerment, based on negotiated and agreed values and principles. It would necessarily entail both teachers and university tutors in the development of a project of self-understanding and social agency involving an examination of its influence and strength, possible exigencies and value basis. It could also extend the person's professional project, beyond education through the exploration of the self, to a wider social world of which the person is a part. The understanding that people have of themselves as social actors, with lived experiences, values and motives, influences their practice of education. The critical discourse which takes place in groups, e.g. the research group referred to above, reflects in its conscious articulation of the narrative each individual's unique lived experiences up to that point. In the group there is the opportunity for reflection on, and some analysis of, the influence of background values in educational practice. The research critique allows judgements to develop about what ought to be integrated into professional actions for improved teaching and learning, e.g. through democratized action research. In this way a wider discourse is created that can realize new forms of social life in schools and beyond.

The argument up to now implies that the CPD of teachers must be focused on the task of educating them to become active in the pursuit of aims which will foster democratic educational values. Teachers and all educators need to be educated to feel confident about their intellectual skills and abilities. They need to have the courage to argue in support of their theories and ideas in a self-determined manner.

To assess the success of such an educational project in courses in universities, course tutors would need to consider how ideological and material conditions for the person's thesis are realized and how successful it is shown to be in demonstrating the relationship between schooling and the ethical and value basis of its curriculum activities. MacDonald (1996) claims that such a process as the one outlined above meets the needs of an open and dynamic system by supporting a process of continuous change. It is not a situation which suits recent government education policies. He presently sees the profession facing a hostile state and a closed system, whose only acknowledged needs are for management and surveillance.

However, I feel the efforts necessary to make a difference to national education systems are only partly achieved within each generation. If we do not make a difference in our own practice and in supporting and modelling some form of dialogic critique within the system, then the possibility of education becoming everyone's, rather than no one's, business will only recede further. Posch (1996) supports my professional stance in his view that the continuous creation of understanding is critical for renewed professional activities in education. He believes, unlike MacDonald, that the social pressure to allow students in schools to experience and create meaning have increased and will overcome the odds even if they are not in line with national governmental policies.

For me this makes the 'extended professionalism' of Stenhouse (1975) even more relevant in such stringent political circumstances. It is through the process of teachers' research-based enquiry that the views of society and its educational system will transform in time.

Conclusion

Initial training in any profession provides a foundation for professional career development. However, education is a distinctive professional enterprise which privileges its graduates to educate future generations and to lead society into ever challenging and changing human projects. It is necessary for teachers and educators not only to question the nature of knowledge, the curriculum and its reproduction, but also to model in their teaching how best this may be achieved through educational practices. Without a detailed understanding of what is really going on in the practice of teaching at all levels in society, a self-understanding on the part of its practitioners, about why and how they are acting in educational endeavours, their functions and problems etc., it will not be possible to change unproductive and unethical practices in schools and other institutions, including universities, in the creation of 'experts of the future'. A critical group process in teachers' professional development through higher degrees, developed on democratic principles, will, however, enable powerful voices to counter and reframe unworthy national educational policies and practices at school, college and university level.

References

DfEE (1992) *Choice and Diversity: a New Framework for Schools*. London: HMSO.

Habermas, J. (1984) *The Theory of Communicative Action. Volume 1, Reason and the Rationalization of Society* (trans. T. McCarthy). Boston: Beacon Press.

Habermas, J. (1987) *The Theory of Communicative Action. Volume 2* (trans. T. McCarthy). Cambridge: Polity Press.

MacDonald, B. (1996) How Education Became Nobody's Business. *Cambridge Journal of Education*, 26(2), 241–51.

MacDonald, B. and Stake, R. (1974) *The first year of a national development programme of computer assisted learning from an issues perspective*. Unpublished evaluation report, Centre for Applied Research in Education, UEA, Norwich.

Posch, P. (1996) Changing the culture of teaching and learning: implications for action research. In C. O'Hanlon (ed.) *Professional Development through Action Research in Educational Settings*. London: Falmer, pp. 61–71.

Stenhouse, L, (1975) *An Introduction to Curriculum Research and Development*. London: Heinemann.

Teacher Training Agency (1997) *Proposals for the Future Use of TTA INSET Funds*. London: HMSO.

13

Teacher control and the reform of professional development

LAWRENCE INGVARSON

This chapter presents a personal perspective on changes in professional development policy in Australia over the past 25 years. The point of departure is taken from the 1973 Karmel Report, *Schools in Australia* (Interim Committee for the Australian Schools Commission 1973). The report, prepared for the incoming Labor government (the first since 1949), had a profound influence on Australian education. The Karmel Committee had been given a wide brief that foreshadowed a more active role for the commonwealth government in school education generally, traditionally a state responsibility. With respect to professional development, however, the report argued strongly that the teaching profession itself should exercise greater control, relative to employers and universities:

> A mark of a highly skilled occupation is that those entering it should have reached a level of preparation in accordance with standards set by the practitioners themselves, and *that the continuing development of members should largely be the responsibility of the profession. In such circumstances the occupational group itself becomes the point of reference for standards and thus the source of prestige or of condemnation.* There are circumstances that make teaching a particular case since the administrative hierarchy within which most teachers work is recruited largely from outstanding practitioners. However, in Australia teachers as an occupational group have had few opportunities to participate in decision making. Their organisations have been traditionally more concerned with industrial matters, including those which affect the quality of services offered, than with the development of expertise, which has been seen as primarily the responsibility of the employer.
>
> (Karmel Report: 123; italics added)

What happened to this exciting Karmel vision? Despite more than 25 years of reports, inquiries and reviews at national and state levels advocating that professional development should become the responsibility of the profession, movement in this direction has been slow. Governments and universities still basically set the in-service education agenda around their goals and priorities. Teachers still come a poor third in the triangular struggle over the allocation of resources and the determination of priorities and purposes for their own professional development.

Nor is it possible to say that the teaching profession has become 'the point of reference for standards and thus the source of prestige or of condemnation' for its members. Attempts to establish independent professional bodies with responsibility for the 'development of expertise' have been thwarted. As a result, development of the teaching profession, as a profession, has been stunted. The profession has yet to build its own infrastructure for defining high-quality teaching standards, promoting development towards those standards and providing recognition for those who reach them; in other words, a professional development system guided by profession-defined teaching standards.

The Karmel image of a professional development system controlled by the profession raises the following questions for this chapter.

- Why has it been so difficult for the teaching profession to gain control over the professional development of its own members, compared with most professions?
- By what means could the teaching profession assume the major responsibility for the nature and direction of professional development for its members in the future?

The Karmel vision for a teacher-initiated in-service education system

The Karmel Report recognized the increasing importance of professional development for teachers in the 1970s, and the difficulty states were having in providing adequate funds to meet the need. It also foreshadowed the need for new teacher associations that organized around issues of expertise and quality rather than, or as well as, traditional industrial matters. Consequently, in allocating dramatically increased funds for professional development, the Karmel Report (p. 120) made a clear distinction between employer-initiated and teacher-initiated in-service education in the following terms:

> There will always be a need for conferences and courses in which the initiative will rest with the employing authority and through which it will seek to induct teachers into new knowledge and methods . . . While essential, such conferences and courses cannot make more than a limited contribution to the teachers' professional growth, because they

> are too short and insufficiently searching in their theoretical content to increase his capacity to consider rationally alternatives on his own initiative and because they are often someone else's diagnosis of what he requires.
>
> Consequently, there is a need for other approaches which move outward from the teacher's own experience and are based on his own developing conception of what it might mean to be a competent practitioner. Such alternatives recognise that while some teachers are obviously more skilled than others, there is no single pattern to which good teachers conform. The objective of this approach to growth is to help the teacher become progressively more sensitive to what is happening in his classroom and to support his efforts to improve, assisted by theoretical studies arising from his needs as he perceives it.
>
> The teacher is the initiating force in such an approach to in-service education, which is more likely to be followed in schools and systems where the essence of curriculum development and review is new thinking on the part of teachers themselves as well as their appraisal of others.

In making this distinction, the Karmel Report made it clear that in-service education embraced wider purposes than helping teachers to keep up with government- or employer-initiated policy changes. In-service education should also be about helping teachers keep up with 'new thinking on the part of teachers', still a rather presumptuous notion to many. This meant that teacher expertise and research could become the reference point for standards and the basis for setting the agenda for in-service education and shifting its control into the hands of the profession. The report recognized that in assuring quality teaching and learning, governments must inevitably rely on a culture of collective responsibility for standards from within the profession itself; a culture of commitment, not compliance.

In 1973, Karmel identified the large, monolithic state education department bureaucracies as a barrier to reform, and argued for devolution of responsibility to the people involved in the actual task of schooling and greater community participation in school governance. Today, ironically, we have what are called self-managing schools in the public school system, but arguably even less opportunity for teachers to define and pursue their own professional development goals, except those that fall within the goals of centrally framed school charters and curriculum.

We are still struggling, therefore, to find satisfactory answers to the questions about control raised above by Karmel. But there are signs of change. This chapter argues that although progress towards the Karmel vision has been slow, we now have a clearer idea of the conditions that need to be in place if the teaching profession is to exercise a leading role in the professional development of its own members. Key to gaining control over professional development is the capacity of teacher associations to define what their members should know and be able to do, based on core educational values; that is, to develop standards for highly accomplished teaching across specific areas of the curriculum.

Teaching standards make it possible for the profession to establish its own professional development system geared to helping teachers to reach those standards and providing recognition and certification for those who do. Some of the roots of this idea go back to the vision of professional development that came out of the work of the UK Centre for Applied Research in Education (CARE) in the 1970s, around the time that the Karmel Report appeared in Australia.

Teacher development as the pursuit of profession-defined standards

The educationists at CARE arguably redefined the meaning of teacher development as the pursuit of professional values. They recast the role of teachers in relation to in-service education. In-service education was no longer just courses put on for teachers as an audience. Professional development was the outcome of teacher engagement in authentic and challenging professional tasks such as curriculum research. These tasks brought teachers together to extend pedagogical and curriculum knowledge about how to implement core educational values and professional purposes. And, in relation to national curriculum reforms, teachers came together not as passive implementers, but as critics, evaluators and shapers of ideas in the reform proposals (Stenhouse 1975).

A key feature of these tasks was that the agenda was based on educational values and images of quality learning that were developed by, and irresistible to, teachers. Teachers in the Humanities Curriculum Project and the Ford Teaching Project, for example, were guided in their research by professional values or standards concerning the obligation of teachers to promote learning through discussion and independent reasoning. Professional development in these CARE projects was the result of engagement by teachers in networks and communities with a mutual desire to learn how to bring their values closer to their practice. By documenting this experience (MacDonald and Elliott 1975), teachers extended current knowledge about pedagogy, and this knowledge in turn provided a framework for the professional development of other teachers. CARE's research showed how the agenda for professional development could be driven by relatively stable professional knowledge and values, not merely swings in government policies and priorities.

Although the people involved would not have used the term, CARE projects showed how professional development could be organized around teaching standards. CARE's action research was essentially standards-guided curriculum evaluation and professional learning. CARE researchers like Elliott and MacDonald were assisting teachers to formulate and document their own knowledge base from research on significant aspects of educational practice, such as how to promote productive discussion of controversial social issues. The rationale for professional development became the need to keep up with professional knowledge and expertise, not just pressure to implement government-initiated reforms. It was assumed that the scope of professional development was necessarily wider and more long term than goals framed by government policy of the day.

An early image of standards-driven professional development

I remember attending a conference of the National Association of Teachers of English (NATE) in the UK in the early 1970s. This teacher-run conference was rich with new ideas about the teaching of English, especially the role of language in learning. Debate from conference sessions spilled over regularly into nearby bars and eating places. While people such as James Britton, Harold Rosen and Douglas Barnes fuelled the debate with their presentations, the greatest excitement came from the sessions run by groups of teachers on issues arising from their own teaching of English. In some of these sessions, discussion focused on pedagogical issues that had arisen for teachers who were attempting to implement values and teaching standards underpinning Lawrence Stenhouse's Humanities Curriculum Project (MacDonald and Rudduck 1971).

It was a revelation to see so many enthusiastic teachers leading sessions based on detailed descriptions and analyses of their own teaching, backed up by audio- and video-tapes and transcripts of classroom dialogue. Though obviously highly experienced and sophisticated, these teachers were still learning and wondering about their teaching; for example, about the ways in which they inadvertently dominated classroom discussion among 13-year-olds about a challenging Roethke poem, and what they might do to promote the kind of talk and understanding they valued. These teachers were revealing their ongoing uncertainty about their teaching, and thereby being accountable to colleagues, in ways I knew were beyond my confidence and capacity. But their candour evoked a sympathetic response in fellow teachers. It acted as an invitation to join them in the excitement of their experimentation.

In retrospect, what attracted me most about this conference was the image of teaching these teachers personified. They represented the three faces of professionalism; commitment, empowerment and accountability. They saw teaching as something teachers continually questioned and learned about, not a finished product. Their learning was clearly driven by educational values, or standards, they held dear, but it was also clear that the teachers were changing and deepening what they valued as a result of their analyses. Their development was driven by a natural desire to increase their competence – to do a better job. It was also guided by images of quality practice that had evolved from within their professional community. They did not think of their role as mere implementers of a curriculum prescribed by government. They were leaders in curriculum reform. As a consequence, they were setting a long-term agenda for professional development based on images of quality teaching and learning in English. These English teachers were part of ongoing conferences, debates and research within the NATE community about language and learning from the mid-1960s to the mid-1970s. Their work undoubtedly contributed to the professional knowledge and practice of others through publications, further conferences and local networks of teachers. I have been told that NATE conferences no longer attract the numbers they did back then, which is regrettable if it is true. This makes one wonder whether those teachers remained in teaching – and whether teaching is as capable of attracting and retaining people with similar dispositions today.

Elliott (1993: 65) argues that activities such as the NATE programme above 'did not simply emerge from academia, but constituted an articulation of a professional culture that emerged amongst teachers engaged in school-initiated curriculum reform during the 60s and 70s.' That culture struggled over the following years, receiving virtually no official recognition among UK policy makers as a basis for initiating significant educational change. Sources of expertise or authority other than central executive government, such as professional associations, were seriously marginalized (MacDonald 1996). Education bureaucrats looked increasingly to managerial and market mechanisms for quality assurance, rather than enhancing professional models of control and accountability (MacDonald 1978).

Two things stand out now about the NATE type of in-service activity in the 1970s. Although teachers set the agenda, little was done to formalize the developing knowledge base and to articulate a working consensus on what English teachers should know and be able to do into a set of advanced standards for teaching English. There was a tendency to equate standards with standardization of practice. The incentive structure for this kind of activity was weak. It did not have the capacity to engage most teachers and retain the best in teaching positions. There was no system for assessing and certifying teachers who demonstrated their professional development, and who were, presumably, worth more *as practising teachers*. Recognition, in terms of further career stages and salary for those who reached higher standards of practice, was absent, unlike in most comparable professions.

In similar vein, Elmore (1996) has drawn attention to 'the problem of scale' in educational change: few reforms in the twentieth century ever managed to engage more than about 20–30 per cent of teachers in 'ambitious' practices. Most reach only those 'teachers who are intrinsically motivated to question their practice and look to outside models to improve teaching and learning' – and these teachers seldom influence their peers widely (Elmore 1996: 16). The prevailing attitude in teacher culture is that successful teaching is an individual trait rather than a body of professional knowledge and skills deliberately acquired over the course of a career. To address the problem of scale, Elmore (1996: 18) calls for the creation of 'strong professional and social normative structures for good teaching practice that are external to individual teachers and their immediate working environment, and provide a basis for evaluating how many teachers are approximating good practice at what level of competence.'

The control of professional development: an overview of the past quarter-century in Australia

From a charitable perspective, it is possible to see the quarter-century of federal in-service education policies in Australia since Karmel as a series of well intentioned strategies for increasing the responsibility that teachers exercise over their own professional development that failed. These policies met with considerable resistance from state-level employing authorities. The Karmel Report itself saw the UK idea of teachers' centres as the primary vehicle for supporting and promoting in-service education initiated by teachers, and provided funds for 14 self-governing centres to be established. But several state education departments responded by setting up their own teachers' centres, controlled by their inspectors, to freeze them out. (While a few of the Karmel initiated centres still survive, few traces of department centres can be found today.)

While universities, state governments and other employers voiced agreement with the Karmel sentiment of 'valuing teacher initiatives in programs designed to increase their competence' (p. 123), in practice they were in a much better position in the 1970s than teacher organizations to take the initiatives that led to control of new commonwealth funding and maintenance of the status quo in terms of who set the agenda for in-service education. Using politically oriented models of evaluation emerging in the early 1970s (MacDonald 1976), Ingvarson (1977) describes how the aspiration of the Karmel Report to value 'teacher initiatives in programs designed to increase their competence' became transformed into a bureaucratically controlled programme of traditional short in-service education courses *for* teachers.

Four years after the Karmel Report, the Commonwealth Schools Commission (1978) reiterated the Karmel view that 'the teaching profession should take a leading part in directing its own improved functioning' (p. 89). This time it shifted the strategy to school-focused in-service education as a means for increasing teacher responsibility over professional development. However, despite support in principle from state employing authorities, this strategy also met with resistance for some years. The main stumbling block was the desire by employing authorities to retain central control over the disbursement of federal funding.

A quarter of a century later, most state schools now have their own professional development budgets, but this devolution has not meant that the profession has increased the part it plays in directing its own improved functioning. In Victoria, for example, these budgets are allocated mainly to activities delimited by the charters of self-managing schools, and these charters, in turn, are heavily shaped by state government priorities. The original conception of school-focused in-service education in the service of an accountable professional community has shifted to that of management-controlled *staff* development in the service of implementing centrally determined objectives.

During the 1980s and 1990s, federal interest in funding special purpose programmes like the Schools Commission's Professional Development Program waned as state governments were perceived to have used these programmes to fund their own in-service priorities and to reduce their own spending on professional development. In response, federal governments increasingly specified the objectives to which each state's programme funds could be directed. As part of the 1993 election campaign, the threatened federal Labor government made a sudden and dramatic commitment to provide $60 million for a National Professional Development Program (NPDP) for teachers over the following three years. (In cooperation with teacher unions, it also supported the establishment of a national professional body for teachers, the Australian Teaching Council.) The Minister for Education proclaimed that the NPDP should 'focus on providing teachers with the opportunity to play a central role in determining their own professional development needs' (Beazley 1993: 13). But, at the same time, the minister specified that the funds could only be spent on courses to implement commonwealth government specified objectives, or emerging 'national priorities', such as national curriculum frameworks.

In fairness, however, the NPDP went further than any previous commonwealth programme in allocating funds and responsibility to national teacher organizations such as subject associations and teacher unions to meet these objectives. Funding to states under the NPDP was now conditional on evidence of collaboration between teachers' organizations, universities and employers in developing proposals. While state governments still claimed the right to appropriate first all the federal funds coming to their state, and then to determine how those funds would be allocated, state level teacher and subject organizations did gain greater discretion and confidence over the spending of larger amounts of government funding for in-service education than they had had in the past.

Once teacher organizations gained greater responsibility they began to spend NPDP money more and more judiciously. Some teacher organizations, such as the Australian Science Teachers Association (ASTA), began to go further. In order to take on greater responsibility for the professional development of science teachers, ASTA decided it was necessary to develop its own goals for professional development. These would be based on images of high-quality learning in science and would describe what teachers needed to know and be able to do to promote that learning. These 'standards' would provide a clearer sense of purpose and sequence to the professional development programme.

Consequently, ASTA used part of its NPDP funds to commission a report on teaching standards, and its possible future role in applying these to the registration of beginning teachers and the evaluation of teachers for advanced certification and promotion purposes (Ingvarson 1995).

After the 1996 election, the incoming coalition government decided to discontinue the NPDP and any further support for the development of an independent national professional body for teachers. Federal funding for professional development was reduced significantly, and the purposes to which funds could be put underwent another major shift to serve new political objectives, such as a national literacy programme. It became clear that the Karmel aspiration for a stable professional development system geared to the long-term development of expertise in teaching had been thwarted once more. In fact, it was unlikely ever to be realized if the profession was to wait for governments, or universities for that matter, to take the initiative in delegating responsibility to teachers' own professional bodies for the operation of such a system.

How can the teaching profession gain a major responsibility for the professional development of its members?

The authors of the Karmel Report clearly believed in the importance of empowering teaching as a profession. Recent research confirms the importance of strong professional community to the improvement of teaching (Louis *et al.* 1996). There are two conceptions of empowerment however. It can be seen as something *given* or delegated to teachers by government or bureaucratic management, or something *taken* or developed by teachers themselves, through, for example, the development of professional knowledge and expertise. Australian experience over the past quarter-century shows that empowerment will have to be taken.

If teachers are to gain responsibility for establishing their own professional development system, their organizations must demonstrate the capacity to establish standards for highly accomplished teaching, and valid methods for assessing and certifying teachers who reach them. Over the past ten years, several professional associations have demonstrated that the profession has the ability to reach a consensus on standards for high-quality teaching. The best known examples so far are the work of subject associations in the USA, most notably the National Council of Teachers of Mathematics (NCTM 1991). These subject- and level-specific standards provide exciting and challenging descriptions of high-quality teaching in specific subject areas, as Stenhouse attempted to do for the 'humanities'. They go far deeper into the nature of what it means to teach well than the generic lists of criteria and competencies typical of most managerial models for teacher appraisal and evaluation. These standards indicate that the profession has the capacity to lay down its own directions and goals for the professional development of its members. They are stable, long-term, expertise-based guides to fellow teachers about what their profession expects its members to get better at and the quality of learning opportunities they should be able to provide.

A *standards-guided professional development system* is proposed as a means to realize the Karmel vision to reform professional development and move its control into the hands of the teachers' professional associations. This system is described in greater detail by Ingvarson (1998a; 1998b).

While the details are yet to come into focus, the key components of this system include:

- *teaching standards* based on professional values that provide the goals and the major milestones for professional development over a long-term career in teaching;
- staged career paths that provide *incentives* for all teachers to attain these standards and recognition for those that do;
- an *infrastructure for professional learning* that enables teachers to gain the knowledge and skill embodied in the teaching standards;
- a credible, voluntary system of *professional certification*, based on valid performance assessments, for teachers who have attained the standards.

In this standards-guided system, teachers' professional bodies develop teaching standards for career advancement *as practising teachers;* for example, to master teacher and leading teacher levels. They also develop and operate a voluntary system for assessing teacher performance for professional certification. Teacher associations, in collaboration with employers and universities, provide appropriate development opportunities for teachers to reach the standards and, eventually, to prepare for certification by professional bodies. Attainment of these standards, as validated by performance assessments developed by the professional body and conducted by trained peers, is regarded by employing authorities as a prerequisite for promotion through a series of three to four career stages over the period of a teaching career. The most thoroughly developed example in the world of a national professional body for developing standards and performance assessments for advanced certification is the National Board for Professional Teaching Standards (NBPTS 1989) in the USA.

A system for professional development based on profession-defined standards has the potential to overcome widely recognized weaknesses in the traditional in-service education system for teachers: the lack of clarity about what teachers should get better at and the lack of extrinsic incentives for development built into the career structure. A major weakness in the traditional in-service education system has been the prevalence of brief, one-off courses and the lack of coherent sequences of professional development experiences over several years designed to assist most teachers to reach challenging teaching standards. Another has been its failure to 'engage' the bulk of the profession in the enterprise of professional development and to create a sense of ownership for its purposes and quality, a reflection of the relative powerlessness of teaching as an occupation in relation to its own professional development.

The emerging standards-guided system is complementary to, not a replacement for, the in-service education system that employers should provide to support the implementation of changes and reforms *that they initiate*. That, properly, should remain the responsibility of employers to fund fully, but, as in any profession, employing authorities cannot, and should not, be expected to take responsibility for all professional development. The emerging system is an acknowledgement that, as in any profession, professional development is more than keeping up with changes initiated by governments and employing authorities.

The standards-guided system aims to provide more powerful incentives for professional development, *as teachers*. It operates on a different economy from the traditional employer-funded system. Teachers invest in their own development in the knowledge that evidence of professional body certification is a prerequisite for major salary rises and career steps with employing authorities. The new system aims to encourage more good teachers to remain in teaching by bringing professional development and career development together. It bases career stages primarily on demonstrable advances in professional knowledge and skill, rather than selection for specific jobs in a career ladder hierarchy, thereby reducing negative effects of competition for limited promotional positions. In these respects the pay system in teaching is attempting to catch up with best practices in other organizations that employ professionals. These seek to bring career structures and pay systems into closer alignment with the central objectives of organizations (Lawler 1990). In the case of schools, this means that the pay system needs to reflect the fact that it is primarily good teachers who make good schools, rather than the reverse. Odden and Kelley (1997) describe examples of emerging pay systems designed to recognize the central value to schools of teachers who have reached high professional standards and to promote the building of professional learning communities.

Essential to the new system has been the development of valid methods for teacher assessment by an external professional body that are acceptable to employers as well as teachers. It is difficult to argue for greater value to be placed on teachers' work without credible methods for assessing its quality. Major progress has been made over the past ten years by professional bodies, such as the NBPTS, in developing more valid methods for assessing teacher performance using portfolio and assessment centre exercises (Pearlman forthcoming). Most schools and principals cannot expect to provide the expertise to assess advanced teacher performance validly across all subject areas with the same rigour as a professional body such as the NBPTS. And research indicates that teachers believe that the process of preparing portfolio evidence for certification by an external professional body such as the NBPTS has proved to be one of the most powerful avenues for professional development they have ever experienced (La Russa *et al.* 1995; Ingvarson 1999a; Wolf forthcoming).

A standards-guided professional development system like the NBPTS is beginning to overturn old assumptions about who provides in-service education and how and where professional development takes place. In the USA, teachers and their professional bodies are increasingly setting up their own support networks within and across schools to help each other develop towards NBPTS certification. These networks are working towards attaining profession-defined standards in multiple ways. Case methods (Shulman 1992; Barnett and Ramirez 1996), for example, when they focus on teaching standards, are proving to be an excellent basis for building professional communities. Teachers and their organizations are still making use of traditional providers such as universities in the new system in the preparation of their portfolios, but the relationship is more like that of a service provider contract between equals in which teachers set the agenda.

The ASTA has now begun a project to develop advanced standards and performance assessments for science teaching, but on a smaller scale than the NBPTS (Ingvarson 1999b). The project will seek to conceptualize the main dimensions along which science teachers develop and improve their practice. It is hoped that these standards will provide the ASTA with a relatively stable framework for planning the professional development programme it offers to its members. The aim of this project will be to conduct the research and development necessary to establish a national voluntary system for the certification of teachers who have reached advanced professional standards for teaching science. The ASTA project has already received support in principle from most major state employing authorities and teacher unions.

Conclusions

Australian experience since the 1973 Karmel Report demonstrates that no one will give control of the professional development system to the teaching profession on a plate. Professional empowerment in this area will not be given; it will have to be taken. If teachers want control, they must assume the right to get on with building their own infrastructure for defining high-quality teaching standards, supporting development towards them and providing certification for those who reach them. Teachers will need to build their own strong national professional body to coordinate this infrastructure, one that embraces all teacher associations and stakeholders. If this infrastructure for a standards-guided professional development system is constructed in collaboration with governments, employing authorities, unions and universities, it will have the capacity to remedy major weaknesses in the traditional professional development system.

The Australian experience shows that we cannot, and perhaps should not, expect governments to provide a professional development system designed to encourage most teachers to progress over the long term towards profession-defined standards for high-quality teaching and learning. While it would be in the interest of government to encourage such a system, there is no need for government agencies to provide or control it.

Teacher organizations are recognizing they must demonstrate their capacity to be explicit about quality learning and teaching if they are to be taken seriously in national policy debate and to counter policies designed to deprofessionalize their work (Kerchner *et al.* 1997). Current policies for self-managing schools, which devolve quality assurance and staff management functions to school management teams, leave teachers and their national organizations outside debates about standards and expertise in teaching. The basis for defining the goals for professional development is in danger of narrowing to school charters and duties-based teacher appraisal schemes. These policies overestimate the effectiveness of managerial models of control over teachers' work, and they underestimate the capacity of professional culture and networks to influence what most teachers actually think and do. They fail to understand how responsibility harnesses commitment, an insight at the heart of Karmel's advocacy of a profession-controlled in-service education system based on professional teaching standards.

References

Barnett, C. and Ramirez, A. (1996) Fostering critical analysis and reflection through mathematics case discussions. In J. A. Colbert, P. Desberg and K. Trimble (eds) *The Case for Education: Contemporary Approaches for Using Case Methods*. Boston: Allyn & Bacon.

Beazley, K. C. (1993) *Teaching Counts: A Ministerial Statement*. Canberra: AGPS.

Elliott, J. (ed.) (1993) *Reconstructing Teacher Education: Teacher Development*. London: Falmer Press.

Elmore, R. (1996) Getting to scale. In S. Fuhrman and J. O'Day (eds) *Incentives and Systemic Reform*. San Francisco: Jossey-Bass.

Ingvarson, L. C. (1977) In-service education since Karmel. In A. D. Spaull (ed.) *Australian Teachers: Colonial Schoolmasters to Militant Professionals*. Melbourne: Macmillan.

Ingvarson, L. C. (1995) *Professional Credentials: Standards for Primary and Secondary Science Teaching in Australia*. Canberra: Australian Science Teachers Association.

Ingvarson, L. C. (1998a) Teaching standards: foundations for professional development reform. In A. Hargreaves, A. Lieberman, M. Fullan and D. Hopkins (eds) *International Handbook of Educational Change*. Dordrecht: Kluwer Academic.

Ingvarson, L. C. (1998b) Professional development as the pursuit of professional standards. *Teaching and Teacher Education*, 14(1), 127–41.

Ingvarson, L. C. (1999a) The power of professional certification. *Unicorn*, 25(2), 52–70.

Ingvarson, L. C. (1999b) Science teachers are developing their own standards. *Australian Science Teachers Journal*, 45(4), 27–34.

Interim Committee for the Australian Schools Commission (1973) *Schools in Australia: Report of the Interim Committee of the Australian Schools Commission (the 'Karmel Report')*. Canberra: Australian Government Publishing Service.

Kerchner, C. T., Koppich, J. E. and Weeres, J. G. (1997) *United Mind Workers: Unions and Teaching in the Knowledge Society*. San Francisco: Jossey-Bass.

La Russa, A., Dagley, P. and Capie, W. (1995) The use of teacher constructed portfolios in a National Teacher Assessment System. Paper presented to the Annual Meeting of the American Educational Research Association, San Francisco.

Lawler, E. E. (1990) *Strategic Pay: Aligning Organizational Strategies and Pay Systems.* San Francisco: Jossey-Bass.

Louis, K., Marks, H. and Kruse, S. (1996) Teachers' professional community in restructured schools. *American Educational Research Journal,* 33(4), 757–98.

MacDonald, B. (1976) Evaluation and the control of education. In D. Tawney (ed.) *Curriculum Evaluation Today: Trends and Implications*. London: Macmillan.

MacDonald, B. (1978) Accountability, standards and the process of schooling. In T. Becher and S. Maclure (eds) *Accountability in Education.* Windsor: National Foundation for Educational Research Publishing Company.

MacDonald, B. (1996) How education became nobody's business. *Cambridge Journal of Education,* 26(2), 241–9.

MacDonald, B. and Elliott, J. (eds) (1974) *People in Classrooms.* CARE Occasional Publications No. 2. Norwich: Centre for Applied Research in Education, University of East Anglia.

MacDonald, B. and Rudduck, J. (1971) Curriculum research and development projects: barriers to success. *British Journal of Educational Psychology,* 41(2), 148–54.

National Board for Professional Teaching Standards (1989) *Toward High and Rigorous Standards for the Teaching Profession.* Detroit: NBPTS.

National Council of Teachers of Mathematics (1991) *Professional Standards for the Teaching of Mathematics.* Reston, VA: NCTM.

Odden, A. and Kelley, C. (1997) *Paying Teachers for What They Know and Do: New and Smarter Compensation Strategies to Improve Schools.* Thousand Oaks, CA: Corwin Press.

Pearlman, M. (forthcoming) An architecture for NBPTS performance assessments. In L. C. Ingvarson (ed.) *Assessing Teachers for Professional Certification: The National Board for Professional Teaching Standards.* Greenwich, CT: JAI Press.

Schools Commission (1978) *Report for the Triennium 1979–81.* Canberra: Schools Commission.

Shulman, J. H. (ed.) (1992) *Case Methods in Teacher Education.* New York: Teachers College Press.

Stenhouse, L. (1975) *An Introduction to Curriculum Research and Development.* London: Heinemann.

Wolf, K. (forthcoming) Effects of the National Board for Professional Teaching Standards Certification Process on Teachers' Perspectives and Practices. In L. C. Ingvarson (ed.) *Assessing Teachers for Professional Certification: The National Board for Professional Teaching Standards*. Greenwich, CT: JAI Press.

Overview

14

Towards a synoptic vision of educational change in advanced industrial societies

JOHN ELLIOTT

Education and economic success: what's the connection?

Everyone in education within the Western European democracies is into school improvement in some form. Politicians tell us that it is vital for the economic well-being of our nation state. Global competitiveness, they have decided, depends on it. So how do our politicians draw these conclusions about the relationship between the economic goals of the nation and education?

House (Chapter 1) identifies four ways in which economic concerns shape educational policies. First, economic conditions within society influence policy by constraining or encouraging government spending on education and effecting social consequences, such as increasing inequalities of wealth, which present problems for schools to handle. Second, the object of certain educational policies may be to make schools more cost-efficient and productive. Third, education and economic development are presumed to be closely linked. It is taken for granted, House argues, 'that more or better education leads to improved technological capabilities and better jobs.' Fourth, 'economic concepts and metaphors permeate educational thinking.' For example, educational policies are formulated in terms of a need for schools to create and respond to 'markets'.

House identifies four errors which correspond to these influences: 'misunderstanding the economic system; misunderstanding the educational system; misunderstanding the fit between the two; and misapplying economic concepts.' All four errors, he contends, 'are abundant in education', while he points out his belief that economic concepts can be 'productively applied' to education. In his chapter he develops an *error theory* of educational policy making to explain why 'government policies are usually (but not always) counter-productive'.

> Frequently, they do not result in better education or improved productivity. A series of educational failures litters the reform path. None the less, misguided policies continue to be advanced and to secure high-level support. Policy should be based on the way educational institutions actually function if there is to be hope of better and more productive schools.

I want to focus here on the link between education and economic development, and the presumption that a country's economic productivity is directly related to levels of student achievement in schools. Raising standards in schools, it is assumed, will improve the technological capability of the country and create better jobs for people as a result. House, on the other hand, argues that there is evidence to suggest 'that education is led by jobs rather than the other way round'. The assumption, I shall argue, does indeed correspond to House's third category of error. It fails to understand the relationship between economic development and educational practice. I shall argue that the relationship is basically mediated by the way in which the cultural context of schooling shapes the educational process.

Let me start by looking at the assumption built into the current policy-making practice of international benchmarking. First, one identifies another country that appears to be successfully competing against one's own in the global market place. Recent UK favourites for benchmarking consisted of countries located on the pacific rim: Taiwan, Japan, Hong Kong, Singapore, South Korea. Second, one identifies some of the ways in which this nation state differs from our own. It appears that one major difference lies in levels of educational achievement as these are measured by tests for basic numeracy and literacy. Third, one draws the somewhat sweeping conclusion that differences in educational achievements, quite narrowly defined ones at that, explain differences in the economic performativity of nation states. In the latter part of 1997 this 'theory' became somewhat contestable when the Far Eastern economies plunged into crisis. Whether this is a short- or long-term condition is not clear, but at the time of writing (early 1998) one very rarely hears UK government ministers, as they did in the recent past, making unfavourable comparisons with educational standards on the Pacific Rim as part of their rationale for driving standards up. Perhaps it will become necessary to invent new benchmarks to legitimate policy if the condition in these countries turns out to be chronic, despite their standards in schools remaining high. In any case, the 'theory' that differences in educational standards explain differences in economic performativity begs all manner of questions when it is used as the basis for educational policies aimed at driving up standards. So what are the questions begged?

One fundamental question is: what are policy makers talking about when they talk about *educational standards* and attempt to use them to make international comparisons? MacDonald (Chapter 2) argues that there is no such thing as a set of independent standards against which to measure the educational performance of students. Yet, he points out, standards are a powerful construct in contemporary educational debates, conveyed, however unwittingly, by ministers and government officials to an often gullible public.

MacDonald contends that so-called international comparisons, used by politicians and government officials to 'bolster their arguments' about standards as a means of justifying state intervention in the business of education, are largely bogus. One cannot abstract standards from the social contexts in which such measures are constructed, he argues, and he cites the OECD's long and inconclusive quest for valid comparisons. Ministers, he points out, appear to be undaunted by the difficulties in such a quest.

Given the fact that educational achievements are assumed to be directly linked to a country's economic productivity, it is hardly surprising that such difficulties are 'glossed over' by politicians. To acknowledge them would begin to destabilize the ideological basis of the standards debate. In this context the need to compile league tables for the purposes of international and intranational comparisons becomes a political imperative and will override any concerns expressed by academics about the validity of measures. Those who exercise power in the construction of the standards debate want to hear the 'good news', not the 'bad news', about validity. Hence, there is a dilemma for school effectiveness researchers, who on the one hand self-deludedly collude with the political construction of the standards debate and on the other quibble about the way politicians refuse to listen to their cautionary tales and draw unwarranted and rash conclusions from their findings. A little self-knowledge would have gone a long way.

Let us look at a further question 'begged' by the assumption that educational achievement in schools can be directly linked to a country's economic productivity. Does the value of education reside primarily in its instrumentality for pursuing the economic goals of society? The assumption that it does is challenged by both House and MacDonald. House claims that in most countries now educational policies are predominantly formulated to achieve economic goals. Moreover, he argues that they often don't work because they lack 'sufficient understanding and appreciation of educational institutions' and consequently ignore the complexity of educational practices, which are shaped by 'many influences other than government policies'. House is not arguing against education serving economic goals, but that when the latter are made the exclusive focus of schooling a self-defeating mismatch is created between policy and practice. In this situation policy often runs counter to practice or has the reverse effects to what was intended. 'Policies intended to increase productivity often decrease it. It is as if suggestions for improving productivity in the auto industry were made without detailed knowledge of how cars are assembled.'

Given the ineffectiveness of policies which ignore the complexities of teachers' work in schools, why, House asks, are such mistaken policies perpetuated by governments as one succeeds another. Because, he replies, they are 'too wedded to powerful interests with misleading ideologies and simply misinformed'. One such ideology is connected to House's fourth error and its social consequences; namely, the totalizing use of market concepts like 'freedom' and 'choice' to legitimate the restructuring of the whole of the social order in terms of market relations. The outcomes are the increasing isolation and disaffection of individuals from traditional forms of social affiliation and control and the increasing dependency of the state on the private sector for buying off social aggression with material enhancement. House argues that 'As market relations destroy communal and traditional bases of support, the government must rely on material means of securing compliance. This means government becoming more dependent on business enterprises, which produce the wealth in capitalist societies.'

While it seems to me that MacDonald's account of educational policy making is broadly consistent with House's view that economically driven government policies are largely ineffective because they misunderstand the complexities of teachers' work in schools, he highlights the damage such policies are causing in the UK. They incapacitate schools from making a constructive response to a diversity of educational needs within society as these are articulated by 'countervailing and mediating interest groups', and in so doing undermine the functions of education in a pluralistic democracy. Furthermore, echoing Schostak (Chapter 3), MacDonald depicts how government in the UK, irrespective of party, now has a tendency towards 'paranoia' in its attempts to undermine and prevent any public critique by those involved in implementing policies. All this explains for MacDonald the fact that in the UK the effect of policy making has been to turn education into nobody's business.

Suppose any differences in economic productivity between European and Asian countries are best explained in socio-cultural terms. Fukuyama (1992), in the *End of History and the Last Man*, argued that the economic success of Asian countries can be explained not simply by the borrowing of Western business practices, but also by the retention of elements of Confucian culture and their integration into a modern business environment. He also argued that this retention 'produces tremendous pressures for conformity that children in such cultures internalise at a very young age', which may indeed explain the perception that Asian children achieve higher levels of attainment than their Western peers.

The connection between high levels of attainment in schools and the former economic success of Asian societies may have had less to do with the economic utility of the knowledge and skills learned in schools than with the operation of the work ethic embedded in traditional Confucian values and beliefs. Schooling may have contributed to economic performativity in Asian societies by reproducing and reinforcing the traditional culture and its associated work ethic in a form that can be subsequently integrated into a modern business environment; a process which recent events may have shown to be insufficient to sustain long-term economic growth in the global market.

We might, therefore, argue that the primary goal of schooling in Asian societies is to socialize children into the basic values and beliefs which define Confucian culture. The standardization of learning outcomes is a device directed to this socio-cultural goal rather than a specifically economic one.

A major reason for the past economic success of Asian countries may reside not so much in the formal curriculum, in the utility value of the knowledge and skills pupils learn at school, as in the 'hidden curriculum' which transmits certain cultural values and norms, e.g. a strong work ethic, deference to elders and obedience to authority, and the investment of value and worth in groups rather than individuals.

The problem with the 'educational theory' that Western politicians tend to use to connect a country's educational achievements with its economic success, or lack of it, lies in the assumptions of traditional liberal economic theory that underpin it. As Fukuyama (1992: 225) points out, such theory views work as essentially unpleasant and instrumental to the satisfaction of desire. The implication for education is that pupils will work hard at school to achieve results because they perceive these results as giving them the knowledge and skills they need to get a good job which pays well and thereby contributes to their material well-being. Hence, Western governments tend to reform and update curricular provision in terms of core knowledge and skills which are perceived to have economic utility for both individual pupils and society in general. However, Asian children will work hard at school to achieve results not simply because their achievements are perceived to have utility value for their future economic well-being, but because they are a condition of securing recognition and status for the individual as a member of the work group (the class).

Fukuyama contrasts the human desire for recognition with desires that stem from rational self-interest. The former, he argues, can be located in that part of human nature which Plato called *thymos*, and which experiences 'the need to place *value* on things', including in the first instance 'one-self', 'but on the people, events, and things' which surround one as well. The problem with the traditional liberal economic theory of Western societies, Fukuyama contends, is that it disregards the need of human beings to find worth in themselves in a form which transcends their material well-being, and to have that worth recognized by others. The source of such self-esteem resides in moral/spiritual identities available within the social culture.

Could it be the case then, that the key to 'improving' schools in the liberal democratic societies of the West lies in the extent to which the curriculum, and the pedagogical processes by which children are engaged with it, provides students with opportunities to secure recognition of their worth as individuals, in a form which is congruent with the basic values from which people derive their sense of worth. The emergence of the liberal democratic state expresses the need of individuals, in the absence of traditional forms of social authority, to have not just their material desires satisfied but also their desire for recognition as autonomous and free agents capable of shaping the conditions of their existence in civil society.

On this account of the relationship between liberal economics and liberal politics, it becomes clear that liberal democracies are weakened when the policies of their politicians are solely concerned with economic productivity.

In these circumstances, as House points out, governments increase their social control over the citizenry. The spread of market relations in society, and the consequent decline of traditional social institutions, accompanied by increasing social disarray, pressurizes governments to 'buy off' their citizens with the promise that their policies will provide them with even more material benefits. This strategy of securing the compliance of the citizenry to the government's economic policies contradicts the idea of a liberal democracy as a social order which affords equal recognition to the citizenry as autonomous and free moral agents, capable of participating in the construction of the policies that shape their lives. The outcome is what MacDonald calls 'a residualized democracy' which effectively restricts the substantive democratic participation of the citizenry to the franchise.

In a political context where policy subordinates liberal democratic social orders to the imperative of economic productivity, the educational system, as House points out, becomes one of the factors of production and is restructured in the form of market relations. In his chapter, MacDonald exposes the social consequences of subordinating schooling to the 'economic growth' imperative. The New Right ideology, he argues, with its proclamation that there is 'no other way' has resulted in:

> the reappearance of destitution on the streets and lanes of our urban and rural ghettos. Wealth creation meant that in 1992 Britain overtook the USA in boasting the widest gap between rich and poor of all the developed countries . . . it may be worth asking: was not mass education, now a century old, meant to change all that and was not social science, of similar age, expected to supply the blueprint?

What spaces exist, we might ask, for schools to educate the mass of students in ways which respond to the need of individuals in liberal democratic societies to secure equality of recognition as autonomous and free moral agents? In other words, I am asking about the possibility of schools supporting the development of students as 'enterprising people'. If it is possible, then such development, as an aim of education, would be justified in terms of preparing students to become citizens in a liberal democracy as opposed merely to fostering their material well-being.

Given the primacy I have argued for a particular socio-cultural goal of education in liberal democratic societies, it is still appropriate to ask what economic pay-off this will have for such societies. In advanced industrial societies the restructuring of large hierarchical business organizations into smaller, more flexible units which outsource many jobs and use more part-time and temporary labour in response to dynamic markets makes it increasingly difficult for schools to fulfil their traditional functions of allocating careers to students. Careers are on the decline, jobs and their related knowledge and skills are continually changing and countries are developing life-long learning policies. Individuals are increasingly portfolio people, having continually to recreate their own work futures in response to changing circumstances. In this context, schools will need to change to provide opportunities for students to learn how to take more control over both the social and economic conditions of their existence in an increasingly complex and dynamic society. If liberal democracies are to work economically as well as socially, they require an active rather than a passive citizenry.

The culture of schooling in Western liberal democracies and the problem of supplying students with the motivation to learn

The socio-cultural purposes of education in liberal democratic societies will differ from those which still obtain in societies where Confucian culture remains a dominant influence. Within liberal democratic societies there is the expectation that the individual is worthy of recognition and respect, not by virtue of his or her membership of a group and conformity to its customs and rules, but by virtue of his or her capacities for autonomous thought and action. This includes capacities for choosing the values he or she will live by and for creating the social and political conditions in which they can be realized.

Yet liberal democracies in the West have been reluctant to institutionalize in schools the bestowal of recognition and status on pupils by virtue of their capacities for autonomous thought and action. Deference to elders may not be expected to continue throughout one's adult life in the contemporary industrial societies of the West, but it is expected to continue throughout the period of formal schooling, and the model of authority relations employed is essentially one of paternalistic authority. As Fukuyama (1992: 239) argued, the emergence of modern liberal democracies in the West represented a break from this model of authority relations, but it seems that the break did not occur in the domain of schooling.

The reason for this is not hard to find. It stems from a belief embedded in the philosophy of the Enlightenment, which makes the accumulation of objective knowledge a condition of emancipating the individual from the blind prejudices and desires which shape mundane human existence. According to this philosophy, the autonomous person is the individual who grounds his or her thinking and actions in the reasons furnished by objective knowledge, knowledge accumulated and organized in the forms of the academic subjects and transmitted by deferring to the authority of subject experts. The bestowal of recognition and status on individuals as autonomous subjects must await the outcome of the process of schooling as signified by the issuing of academic credentials to leavers. It is not viewed as integral to the process itself.

Despite the erosion of the emancipatory narrative, which some scholars regard as marking a transition from modern to postmodern societies, schools continue to operate as if knowledge can still be regarded as an objective mirroring of reality. In doing so, it appears to produce 'fixed standards' for measuring educational achievements. Such a view of knowledge is perpetuated because it becomes imperative for educational policy dominated by economic productivity as *the* goal of education. This is why standards-driven educational reforms embody the same view of knowledge as that embodied in the traditional subject-based curriculum. Although MacDonald acknowledges that in this sense nothing has changed in the UK, in another sense what has changed is the government's capacity to employ power-coercive devices for undermining educational change which destabilizes the traditional view of knowledge. In particular, he notes the demise of the Schools Council, a national body representing the interests of central and local government and teachers, as a destabilizing influence.

> Some will maintain that nothing has changed, that what Goodson (1988), following Bernstein, calls 'the deep structure of curriculum, differentiation linked to a social base', has merely been made more transparent. This is true as far as it goes. The traditional route to higher education has been maintained for those whose expectations, aspirations and stomach fit them for the climb: for the rest, basic skills plus the rudiments of patriotic history, parochial geography and socially sanitized science. But the 'plus ça change' conclusion is insufficient. What the government has done in dismissing the Schools Council for 'mediocre' performance was to dismiss its mission. That was, in general terms, to prepare for the raising of the school leaving age . . . by making the curriculum and pedagogy, particularly of the secondary school, more engaging and more relevant to the life of the average pupil. That involved a more liberal reinterpretation of subject matter, thematic integration of disciplines around human issues, more enquiry-based learning, more child-centred approaches. It was not the conservatism of teachers that frustrated the full realization of these efforts, but the conservatism of their own, and their governing, institutions.

What schools cannot do, in a traditional view of knowledge, is to bestow recognition and status on pupils for exercising autonomy within the learning process, since this view regards knowledge as static and passively acquired on the basis of authority rather than dynamic and actively constructed through inquiry. What the now defunct Schools Council tried to do was to support schools in bringing about change which is consistent with the latter view of knowledge.

If the traditional view of knowledge, reinforced by government policy and legislation, continues to be deeply embedded in school cultures within liberal democratic societies, then schools will fail as educational institutions, not because they are failing to maintain 'standards' but because they are failing to supply the culturally appropriate form of motivation for pupils to learn. The basis for such motivation resides in bestowing recognition and status on pupils as autonomous learners. The valuing of individual autonomy is deeply embedded in Western culture but becoming detached from the belief that the prior acquisition of stocks of universal and objective knowledge is a condition of its realization. This is why traditional education no longer supplies motivation for individuals who seek recognition as autonomous persons. As MacDonald points out, policy interventions in Britain during the 1990s, have done little to replenish the supply of motivation and, indeed, have done much to exacerbate it.

> What was readily available, at a price, was the so-called effective schools movement, and the schools improvement service, both academically led, managerially oriented 'solutions' to the problem of achieving government-set targets. Many schools signed up for these offerings, only to find that the wrappings of the curriculum could not for long disguise the poverty of the merchandise. As we reached the end of the decade the problems mounted. They began with a rush of early retirements on the part of teachers and demands by headteachers for greater powers of exclusion over recalcitrant and alienated pupils, and they ended with a crisis of teacher recruitment.

It is doubtful if political authorities in the West can drive up standards in schools, despite their claims. Fukuyama (1992: 238) has argued that the groups in traditional Confucian societies that are critical in sustaining the work ethic – parents, teachers and business organizations – are also critical as the basis for political authority. They reinforce the authority of the rulers over the ruled. Are parents, teachers and members of business organizations in liberal democracies in a position to collaborate with government-led strategies for driving up standards in schools? Can they exercise over pupils the kind of paternalistic authoritarianism that commands the degree of deference observed in some Asian schools? I think not, in which case schools in liberal democracies may always appear to be underachieving in comparison with Asian schools in the light of traditional academic measures of achievement. However, this need not imply that pupils cannot be motivated to learn within liberal democratic societies in ways which have positive spin-offs for their economies. It does mean that political authorities in such societies should avoid attempting to imitate the paternalistic authoritarianism which appeared to work in the past and may still appear to work within some Asian societies, as a basis for school improvement.

We only have to look at some of the education policies launched by the UK's 'New Labour' government to realize that they constitute an ill-conceived attempt to reinvent a form of paternalistic authoritarianism in the field of education. It is busy developing highly centralized policies for driving up standards in schools that are based on a very paternalistic model of authority relations. Many are framed by an expectation that children should defer to their parents and teachers, e.g. home–school contracts as a method of controlling the behaviour of children at school.

Analysing the changing social context of schooling

In my view, one the most coherent visions of educational change, which is grounded in a comprehensive analysis of contemporary social and economic change in advanced industrial societies, stems from a range of school development initiatives launched by Peter Posch and his associates at the University of Klagenfurt. The strategic vision for school development outlined by Posch (Chapter 4) provides a marked contrast to the dominant standards-driven model of school improvement, because it places at the centre of development the need to bestow recognition and status on pupils for exercising autonomous thought and action. The examples he provides illustrate the significance for Posch of contemporary and locally situated environmental issues, rather than the traditional school subjects, as a curriculum strategy for transforming the culture of teaching and learning. The traditional subjects have become associated with abstract universal knowledge (detached from the personal and social experience of pupils), authority-based teaching, and passive learning. A curriculum which focuses on local environmental issues provides a context in which knowledge can be viewed as locally situated truth, schools as agencies for its construction and therefore integrated into their local communities, teaching as enabling pupils to influence the conditions of their lives, and learning as an active process in which pupils display dynamic qualities associated with the exercise of initiative and judgement in unstructured situations.

Posch's perspective on school change, in contrast to the standards-driven school improvement perspective, fits what I have called a pedagogically driven perspective on educational change. Such a perspective focuses on broadly conceived school development processes. In the light of this distinction, Posch's thinking deserves a fuller account which locates his chapter in this book within his wider body of work. Providing such an account will enable me to explore the links between Posch's ideas and the various images of educational change presented by other contributors to this book.

In his chapter, Posch highlights two closely connected developments in industrial societies which have implications for the culture of teaching and learning in schools. He has elaborated on these elsewhere (Posch 1994a: 154–5). The first is the growing *complexity* of the interactions between human beings and their environment, made possible by an increasing array of technologies, or cognitive limbs, which enhance their capacity 'to access, store, process, use and communicate information'. This complexity implies a number of major changes in the social conditions governing human existence. Because the effects and side-effects of complex human interactions become less foreseeable and controllable, human existence in society is increasingly put at risk. Technological development carries both life and death potential for individuals. It is here that Posch's social analysis echoes Beck's (1992) analysis of advanced societies as risk societies.

The difficulties in predicting and controlling the effects of human interactions in complex societies also render centralized power structures problematic because they reduce their problem-solving capacity. Hence, argues Posch, there is a paradoxical tendency of governments, as illustrated, for example, in the 'privatization' of the public services, to decentralize power as a means of controlling the diversity of influences operating in society.

Posch (e.g. 1994a: 154–5) points out that this tendency towards greater decentralization of power is not simply a linear process, because it operates in the context of a tendency for individuals to call the legitimacy of social authorities into question and step out of society (interpreted as a predefined structure of rules and practices that are legitimated by reference to some external authoritative source) into a diversity of subcultures and practices. This active defection of individuals from the established social order threatens social continuity and cohesion, which can only be re-established by devolving social responsibility more and more to the level of the individual.

The second development in industrial societies cited by Posch is the *process of individualization*. The devolution of power from the centre tends to progress through phases depending on the level of complexity that society has to cope with (Posch 1994a: 154). At a certain level complexity can be handled by devolving power to subgroups and cultures in the society when the centre is no longer able to control the emerging diversity of values and practices. But there comes a point, argues Posch, when there is such a diversity of subcultures, and perspectives on issues within subcultures, that responsibility for developing strategies which enable human beings to cope with and adapt to the conditions of their existence has to be devolved to the smallest possible social unit, that of the individual (Posch 1994a: 155). This process of individualizing responsibility represents a late stage of human development for Posch, the culmination of the promise of the European Enlightenment 200 years earlier, which he summarizes in the words of Fend as 'the right, duty and possibility to use one's mind without being led by someone else, and to shape one's life in one's own terms' (Posch 1996: 2).

Together, increasing complexity and individualization of responsibility, provide the conditions in which liberal democratic social orders emerge and develop. According to Posch, the development and growth of democratic structures as a means of ordering society may be interpreted as a strategy for coping with the complexity of industrial societies; a complexity which brings increased risks to individuals, a marked decline in the problem-solving capacities of centralized power, and severe reductions in the legitimate power of externally defined rules and norms.

Posch clearly regards increasing complexity and growing individualization as global changes taking place across the industrialized world, leading to the development of liberal democratic social orders as the global norm. Such a state of affairs has been represented by Fukuyama as the end of history, and its ultimate unit of value, the autonomous individual, as the last man.

One might argue that the cases of prosperous industrial societies in Asia, which retain a capacity to maintain highly centralized power structures within very minimalist conceptions of a democratic social order, contradict the thesis of Posch, and indeed of Fukuyama, that human development is moving inexorably in the same direction across the industrialized world, towards the mutual recognition of the individual as the ultimate source of value. Could it not be the case that increasing complexity and the growth of individualization are not simply the consequences of technological development, but also the realization of values which embedded themselves in European cultures 200 years previously during the 'Age of Enlightenment'? To what extent can these Enlightenment values be globalized, as Posch assumes, particularly in relation to Asian societies? Fukuyama claims that there are contrary tendencies in this respect. He writes:

> On the one hand, Asia's increasingly cosmopolitan and educated populations can continue to absorb Western ideas of universal and reciprocal recognition, leading to the further spread of formal liberal democracy. Groups will decline in importance as sources of thymotic identification . . . On the other hand, if Asians become convinced that their success was due more to their own than to borrowed cultures, if economic growth in America and Europe falters relative to that in the Far East, if Western societies continue to experience the progressive breakdown of basic social institutions like the family, and if they themselves treat Asia with distrust or hostility, then a systematic illiberal and non-democratic alternative combining technocratic economic rationalism with paternalistic authoritarianism may gain ground in the Far East.
>
> (Fukuyama 1996: 242–3)

Fukuyama clearly believes that the development of a new Asian authoritarianism will constitute a temporary historical trend in the evolution of Asian societies, since the empire of deference it represents, while possibly bringing unprecedented prosperity, will, in perpetuating the childhood of the citizenry, ultimately fail to satisfy the need of all human beings to be recognized as individuals capable of moral agency and choice in shaping the conditions of their existence.

Curriculum development and the challenge of social change

It is in the light of the above analysis of the growth of complexity, individualization and democratic structures in industrial societies that Posch identifies four main cultural challenges which face schools today (Posch 1994a: 156–7):

- negotiation of rules;
- social continuity;
- the development of dynamic qualities;
- a reflective and critical stance towards knowledge.

Negotiation of rules

How can schools respond to the breakdown in the wider society of traditional social structures in the form of rules and norms governing relationships in the primary institutions of society. Such rules and norms can no longer be enforced on the basis of paternalistic authority because they have lost the external legitimacy authority has traditionally appealed to, whether this be via an appeal to the Will of God or to Reason. Yet no society can survive without rules and norms, and Posch argues that in the future they will have to be constructed in negotiation with those who are subjected to them. He claims that the pattern of authority relationships in families has changed significantly over the past thirty years. What is allowed or not allowed has increasingly become more a negotiated matter than the outcome of lone parental decisions.

Yet Posch contends that children and young people come to school and are 'confronted with a culture of predefined demands' without 'space for negotiation'. They increasingly experience a clash between two cultures, one in the family and the other in school. Schools appear to be stuck in a time warp, unable to cope 'with a social development in which negotiation of rules and norms is gaining in importance'. The prevalent culture of teaching and learning in schools is 'still attuned to a relatively static society, in which the necessary knowledge, competencies and values are redefined and stored in curricula, tests and accredited textbooks.' It is a culture of predefined demands which reinforces and reproduces traditional patterns of authority relations, and leaves few social spaces in which students and teachers can renegotiate the rules and norms which structure their interactions. The challenge for schools is to take responsibility for curriculum initiatives which create such spaces and thereby enable pupils to negotiate new pedagogical conditions which recognize and value their capacities for autonomous learning.

School development in this context will involve developing strategies for changing the balance within the curriculum between the transmission of abstract systematic knowledge, compartmentalized in terms of traditional academic subjects, and the encounter with what Posch calls low structured situations (e.g. Posch 1991). Such situations are low in structure because 'the problems to be solved have yet to be clearly defined' and therefore differ from the normal situation in classrooms, where pupils are presented with 'prestructured and systematic information' (Posch 1991: 16). The inclusion of low structured situations in the curriculum makes pupils' learning experiences realistic, because they are the kinds of situations they encounter in everyday life and therefore they connect learning to personal experiences and concerns. Developing an understanding of these low structured realistic situations requires a holistic approach to learning which cuts across disciplines and involves skills that cannot simply be limited to those involved in the passive acquisition of a stock of knowledge. These low structured situations require pupils to develop 'personal points of view and value judgements in the presence of ambiguity and controversy', and this involves developing such reflective skills as the careful weighing of evidence and listening with tolerance to alternative points of view. Changing the curriculum to give greater importance in the learning environment to these low structured situations creates the social spaces in which pupils and their teachers can begin to reconstruct the culture of teaching and learning in ways which recognize and value pupils' capacities for independent thought and action.

Posch's arguments for changing the curriculum to accommodate the low structured situations young people encounter in everyday life reflects the influence on Posch's thinking of the ideas of the British curriculum theorist Lawrence Stenhouse. Stenhouse's Humanities Curriculum Project (1967–72; see Stenhouse 1970) designed a curriculum which focused on social situations that raised controversial issues in society. It challenged teachers to reconstruct pedagogically the culture of teaching and learning in their classrooms and schools in the light of certain aims and criteria. These referred to values that were to be embedded in the process of education rather than specific knowledge objectives, e.g. enabling students to form their own value positions through a reflective discussion of evidence in which the teacher: adopted a procedurally neutral stance by refraining from using his or her authority position as a platform to promote his or her own views on socially controversial issues; protected a divergence of view; ensured that minority opinions were represented; and accepted responsibility for standards of reasoning within the discussion by requiring students to support their judgements and views with evidence. Stenhouse called such a design framework a process model, in contrast to the objectives model, with its emphasis on the pre-specification of knowledge content (see Stenhouse 1975). As Schostak points out, such a model stemmed from a view of education as a democratic process in which the views of all are recognized as worthy of equal regard. He writes:

> The democratic impulse was sown by HCP through a radical undermining of traditional teacher/knowledge authority patterns by the instigation of the concept and practice of the 'neutral chair'. In the position of the 'neutral chair' the teacher would set the rules for rational debate but could not provide the content for that debate. Rather, children were to discuss, employing evidence, key controversial issues . . . In this fashion, opinions were raised, challenged and debated in ways which set people in relations of equality rather than dominance and submission.

Posch argues that the transformation of the culture of teaching and learning at the classroom level also has implications for change at the level of the school. Giving greater importance in the curriculum to low structured situations implies a shift in the role of schools in society, away from an exclusive emphasis on the top-down transmission of systematic knowledge towards a role which enables students to actively construct local truth as a resource for informing intelligent debate within their communities. School development therefore involves a shift of emphasis from giving priority to the transmission of systematic, compartmentalized, knowledge to the active construction of locally situated knowledge. Only through such a shift of emphasis can pupils begin to experience teaching and learning in schools as an open process which recognizes, values and develops their capacities to shape the conditions of their existence. It is a shift which is entirely consistent with preparing pupils to accept the responsibilities of active citizenship in a liberal democratic social order, a point which Stenhouse (1970) also argued in relation to HCP.

All this explains why curriculum reform is so significant in Peter Posch's thinking about school development. Curriculum space must be found for the study of social situations which pupils confront in their everyday lives, and in which they will be expected to exercise individual initiative, responsibility and judgement as citizens in a liberal democracy.

The process model of curriculum development, employed by Stenhouse in relation to the study of socially controversial issues in general and by Posch specifically in relation to environmental education, is seen by Schostak as a strategy for radically destabilizing the traditional culture of schooling and transforming it into an educative culture. The key image of educational change for Schostak is getting teachers and their students to 'go off the rails' and play the education game by different rules. Stenhouse's 'derailing' strategy was to get them to play the game of neutral teacher, while Posch's was getting them to play at constructing local truth about our environment for local use, as opposed to transmitting universal truth for little immediate use. Interestingly, both Stenhouse and Posch justified their 'derailing' strategies by appealing to local school communities. Stenhouse argued that parents would have a right as democratic citizens to object to a teacher who used his or her authority to promote socially controversial value positions that contradicted their own, as opposed to fostering through discussion mutual understanding and regard of different positions. Posch justified local knowledge as something constructed with the community for its use.

Posch's epistemological notion of local truth connects with the view recently expressed by another curriculum theorist he has been associated with, the American science educator Myron Atkin. In this book, Atkin (Chapter 6) argues that science as a knowledge production process is itself being reshaped in advanced industrial societies in the light of the practical situations and issues individuals and communities confront. Increasingly, the quest of science is not an abstract knowledge of universal principles but the need to help the citizenry act 'wisely and well' in particular circumstances. Atkin argues that the image of science is shifting from 'the abstract to the concrete, from thought and reflection to action; from the timeless to the timely.' Such a shift is consistent with changes in some teachers' image of the purposes of science teaching, as they respond to an increasingly varied student population by making science of 'greater immediate relevance to the students'.

Atkin's analysis perhaps indicates a general trend in the way knowledge is being socially constructed in a fast-changing world, i.e. in collaboration with user groups who need a knowledge base to inform their judgements and decisions in particular social situations. In this context the construction and organization of knowledge is shaped by the values of practical 'relevance' and 'utility', 'accessibility' and 'immediacy'. They imply that all knowledge is to be treated as situated and provisional rather than timeless and fixed.

Schostak also acknowledges the social context of this epistemological transformation when he argues that 'Ahead are the post-modern tracks of information flows so fast that they not only cut up the world into domains battled over by federations and coalitions of states and multinationals, but striate the world, making changing alliances hard to focus on, let alone try to control.' To elaborate on Schostak's railway track metaphor, one might argue that the traditional knowledge tracks (subjects) – a set of straight lines with few intersections and each leading to a terminal at the 'end of the line' – are quickly disappearing and giving way to a dynamic interlocking system in which bits of track are constantly being rearranged and the interconnecting points constantly changed. It is a system with no terminals, and the stations in it are strictly mobile structures which are continuously shifted with the rearrangements of the system; new bits of track are laid and old bits removed, and the points of intersection changed.

According to Schostak, 'when things change so quickly that their duration can no longer be adequately counted in terms of the human heart beat, time itself no longer means anything.' Schooling, he concludes, now stands at the end of time. When events move too quickly to be counted and predicted in society and people's 'futures' can no longer be fixed and constructed for them, systems of power relations like schools are no longer sustainable in the long run. 'There can be no grand narrative concerning what is "good for all". Standardization and its surveillance techniques to create *the* curriculum are patently absurd in a context of change that is so fast, so diverse and so technologically and culturally creative.' Schostak's analysis of social change, summarized by the notion of the end of time, and the challenge it poses for contemporary schooling, is clearly consistent with Posch's analysis. He generates from such an analysis a vision of educational change that is remarkably similar to that of Posch. What sort of curriculum, Schostak asks, is appropriate in a society at the end of time:

> A forward looking curriculum for personal and social development requires principles that facilitate diversity, dialogue and a mutuality of relationship. Such a curriculum cannot have personal meaning unless time is brought into the ambit of an individual's lifetime, an individual's life course; nor can it have social meaning unless there is a community of regard where time is defined as the time to meet, to interact and to develop through dialogue.

Posch's vision of the cultural transformation that needs to be accomplished if schools are to become more responsive to the profound social changes now taking place resonates with Schostak's distinction between schooling and education. The former corresponds with Posch's culture of predefined demands, which leaves little room for negotiation, and the latter corresponds with Posch's vision of teaching and learning as an open process which recognizes, values and develops the capacities of students to shape the conditions which govern their lives.

Schostak, like Posch, argues for a curriculum of 'unstructured situations' which enables students to reflect on their life experiences and to experience education as a democratic process in which they are able to negotiate their own 'agenda for learning'.

> If a key principle of education is to include a sense of mutuality and equality of access to the means, products and processes of cultural action, then the individual, at whatever age, must be included as a decision-making partner in the process. Simply, the child contributes to any agenda through which a curriculum is framed. Including the child as a decision-making partner whose claims are equal to those of any other individual in an arena of debate and cultural action is something rarely considered . . . In this image of what it means to follow a process of education the child is not locked on to a track but is located at the 'points', the place where multiple tracks arise . . . The child is at the point . . . where tracks may be switched, where it is always possible to challenge and pursue alternatives.

The railway track metaphor, with the child located at its 'points' rather than on its 'tracks', imaginatively captures the kinds of 'unstructured situations' that cut across the disciplines, but which the student is expected to use as 'resources for thinking' in the process of constructing 'local knowledge'.

However, I would contend that the images of change – from schooling to education – portrayed by Posch and Schostak are not reflected in many countries' current responses to the postmodern condition of their societies. In these countries (e.g. the UK) standards-driven school improvement preserves the curriculum in a dream world of discrete knowledge tracks stretching out towards timeless terminals (standards) and punctuated by a series of stations at which progress along the way is assessed and recorded. It is a dream time curriculum conjured up from a fast vanishing world and increasingly disconnected from the way knowledge is becoming constructed and organized in advanced industrial societies.

Whereas both Posch and Schostak locate their visions of educational change in the profound changes taking place in society, Schostak highlights, in a way Posch does not, the 'paranoid' responses of policy makers, aimed at 'purifying' the school curriculum of elements that threaten to destabilize the traditional culture of 'predefined demands'. Schostak probably does so because he is located in a national policy context within the UK which might justly be described as 'paranoid' compared with Posch's policy context. For Schostak, the paranoid curriculum, albeit labelled 'reform', responds to social change by looking back to 'a golden age of basics', and this is exactly how educational policy makers in the UK appear to be responding to a speed of social change which threatens to take the future of the nation's children out of their sphere of control.

Social continuity

Increasing individualization and defection from traditional social structures destabilizes the established social networks in society, and presents the problem of how human beings can experience continuity in their relationships, as opposed to treating others as merely instrumental to the satisfaction of their immediate needs and desires. For Posch, the challenge to schools is to create situations which provide pupils with opportunities to cooperate with others in pursuing mutually agreed social goals. In responding to this challenge, schools will be involved in developing new kinds of social networks, dynamic as opposed to static networks inasmuch as they are constituted by the mutual recognition of the individual as an autonomous person who freely cooperates with others on the basis of a shared concern for the social good (see Chapter 3).

The essential feature of dynamic networks, writes Posch (1996, see also 1994b), 'is the autonomous and flexible establishment of relationships to assist responsible action in the face of complexity and uncertainty.' They are answers to the specific characteristics of low structured situations:

- they call for specific knowledge and not simply general knowledge to cope with them;
- this specific knowledge can only be generated within the situation by those who, through their actions, are involved;
- specific knowledge is not applied instrumentally to actions but expresses itself holistically in action in relation to people's value positions and feelings.

The need to construct dynamic learning networks as an educational implication of advanced industrialization, and founded upon the mutual recognition of autonomous individuals as agents of their own learning, is also acknowledged by Schostak when he refers to 'a forward looking curriculum for personal and social development' having no social meaning 'unless there is a community of regard where time is defined as a time to meet, to interact and to develop through dialogue.' Such communities of regard, I would argue, flow from learning networks constructed for the purpose of sharing information and experience on the basis of shared needs and common interests. Their dynamism resides in their capacity to respond to the changing needs and interests of individuals, by expansion, contraction, interlocking with other networks etc. As a form of social organization they are clearly consistent with Schostak's image of the relationship between postmodern information tracks and how the individual is appropriately positioned in relation to them.

The selection of environmental education as the curriculum reform context for many of the school development initiatives Posch has been involved with is not an arbitrary one. Environmental issues directly impinge on young people's lives and futures and are of great personal and social significance. Yet practically useful knowledge cannot be acquired simply via the transmission of abstract systematic knowledge organized in specialized subject categories. Environmental issues display all the characteristics of the complexity Posch identifies in the social context of contemporary schooling. Environmental knowledge needs to be actively constructed at the local level by learners in relation to their personal experience of their environment and their interactions with other people in the situation. Its construction requires teachers and pupils to participate in the formation of dynamic learning networks which break down the boundaries between the school as an organization and the local community. The curriculum reform context of school development unfreezes the school in relation to the community. It brings the school into the community and the community into the school. The school develops as a node in a dynamic local learning network. The idea of the school as a dynamic social network which crosses the traditional boundaries between school and society also figures in Brennan and Noffke's (Chapter 5) accounts of school development programmes in Australia and the USA. I return to them below.

School-based curriculum change initiatives which focus on low structure situations, the generation of locally useful knowledge in relation to such situations and the formation of dynamic learning networks which cross the traditional boundaries between schools and their communities; these constitute aspects of school development strategies which respond to the two challenges of social change – negotiating new educational ground rules and norms with students and establishing new forms of social relationships – considered above. They provide a context for the next two challenges outlined by Posch.

The development of dynamic qualities

Since the complexity of social life promotes a decentralization of decision making in advanced industrial societies, more and more citizens, argues Posch, will have to take responsibility for their actions in low structured situations. Central authorities will become increasingly dependent on individual and group initiatives at the local level. This has implications for the kinds of competencies schools should be developing in the young. It challenges schools to change the current emphasis on a curriculum structured by systematic knowledge because it places pupils in a passive and compliant role within the learning process. What is needed is a curriculum which supports the development of dynamic qualities, because it gives the young opportunities to define problems and exercise initiatives in proposing actions for which they are prepared to accept responsibility in the face of uncertainty and risk.

According to Posch (1994a: 156) schools need to recognize the 'growing quest among the young to be taken seriously, to be able to influence their conditions of life and to leave traces in the world.' He cites the articulate skinhead who rephrased Descartes's famous statement as 'I throw stones, therefore I am.'

Interestingly, Posch is challenging schools to foster dynamic qualities which are normally associated with entrepreneurial wealth creation, in the context of wider social goals associated with integrating the development of students as autonomous individuals with their development as morally responsible social beings. In doing so he is challenging schools to play a formative role in reconstructing liberal democratic society in ways which resolve the tension between the processes of individualization and social cooperation for the sake of the common good.

A reflective and critical stance towards knowledge

Increasing consciousness of risks (e.g. to health and the environment) throughout advanced industrial societies promotes both a desire for more scientific knowledge and a more critical stance towards it. For Posch this implies that what counts as important knowledge can no longer be left to traditional authorities alone. It must be determined by individuals and groups operating in local contexts of action. Increasingly, truth has to be negotiated at the local level. Confidence in knowledge will depend less on methodology – procedural rules, data and methods – and more on local processes by which knowledge becomes an object of critical reflection and discourse in the light of people's experience of a concrete situation they confront. The challenge for schools, argues Posch, is to involve their pupils in critical inquiries into low structured situations which require an appreciative *and* critical stance to knowledge. This again reflects one of the central pedagogical aims of Stenhouse's Humanities Project and is also central to Schostak's idea of education.

Meeting the challenges of social change along the dimensions of schooling proposed by Posch and other contributors to this book – curriculum, pedagogical, organizational and teacher development – schools will not only make a significant contribution to the development of new forms of social solidarity in liberal democracies but, in doing so, also contribute to their capacities for economic growth. The synoptic vision of educational change outlined above shows us a possibility for reconciling the socio-cultural and economic goals of schooling. We do not have to embrace paternalistic authoritarianism to make our educational systems in the West better serve our economic goals.

Social and educational change: how are they linked?

What is the nature of the link between the social changes taking place in advanced industrial societies and the vision of educational change shared by many contributors to this book? One should be careful about assuming social determinism in this respect, i.e. that the social changes described will inevitably result in the educational changes envisioned. The link presumed by Posch, Schostak and other contributors is a normative one. They presume that a liberal democratic social order is the best way of organizing a society undergoing such changes and that the most appropriate educational response to such changes will be one informed by liberal democratic values. However, they clearly believe that the social changes taking place in advanced industrial societies have destabilizing potential for traditional schooling and, viewed in the light of liberal democratic values, provide new opportunities for educational change.

The growth of complexity and individualization in society does not necessarily imply that individuals will take responsibility for shaping the conditions of their existence. The task of education in a truly liberal democratic order should be to help them do so. At the end of time individuals may feel as powerless to control their destiny as they did when their life course was largely fixed and shaped by the power relationships which obtained in more stable and less dynamic societies. In the 'chaos' of postmodern or advanced industrial societies individuals, as Posch acknowledges, may feel more powerless, adrift, insecure, socially isolated and marginalized than ever before.

The end of time does not imply the end of coercive power relations, just their recasting in forms that make them difficult for individuals to discern in the surrounding chaos. I have, for example, argued that the ideal of the market society constitutes a form of coercive social power legitimated in terms of such liberal concepts as giving individuals freedom and choice. Within such societies individuals are socially constructed as units of infinite consumption to meet their primary goal of economic productivity (see also House and MacDonald in this volume). As Fukuyama has argued, Anglo-Saxon liberal theory has dominated the discussion of human rights in Britain and the USA. It is grounded in an acknowledgement of the desiring and self-interested part of the human soul for physical and material satisfaction. The growth of industrialization and markets may well explain the changes Posch describes and Schostak characterizes as the end of time, and in turn be explained, as Fukuyama argues, by the need of human beings to satisfy their desires. However, markets not only are shaped by human wants and desires but also have the power to recreate continuously the wants and desires which shape them. In this respect they constitute structures of domination.

The social changes analysed by Posch, Schostak and others may not significantly extend freedom and choice in a form which empowers individuals as moral agents who invest value and worth in themselves and others. It is not the end of history. Fukuyama grounds his thesis about the latter in Hegel's view that history is about the struggle of human beings for recognition of their value and worth. What makes the emergence of liberal democratic social orders the end of history is not that they are the best possible arrangements for satisfying everyone's wants and desires but that they are the best possible arrangement for resolving people's struggle for recognition of their dignity and worth. However, Fukuyama argues:

> The social changes that accompany advanced industrialisation . . . appear to liberate a certain demand for recognition that did not exist among poorer and less educated people . . . people begin to demand not simply more wealth but recognition of their status. If people were nothing more than desire and reason, they would be content to live in market oriented authoritarian states . . . But they also have a thymotic pride in their own self-worth, and this leads them to demand democratic governments that treat them like adults rather than children, recognising their autonomy as free individuals.

We should not presume that the relationship between social change in industrial societies and the emergence and spread of liberal democratic social orders is a causal one. The latter is not an inevitable consequence of the former, for if Fukuyama is right, it is people's struggle for equality of regard, for reciprocal recognition, which directs the development of liberal democratic social orders and not their desire for material wealth and prosperity. The latter merely establishes certain possibilities for effecting a resolution, perhaps, as Fukuyama would claim, a final resolution, to the struggle.

If the goal of 'education' in liberal democracies remains primarily linked to 'economic productivity', rather than the socio-cultural goal of enabling individuals to shape the social and economic conditions of their lives, then schools will not respond to the challenges Posch has identified, and this can only be to the detriment of a healthy and vital liberal democracy. The alternative to the vision of educational change outlined in this book is standards-driven school improvement and Schostak's paranoid curriculum.

The paranoid curriculum is designed to eliminate threats to a dominant order over the way students think about their world and themselves within it. Such threats stem not only from those promoting competing predefined curriculum pathways, but also from the resistances students construct against having their thinking and being entirely shaped by these structures. The alternatives for students are either to adopt, and thereby repress, aspects of their experience or to reject the categories which define the experience of schooling. Schostak writes: 'Through the adoption or rejection of such processes of categorization, the image that one has of one's self, one's powers of agency and the objects of one's private world is systematically constructed either in conformity to a given process of schooling or as a resistance to it.'

The paranoid curriculum consists of a set of control mechanisms designed to eliminate alternative ways of organizing experience and the resistant effects of what Schostak calls 'waste products' or 'residuals'; aspects of the experience of individuals which are deviations from the predefined standardized pathways and which form the basis for 'the politics of the "left out" ', the 'forbidden discourses' that manifest themselves in the various forms of students' resistance to, and disaffection from, schooling. Such a 'curriculum' is constituted by a particular kind of learning relationship between a dominant individual or group and a subordinate individual and group, which is structured by a systematically organized set of surveillance and control mechanisms. These are designed to overcome the 'resistances' that stem from 'residuals' and thereby secure compliance with the dominant predefined pathways represented by curricula and courses.

The paranoid curriculum, conceived as a totalizing system of surveillance and control, appears to represent for Schostak coercive power in its most developed form. He clearly sees the 'educational reforms' over the past ten years in the UK as exemplifying the construction of such a system. He writes:

> Policy makers in the UK are currently attempting to engineer politically a dominant definition of schooling that will act as a 'standard'. This is being engineered through the mechanisms of a national curriculum, national testing and inspections. In general, it can be said that a considerable amount of resource appears to be going into trying to school people of all ages to follow certain pathways . . . and thus counteract those paths considered subversive, deviant or simply frivolous.

In his account of the paranoid curriculum Schostak provides us with a description of school improvement in the UK: the process of driving up standards. It is a warning for liberal democracies about the consequences for their basic values of an obsessional concern with 'economic productivity' as the exclusive goal of 'education'.

It is one thing to discover the solution to the human struggle for equality of regard for individuals as autonomous beings. It is another thing to implement it in particular societies with consistency. Even if Fukuyama is right and liberal democratic social orders constitute the direction of history, as he himself acknowledges, some societies may succeed in resisting the implications of arriving finally at their destination.

How, then, is the educational vision of Posch, Schostak and other contributors to this book to be realized in practice? What sort of change is involved, and what are the appropriate strategies for bringing such change about? It is to these questions that I now turn for the remaining sections of this chapter.

School culture as the focus of educational change

Educational change researchers, Finnan and Levin (Chapter 7) argue, have opened the 'black box' of what happens when change occurs in schools and discovered something called 'culture'. The concept of school cultures is central to the image of educational change employed in this project. There can be no significant school change without some kind of cultural transformation occurring. Their Accelerated Schools Project (ASP) is essentially about bringing students 'at risk' of failure – many from low-income and minority groups – into the academic mainstream by transforming the culture of teaching and learning in schools. The direction of this transformation is highly consistent with Posch's vision: namely, to change pedagogical practice in ways which supply motivation to students by acknowledging their generative capacities, and in so doing to bestow on them equality of regard as individuals capable of autonomous thought and action within the learning environment of the school. Central to the ASP is the concept of powerful learning, which Finnan and Levin define as 'authentic, interactive, inclusive and continuous'. They contrast such a learning process, which gives students more control over their own learning, with the 'drill and practice' process which frequently characterizes schools serving 'at-risk' students. This contrast is strikingly similar to Posch's distinction between a learning process which fosters dynamic qualities and one fostering passive qualities.

The educational change strategies used in the ASP focus not so much on learning outcomes as on the basic beliefs and assumptions which underpin schools' cultures and shape the learning process within them. Finnan and Levin classify these basic beliefs and assumptions in terms of five components of school cultures which educational change strategies need to address.

1 *The school's expectations for students.* Some schools have high expectations of their students and some low expectations. Variable expectations tend to be shaped by the basic assumption that less can be expected from students belonging to the lower income groups than from those belonging to the higher income ones. Hence, the former learn by rote using directive teaching methods, while the latter learn to think critically using teaching methods which engage them in intellectually challenging tasks.
2 *Students' own expectations of their school experience.* Variable expectations on the part of students tend to be shaped by beliefs about the value of schooling within their communities for enhancing their life opportunities. Oppositional cultures arise among students in some schools rather than others (e.g. in those serving socially marginalised minority communities) when they perceive their experience of schooling to deny them equality of access to the social and economic 'goods' they desire. Such oppositional cultures are a consequence of school cultures that appear to discriminate unfairly against some sections of society rather than others.
3 *Expectations for adult members of school communities.* These expectations, Finnan and Levin argue, depend largely on the characteristics of students and what is expected of them. Hence, less may be expected of teachers and parents in schools where students are drawn from low-income groups. As a consequence they come to expect less of themselves, lose self-esteem and are reluctant to try new ideas because they won't work with 'our children'.
4 *Beliefs about what counts as acceptable educational practice.* School cultures which foster high expectations of students and teachers will, according to Finnan and Levin, emphasize active learning and challenging curricula.
5 *Basic beliefs and assumptions about the desirability of educational change.* Some schools 'actively and passively resist externally imposed change' because 'the proposed changes do not fit their school culture' and threaten to disempower their teachers and administrators. Other schools are change-

oriented, 'especially if the changes build on the strengths of the existing school culture'.

Finnan and Levin argue that in describing a school's culture one is characterizing the school as both similar to and different from other schools. This is explained in terms of different levels at which cultures are constructed: the societal, local and personal levels. At the societal level there exists, they argue, a culture of schooling, a web of shared understandings about the nature and processes of education which underpin the organizational system members of a society commonly recognize as a school. This societally constructed web of understandings specifies basic beliefs about 'what schools should teach, and how they should be run and organized, who should be teaching in them, and how students should learn and be sorted for the purpose of learning.' They account for similarities between schools.

Schostak's concept of schooling also refers to common features of schools that are underpinned by a societally constructed web of beliefs about their major purposes and the kinds of processes involved in achieving them. However, unlike Schostak, Finnan and Levin offer a formal rather than substantive definition of the culture of schooling. They do not conceptually contrast schooling and education, but imply that the former is a neutral concept that refers to practices which may be judged to be educationally valuable or not. This difference in perspective might be explained in terms of fundamental basic beliefs about schools as social institutions. Schostak perhaps has a tendency to view them as institutions constructed to serve certain sectional and dominant interests in the society. In this context the culture of schooling will constitute an ideological structure which legitimates domination.

Schostak's contrast between schooling and education appears to require radical and disjunctive change. Hence, he tends to use subversive language when talking about change strategies, like 'derailing'. Finnan and Levin, on the other hand, tend to view schools as institutions which are more open to change and to developing their practices in ways which reflect the values of a just and equitable society. Their view is also endorsed by Brennan and Noffke's case studies of two school change projects (Chapter 5). For both Finnan and Levin and Brennan and Noffke the culture of schooling need not legitimate the interests of a dominant group but can be transformed to reflect a democratically constructed consensus about the role of schools in society.

However, as I indicated above, Finnan and Levin do not simply define school cultures by societally constructed beliefs and values. There are aspects of school cultures which are locally constructed and 'moulded by the unique and shared experiences of participants which are influenced by their class, race and neighbourhood as well as the school's history and its leadership.' Brennan and Noffke's case studies also support this view. In addition, Finnan and Levin argue, a school's culture exists at the personal level, inasmuch as it exists not only between individuals, shaping their interpersonal relations, but also in them, by virtue of their personal investment in its constitutive beliefs and values. Such local and personal characteristics, argue Finnan and Levin, account for the uniqueness of specific school cultures.

O'Hanlon (Chapter 12) pinpoints the significance of these multiple levels of meaning embedded in school cultures in her account of helping her group of PhD students, most of them teachers undertaking applied research into policy implementation processes within their schools, to make sense of the evidence they gather: 'it is possible to distinguish multiple layers of value priorities in their articulation and translation of educational policies. Group members tease out different priorities between individuals and schools which are represented and question the basis on which they rest.'

Although Finnan and Levin are less than explicit about the relationships between the basic beliefs which characterize specific school cultures and those generic beliefs which characterize the culture of schooling, it is not difficult to discern the ways they might interact with each other. For example, differences between schools about what can be expected of students tend to be shaped by a generic belief constructed at the societal level that children who come from low-income and minority groups in society are 'low-ability' and therefore little can be expected from them. Hence, a school which changes its beliefs about the capabilities of the students it serves and raises its expectations of them challenges a basic belief embedded in the culture of schooling at the societal level and in doing so threatens its stability as a component of that culture.

To take another example, the difference between a specific school culture which is resistant to change and one which is conditionally open to change can be explained in terms of different basic beliefs about the desirability of change. These different beliefs, however, may both be shaped by a common generic belief at the societal level that discontinuous change is undesirable. Suppose the school whose culture was highly resistant to change no longer believes that change is undesirable because it no longer values much in that culture and wants to transform it radically in ways which are totally discontinuous with it. In other words, it wants to be 'born again'. In this context the attempt to realize a vision of radical change at the local school level will challenge and to some extent destabilize the generic and societally defined belief that educational change is desirable only if it preserves some continuity with present practice. Although Finnan and Levin do not themselves appear to present this belief as open to challenge, the possibility is, I believe, implicit in the way they tend to represent the relationship between specific school cultures and the culture of schooling.

According to Finnan and Levin, the societally defined culture of schooling is more resistant to change than the locally defined characteristics of school cultures because, they claim, 'it exists primarily at an abstract, generalized level in the form of basic beliefs and assumptions about education.' Even when these basic beliefs and assumptions have been eroded within the cultures of individual schools, they may still persist at the societal level. For Finnan and Levin, the strategy for transforming the culture of schooling must therefore be to work at changing specific school cultures at the local level in ways that: (a) transform the basic beliefs which underpin them; and (b) establish a critical mass in the society of such culturally transformed schools as a means of transforming in turn the general culture of schooling which exists at the societal level.

Finnan and Levin's ASP is a good example of what I have called pedagogically driven educational change. It deploys strategies for transforming the basic beliefs and assumptions that shape specific cultures of teaching and learning in ways which recognize and value students' capacities for autonomous thought and action as learners. It stands in marked contrast to 'top-down' standards-driven strategies for school improvement, informed by externally prescribed learning objectives, curricula and instructional systems. The latter strategies cannot effect a transformation of the basic beliefs and assumptions which shape teaching and learning in schools, since many of the same beliefs and assumptions will tend to underpin such strategies. Standards-driven change is surface reform and largely reinforces the time-warped character of schooling at a time when schools need to become more responsive to social change in the wider society.

What Finnan and Levin propose, and illustrate with examples from their ASP, are bottom-up strategies for developing the specific cultures of individual schools in ways which also change the culture of schooling at the societal level. These strategies enable the school to 'take over its own destiny' and initiate cultural change from the bottom up. They include self-review, setting the vision and strategic goals and priorities, participative democratic governance, systematic action research as an approach to problem-solving and a 'powerful learning' pedagogy. Such strategies are consistent with Posch's vision of the school as an initiator of curriculum and pedagogical change, one in which rules and norms are democratically negotiated, and new curricula priorities and goals are set and then implemented via a process of teacher-based action research. They are also consistent with the two projects described by Brennan and Noffke.

Finnan and Levin's distinction between the culture of schooling and specific school cultures enables us to understand further why they appear to be more optimistic about the possibilities for transformative action in schools than Schostak seems to be. If they believe that school practices are exclusively shaped by the traditional culture of schooling, then, given their view that it is highly resistant to change, they might conclude, like Schostak does, that education has little to do with schooling. Finnan and Levin's distinction enables them to articulate a general bottom-up strategy, summarized above, for transforming the culture of schooling by changing specific school cultures.

It is important to appreciate that Schostak's point of view is grounded in a policy context within the UK, where the traditional culture of schooling has been reinforced by power-coercive mechanisms for driving up standards, which impose additional constraints on transforming that culture from the bottom up. In this policy context the bottom-up and pedagogically driven educational change strategies used in the ASP may appear to be less feasible.

Theories of educational change and their implications for strategic action are bound to particular political and policy contexts.

However, Brennan and Noffke's chapter offers a 'bridge' between Finnan and Levin's optimism and Schostak's pessimism. They argue, on the basis of their experience of two educational change projects in Australia and the USA, that schools are a good example of 'contradictory and ambiguous tendencies at work' in advanced capitalist countries. On the one hand, the 'pressures of the globalizing economy' lead to a greater emphasis on standards-driven reforms and schools providing 'more and more standardized accountability information, along lines familiar since the introduction of mass schooling.' On the other hand, schools are also under increasing pressure from the state 'to take up more local responsibility', to be 'more socially just, future-oriented and responsive to community needs'. In the latter respect they echo Posch's analysis of the decentralizing tendencies of States. Brennan and Noffke argue that these contradictory tendencies exist side-by-side, 'interacting and interrupting one another'. In doing so, schools are able to push at 'the edges of self-management policy rhetorics' to open up spaces in which they are able to initiate change; this in spite of the increased constraints that the growth of surveillance and control mechanisms (Schostak's paranoid curriculum) imposes on bottom-up change.

Brennan and Noffke suggest that the spaces opened up by contradictory policies constitute sites not only of resistance to state control, but also, mixed in, conservative attitudes to schooling, reflected in the customary isolation and individualization of teachers' work in classrooms. The experiences of the two projects they report indicated that school-initiated change involves redefining whose business schooling is. It entails rendering the boundaries of schools as communities more permeable and unstable, to include all who have a stake in their work: students and parents as well as teachers, and officials who have a role in implementing state-initiated reforms within the wider educational system. Within the change projects described by Brennan and Noffke, school communities were characterized 'by much more than the local school' and consisted of all those who participated in the processes of action-oriented evaluation within the projects. They write: 'In providing a different way to consider community as centred in joint action, the participants may have developed a sense of being able to affect their local setting, complex as it is.' This participation was not, Brennan and Noffke point out, simply a matter of ensuring the representation of interest groups within a hierarchical and bureaucratic organization.

> It became clear that the understanding of participation as primarily oriented to membership of functional groups (e.g. teachers or parents or administrators) in decision-making was a seriously limited concept, often working against the inclusion of some groups and refusing to acknowledge significant differences among parents and among teachers, not to mention student groups.

The SIP project in Australia involved teachers, students, parents, school administrators and local officials in a process of action-oriented evaluation, which focused on 'the underlying/embedded values' in the practices of schools, thereby 'addressing the fundamental norms by which schools operated, opening up to change the ordering of the system as a whole.' Participants also networked across schools and localities to share experience and information. The latter, Brennan and Noffke claim:

> gave different groupings in schools the opportunity to mix with others as speakers and as audiences, providing important different access to what had previously been largely professional domains of information and professional development. The 'bureaucracy' became 'peopled' rather than an organizational chart – people who were met and interacted with at regular policy development and overview evaluation activities for the initiative as a whole.

This idea of school communities as action-oriented interpersonal networks echoes Posch's idea of dynamic networks as sources of power to transform cultures of teaching and learning at the local level. Within the spaces created by self-contradictory policies, school-initiated change requires the debureaucratization and personalization of relationships and interactions, thereby exposing 'non-predictable lines of fracture and difference' among participants which move across the 'boundaries' between the various 'interest groups' or power blocks. Yet, Noffke and Brennan argue, 'it is only when such difference is accepted and worked with that shared and worthwhile products are derived from the effort put into them.' The mutual acknowledgement of personal differences of perspective is perceived to be a necessary resource, rather than an obstacle, for developing shared values within a democratic community.

For example, the African and African-American Curriculum Project was a local initiative which exposed multiple agendas for change. Multicultural approaches to curriculum change appeared to be at tension with some people's anti-racist agenda, and giving students as individuals equality of regard often clashed with a perceived need for a mandated curriculum and system of testing. Yet, according to Brennan and Noffke, these differences were contained by the shared recognition 'that the formation of communities of struggle around issues of racial justice required a commitment to self-examination'; and, presumably as a result, a mutual willingness to accommodate the perspective of the other in negotiating joint action.

Brennan and Noffke appear to be depicting in their case studies the emergence of school communities as the kind of dynamic, self-reflexive and interpersonal networks that Posch envisions in his theory of educational change. One implication of the emergence of such communities is the destabilization of prevailing power relationships between 'interest groups'. The emergence of debureaucratized and cross-cutting interpersonal networks transcends the categories of 'compliance' versus 'resistance' and 'conservatism' versus 'radicalism'.

Somekh's (Chapter 9) account of the 'learning organization' also appears to imply the emergence of such networks which work with, rather than struggle to overcome, difference. Following Giddens (1994), she uses the phrase 'dialogic democracy' to describe 'relationships ordered through dialogue rather than through embedded power'. Somekh argues that a dialogic democracy does not impose problem solutions on others, however 'rational' and 'well grounded' in evidence they appear to be. Rather, it is a process of identifying and respecting difference, and negotiating solutions, together. Her chapter is about framing an action research methodology for managing organizational change, which has been freed from the imperative to discover the rational solution. Again, her chapter resonates with Brennan and Noffke's account of dynamic interpersonal learning networks:

> Action research, other forms of innovatory work and democratic evaluation have sometimes been justified in primarily Enlightenment terms, bolstering a notion of the critical individual, rationally engaging in choice for progress. This individualistic approach tends to over-valorize dominant groups' understandings of rationality and choice, rather than to emphasize the relation of reflection, action and interaction.

Conceptualizing the relationship between power and consensus in effecting educational change in schools

The kinds of transformational strategies advocated by Finnan and Levin, Brennan and Noffke, and Somekh presuppose the possibility of school communities (teachers, administrators, students, parents, officials etc.) arriving at a new and non-coerced consensus on basic beliefs. In other words, they imply that basic structures of belief and value can be transformed only if all the members of the organization are involved in the process. Their cultural theory of school change differs significantly from the rational-contingency and micro-political theories of organizations described by Altrichter and Salzgeber (Chapter 8), which have tended to shape the dominating discourse of school improvement.

The first 'theory' Altrichter and Salzgeber examine posits organizations as objective structures, which are rational inasmuch as they are designed or constructed to achieve certain organizational goals in response to contingencies operating within their 'environment': the more 'rational' the organization, the more 'efficient' it becomes. Such structures are therefore assumed to be relatively stable and autonomous, and exist independently of the subjective beliefs and desires of the people who work in the organization. Structures exist over and above individuals, shaping their behaviour to achieve the goals of the organization. From this viewpoint, the basis for consensus building is to convince people in the organization of the rationality of the blueprint in a way which secures their willing compliance and therefore commitment to it, irrespective of their subjective preferences and desires. Diverse practices and conflict will be interpreted as a failure in 'communication', a lack of skill in applying appropriate techniques of persuasion.

According to the rational-contingency theory of organizations described by Altrichter and Salzgeber, school improvement is a process of implementing the blueprint, skilfully, i.e. by expending a minimum of energy overcoming any frictions which arise through 'good communication'. Hence, when the 'development' process manifests diverse activities and conflict, it is a sign of faulty implementation strategies being employed, of 'poor communication'.

In my view, standards-driven school improvement processes in the UK are conceived in terms of this theory of organizations as objective-rational structures. For Schostak, as I pointed out above, the use of this theory as a basis for school improvement masks the 'paranoid' and power-coercive nature of the strategies involved.

One characteristic of the production of the paranoid curriculum, according to Schostak, is its claim to rationality: as the mirror in which 'the truth' is perceived for those who comply. The paranoid curriculum aims to eliminate subjectivity in the name of reason, and therefore legitimates its structures of domination as the means of accomplishing some form of 'rational purification' of the individuals being processed, of eliminating the possibility of bias, prejudice and error from their sphere of judgement and decision. In this sense it conforms to a rational-contingency model, cited by Altrichter and Salzgeber, of the relationship between organizational structures and individuals. Schostak's account of the 'paranoid' curriculum suggests that agreements about 'the truths of reason' within systematically organized 'rational' social orders are constituted by relations of domination. 'Truth' and 'reason' are constructed by the dominant order, which leaves no room for the view that they are intersubjectively constructed by free individuals interacting together, with mutual regard/recognition for each other's ideas, to make sense of their world and their role within it. In other words, the 'rational consensus' about goals which legitimates the use of structural power within the rational-contingency model of school improvement is merely masking the will to power. According to Altrichter and Salzgeber, the tacit use of such a theory explains why observers of school development processes are frequently surprised by an apparent absence of consensus, some being 'astounded' by the sheer diversity of activities and the 'irrationality' of their results, while others were 'irritated' by the presence of conflict and even at times 'outright polarization'. Such observations appear to support the micro-political theories which have emerged from some school change studies.

As Altrichter and Salzgeber point out, micro-political theories of organizations tend to view schools as sites best characterized by power struggles. Activities and events are described in terms of the key concepts of 'conflict' and 'domination'. From this perspective, the goals and structure of the organization are inherently unstable as its members, in pursuit of their diverse and often conflicting interests, compete for the power to define the organization in ways which serve them. Structures are the product not of a rational consensus about organizational goals but of 'battles' between individuals and groups as they strategically pursue their conflicting interests within the organization. They constitute sets of power relations inasmuch as they foster the interests of some to the exclusion of the interests of others.

Micro-political theories of organizations leave little room for the idea of structures as objective entities that exist independently of the subjective preferences and desires of people within the organization, because they are constituted to serve one set of preferences and desires to the exclusion of other sets. Since such theories posit structures as 'irrationally' constructed entities, they cannot become objects of rational consensus. They are inevitably viewed as instruments of coercive power and therefore as inherently unstable, since the oppressed will in time develop strategies for resisting and seizing the power of their oppressors.

Schostak's chapter locates the perception of schools as sites of conflictual struggle and power games in different conceptions of schooling. Schooling, he argues, is about socially engineering children for certain social purposes along predefined pathways, called 'courses' or 'curricula', which are defined by 'standardizing categories of "excellence" and "acceptability"'. However, 'since there is not a single social purpose agreed by all, school is a place of contested schoolings that lie in angry opposition or perhaps in ironic play with one another.' He appears to locate many conflictual struggles and power plays in schools as a 'battle for curriculum control'. It seems to me that one implication of Schostak's characterization of schooling is that the actual curriculum structures in place within a school will reflect the outcomes of various conflictual struggles and power plays over the curriculum, not simply within the school but also within the wider society. Such structures may clearly indicate who won the battle for the curriculum, or they may represent an uneasy truce between different interest groups committed to different types of curriculum pathways. Whichever obtains, Schostak's micro-political conception of schooling as processing students along predefined curriculum pathways or tracks implies that such curriculum structures are, inasmuch as they are the outcome of power struggles, fundamentally unstable entities. They produce 'resistances' and sets of unresolved issues which constitute ongoing threats to stability.

Altrichter and Salzgeber point out that micro-political theories of organizations tend to assume that the exercise of structural power is coercive and excludes any possibility of achieving a genuine consensus as a basis for organizational development. They use case study evidence, derived from their study of 'good schools', to challenge this assumption, while at the same time challenging the assumption built into the rational-contingency model that the achievement of a rational consensus about organizational goals is a condition of structural power. They argue that 'the actual relationship between power and consensus' needs to be determined 'in specific empirical cases instead of theoretically presupposing it for all empirical cases'.

One of their case studies depicts a new but experienced teacher being 'pressurized' into adopting an unfamiliar teaching method for first grade students. The method is sanctioned by the headteacher and many staff in the belief that it is the reason for the school's high reputation among parents. The alternative on offer to using the method is the option of teaching a third grade class, but the new teacher prefers to teach first grade. The headteacher and some of her staff offer emotional and personal support to the teacher in overcoming initial difficulties with the method. She proceeds with the first grade class and accepts the practice advised by the head and some staff.

Altrichter and Salzgeber suggest that a micro-political organizational theorist would tend to interpret this situation as one of overcoming a conflict of interest by subtle coercion. Yet the new teacher resisted all attempts by interviewers to get her to entertain such an interpretation. In fact she had over time and with experience become personally committed to the new practice. The case study evidence also challenges the assumption that the achievement of consensus is a rational process. The teacher did not agree, Altrichter and Salzberger point out, to adopt the practice after a Habermas-type 'free and open discussion with the head, staff and parents' which convinced her of its value and thereby resolved the conflict between her view and theirs.

From their case evidence, Altrichter and Salzberger construct an inclusive theory of how stable structures are produced in organizations such as schools, which extends our understanding of consensus to incorporate both the operation of structural power and the subjective preferences and desires of individuals. Within this theory a similar concept of organizational culture to that employed by Finnan and Levin plays a central integrating function and enables us to position the latter's vision of school change in a more inclusive theory of organizations than any of the others discussed by Altrichter and Salzgeber.

Altrichter and Salzgeber argue that stable structures as sources of power in organizations are neither objective-rational entities nor coercive resolutions of conflictual power struggles. Instead, they are created by interactions between members of the organization, which are shaped by implicit agreements at the level of culture about the validity of certain basic principles and norms. Hence, the integration of the new teacher in their case study is not an example of persuading her of the rationality of a certain teaching method, of the authority of the headteacher on matters of classroom practice, of the role of parents in shaping practice. Nor is it an example of the way coercive power subtly operates to overcome conflicting interests by suppressing 'the voice' of the new teacher. Instead, it is an example of the new teacher actively participating in the reproduction of 'the structures' in the school on the basis of assumptions shared with other members of the organization. A distinction has to be drawn between the operation of power as such in organizations and its coercive forms of expression. Structures on this account have both an objective and subjective dimension inasmuch as their overt features constitute manifestations of intersubjective agreements at the level of basic beliefs and norms which define a shared culture.

Shared ideas with the headteacher and staff about 'the legitimate hierarchies and the headteacher's power, the parents' role, the importance of "child-centred teaching" during primary education', lead an experienced new teacher to the school to accept an unfamiliar teaching method 'instead of insisting on the alternative norm . . . i.e. the professional right of teachers to use appropriate teaching methods of their own choice.' Hence, consensus at the cultural level of basic beliefs creates structural power and structural power creates consensus at the level of acceptable practice. The distinction Finnan and Levin make between the culture of schooling and school culture is illuminating in this respect. It is because the new, but experienced, teacher shares certain basic beliefs about schooling with the head and staff of the school she is entering that she is able to be inducted into the school culture without conflict. What the case study portrays is a process of moving to a consensus, which involves compromise but not, despite its 'power-penetrated' core, a conflict of interest to be resolved by the use of power-coercive strategies.

However, Altrichter and Salzberger point out that their account of how power can penetrate and shape a non-coerced consensus does not negate certain features highlighted by micro-political theories of organizations. The new teacher, they argue, actively participates in the reproduction of a certain teaching practice in her classroom. This structure is stabilized through her own agency, and subsequently valued by it, but the outcome of her actions was not her aim from the outset as she interacted with the head and staff of the school. It was an unintended effect of pursuing her own personal interests: wanting to teach a grade 1 class and to get on well with the headteacher and the staff in the school. 'One can be sure', Altrichter and Salzgeber claim, 'that she did not intend to collaborate to stabilize the new method. But this is exactly the effect of what she was doing.' In doing so she also satisfied her own personal interests. The case study illustrates the conditions under which consensus and a stability of 'structure' are achieved in organizations. These refer not only to the operation of non-coercive structural power within organizations, but also to the way in which structures are unintentionally stabilized in the process of individuals pursuing their own personal interests through their interactions with each other. The case study suggests that the achievement of consensus, and the stability of structures it implies, depends both on the reproduction of structural power within these interactions and on individuals feeling empowered in the process.

Altrichter and Salzberger use the metaphor of a game to describe the duality of agency and structure involved in the process of stabilizing overt structures, but to call it a power game risks misrepresenting the case data they provide if it implies winners and losers and the exercise of coercion. The game they describe depicts the points at which structural power and the agency of autonomous, self-interested individuals intersect to produce social consensus and stable structures. Its outcome is not only the reproduction of structures that shape the actions of individuals but the satisfaction of their often divergent interests. Hence, structures can be both constraining and enabling at the same time.

The process of maintaining stable structures in organizations operates at the level of practical rather than discursive consciousness. The new teacher in the case study participated in the reproduction of a certain routine practice in the school, but did not self-consciously articulate to herself or others the beliefs and norms she shared with others in the process. This, however, poses the question of how stable structures become destabilized to effect structural change.

School development and the empowerment of teachers through action research

Central to the vision of Posch for educational change is the empowerment of teachers through action research. His vision of teachers exercising responsibility for school change initiatives depends on the development of their capacities to analyse practical problems and devise and evaluate action strategies aimed at resolving them. For Posch, action research empowers teachers to risk breaking out of their traditional routines, and to accept responsibility for pedagogical initiatives aimed at changing the conditions of learning in ways which prepare pupils to participate as active citizens in a dynamic democratic social order.

Several contributors to this volume articulate a process in which teachers, often in dialogue with students, parents and others in school communities, gather evidence about their practices and critique the assumptions, beliefs and values embedded in them. Such a process, often described as action research, marks a shift from a practical to a discursive level of consciousness. For O'Hanlon it is the learning that takes place at this latter level, rather than simply learning to teach, which is educational for teachers. She argues that the rationalistic assumptions which underpin traditional approaches to professional development have neglected the 'tacit knowledge' embedded in practices and the need for teachers to critique it discursively in the process of initiating change.

> Traditionally, their development has been based upon academic scholarship and intellectual ability, whereas the practical knowledge and experience gained in teachers' careers have been treated as incidental to this focus, and have even at times been dismissed as 'subjective' or anecdotal when used as evidence in written assignments and dissertations.

According to O'Hanlon, the action research process involves more than simply teachers reflexively recovering the assumptions embedded in their practices; it involves locating them within the wider societal context as a basis for critique.

> The professional development of teachers becomes teacher education when a critical theory of the teaching situation allows professionals to

> explain and understand the ways in which teaching is controlled by factors outside the classroom in its societal and political context . . . Educational professionals need to recognize that pedagogy and curriculum knowledge is always problematic, and thus open to scrutiny, critical appraisal and revision. The development of teachers' 'subject' knowledge often overlooks the wider political and national issues which frame it. Debate about pedagogy in largely subject-specific areas overlooks the overall shape of the curriculum and fails to site it in broader complex socio-cultural factors which relate to economic, political and strategic concerns in Western society.

This account of action research as an educational process in which teachers are engaged in developing a critical theory about their practices by locating their underlying assumptions in a broader socio-political context is highly consistent with Finnan and Levin's view that practices in schools are embedded in a societally defined culture of schooling, and illuminates the significance of action research within their ASP initiative as a means of bringing about cultural change in schools. The process O'Hanlon describes is also depicted in Brennan and Noffke's reflections on teachers' involvement in the two school development projects they describe.

> The significant constraints of operations of school systems within the diminishing fiscal capacities of the Western capitalist state continue to loom as a spectre over any reform effort in the public sector. Perhaps such projects serve to bolster optimism of the will to counteract the pessimism of the intellect. Stories about such projects are woven into the oral traditions of school change, providing further opportunities to develop sophisticated reflection and implications for action. Specific individuals recognize how their own settings and activities are shaped by wider contexts, and further understand the mechanisms of that shaping as they press against the constraints. This version of the individual is thus an instance in which 'individual' is defined not only singly but in relation to both community and context. The social constructed, historical nature of schooling and school systems is already apparent at local school sites, partly through the operation of projects such as these.

This extract highlights the relationship in action research between transformative action and understanding the constraints on such action emanating from the wider societal context. Teachers do not first come to understand and critique the assumptions embedded in their practices before attempting to change them. Instead, such understanding is developed interactively with attempts to bring about change. In such attempts teachers become aware of the social mechanisms employed in the wider socio-political context to maintain traditional practices in schools and the cultural assumptions which shape them. Moreover, Brennan and Noffke suggest that this awareness brings a certain self-understanding to teachers; namely, that their personal and professional identities are not simply individually defined but shaped by a socially situated system of belief and value. As Finnan and Levin argue, 'culture' exists as much within as between individuals.

In making the beliefs and values embedded in their practices 'open to scrutiny, critical appraisal and revision' through action research in the way O'Hanlon suggests, individuals lose the illusion of a substantial 'inner self' that exists independently of its socio-cultural context. However, this self-understanding does not render the individual powerless to redefine the self, because it also brings the recognition that the relationship between 'society' and the 'self' is not a deterministic relation. The former does not stand over and against the latter, limiting and controlling its freedom of expression. The 'reflexive self' at the level of discursive consciousness is aware of the duality of agency and structure, of the active participation of individuals at the level of practical consciousness in reproducing the structures that shape their practices, and therefore of the potential power of individuals to redefine themselves self-reflexively by transforming the frameworks of belief and value which underpin these structures. It is also aware that it can only do this in association with, rather than in isolation from, other individuals. Hence, interpersonal networks are significant as enabling structures that support the consciousness raising, critical theorizing and transformative actions which characterize action research as an educational process for teachers, and empower them to counteract the mechanisms which sustain the status quo. Such a process locates the autonomy of the individual in discursive rather than practical consciousness, in a self-reflexive and intersubjectively negotiated self rather than in a substantial and decontextualized self. According to O'Hanlon, it is the task of teacher education to establish a social context, a counter-culture, which fosters and sustains within the teaching profession the development of the autonomous professional self.

> Teacher education concerns the education of teachers into a culture which increases their professional autonomy through the growth of a critical theory of teaching . . . school-based enquiry requires a fostering of educational contexts where teachers can engage in critical reasoning.

However, as the chapters by Pérez Gómez (Chapter 10), Groundwater Smith and Walker (Chapter 11) and O'Hanlon herself demonstrate, enabling teachers to deconstruct and reconstruct their customary practices is no easy task in the face of the mechanisms which, in sustaining the status quo, display little tolerance for any critical distancing from the beliefs and values that shape those practices.

The case studies carried out by Pérez Gómez, into the *practicum* of eight trainee teachers from eight different universities in Spain, throw considerable doubt on the capacity of university-based initial teacher training programmes to provide a social context in which trainee teachers can play a significant role as agents of cultural transformation in schools. His case studies focus on the socializing function of the school *practicum*, an increasingly important element in professional preparation programmes in many countries. Pérez Gómez identifies some of the key factors operating within the *practicum* which militate against the kind of educational process of critical distancing described by O'Hanlon. These factors include:

- the pressures from within the school culture itself on students to adapt to the established forms of classroom practice;
- the personal insecurity and dependency of students in the face of their need to achieve a sense of mastery in a complex and 'alien' environment and to gain respect as teachers within it;
- students' lack of access to alternative theoretical and practical reference points by which to judge what they observe and experience in schools;
- the 'socializing' function of the school-based tutor/mentor and the 'bureaucratic' function of the university-based supervisor;
- the arrangements and procedures in place for assessing students academic and professional learning.

Pérez Gómez concludes that 'the whole of the structure built up around the period of practical training induces the reproduction of dominant forms of teaching behaviour and styles in each particular scenario.' His findings confirm those from other studies of teacher training programmes which have a significant school-based component (e.g. MacDonald 1984; Munroe 1992).

He could find no evidence, in any of the cases, of the university being able to counteract the structural power of the school culture in the course of the *practicum*. The function normally served by the university seminar 'in terms of debate, communication, analysis of problems, stimulation of queries and consideration of alternatives', and one that should be the responsibility of the university supervisor, was in no case evidenced. The role of the supervisor during the *practicum* appears to have been reduced to an administrative function. The effectiveness of the *practicum* as a medium of professional socialization into the prevailing culture of schools, argues Pérez Gómez, is considerably enhanced by the fact that 'the trainees are socialized in the same culture as they themselves experienced for at least 15 years of their lives.'

One need not assume, from Pérez Gómez's account of the 'structural power' of school cultures to shape the practices of teacher trainees in Spain, that he is necessarily portraying a power-coercive process of professional socialization. Pérez Gómez is not claiming that the structural power of school cultures resides in its capacity to compel compliance in opposition to the desires, interests, intentions and will of the students. He points out, for example, that some students reacted defensively to any attempt to get them to achieve 'critical distance' from their practices, and he explains this in terms of the threat it poses to the pleasure and satisfaction they derive from their compliance rather than in terms of any fear of reprisals:

> the satisfactory personal and social relations that student-teachers established with the children they worked with served merely to reinforce the

> prevailing school culture. The pleasure the students derived from pupils' affection made them defer the possibility of asking more demanding questions about the quality of their teaching.

These students appear to be actively rather than passively participating at the level of practical consciousness in defining their professional identities through the socialization process. As such they will not experience the structures which shape their practices in classrooms as constraints. They will only be identified as constraints if and when the students shift to a discursive level of consciousness, by critically distancing themselves from their practices and attempting culturally transformative actions. However, even at this level there is no implication that such constraints will be able to withstand the growth of informed critique and the emergence of a new consensus among a critical mass of 'enlightened' individuals. Much will depend on the extent to which they are reinforced by mechanisms, often emanating from the wider socio-political context, for disciplining and punishing 'non-compliant' behaviour.

Pérez Gómez appears to support Altrichter and Salzgeber's contention that the operation of structural power on individuals in organizations like schools does not necessarily take a coercive form and militate against individuals reaching a negotiated consensus on beliefs and values.

If, as Pérez Gómez claims, an early immersion in direct experience within schools militates against student teachers achieving much 'critical distancing' from their practices and counteracts the influence of the university to this end, then how might one avoid reducing the professional preparation of teachers to mere training, as opposed to education? Groundwater Smith and Walker (Chapter 11) discuss a programme which involves student teachers in a vicarious experience of the realities of schools and classrooms prior to a period of direct experience. The programme involves trainee teachers in a process of analysing case evidence gathered in a particular school that was facing the complexities of social change within its local environment. This teacher education initiative in Australia was stimulated by Barry MacDonald's ideas about the use of case studies of schools in counteracting an early and rapid socialization into conservative practices.

> Barry's concern at Jordanhill [a Scottish Teacher Training College where he worked with Lawrence Stenhouse prior to both moving to CARE as founding members] was that once young teachers were in the schools, they were rapidly socialized by the conservative culture of schooling. So his idea of case study was to give them a sense of alternatives.

At this point it is worth exploring the methodological context of MacDonald's idea of case study in more detail, before we return to the use it was put to by Groundwater Smith and Walker. This is because MacDonald's methodology of case study research embodies similar values and principles to action research, but differs from it in one important respect: its profound scepticism about the capacity of those immersed in the culture of schooling to achieve critical distance without some form of external research intervention to gather and construct databases.

On leaving Jordanhill, to evaluate Stenhouse's Humanities Curriculum Project, MacDonald developed a democratic paradigm for evaluating educational innovation and change which gave a central role to case study research. The basic rationale for case study was the need for educational decision makers and others whose interests are at stake (e.g. teachers, parents, officials and policy makers) to understand the complex social dynamics which shape the fate of innovation and change projects at the level of the school, and which they are either directly or indirectly engaged in. The idea was to use case studies as a means of organizing a free exchange of information about the activities and views of the various parties involved in shaping, mediating and implementing change, which addresses their diverse questions and concerns in a form that cuts across the traditional boundaries controlling the flow of information between them and fosters dialogue and mutual understanding.

MacDonald's case study based democratic evaluation paradigm is not simply a methodology for specialist researchers to use as an instrument for studying educational change. It is best understood in MacDonald's own terms, as a political strategy for accomplishing democratically negotiated educational change by establishing conditions which foster and maintain a critical reflexivity among, and mutually educative relationships between, those individuals and groups who play a role in defining, shaping and mediating young people's experience of schooling in particular contexts. In this light, case studies may be viewed as an organization of evidence about the complexity of educational change contexts in a form which promotes the development of what Somekh, following Giddens, calls dialogic democracy.

Studies of educational change within a democratic evaluation framework acknowledge the complex interactions in particular contexts between local and societal factors and therefore do not confine the boundaries of the case to the locality. This is why evidence about the activities and views of those involved in defining, shaping and mediating the culture of schooling at the societal level will legitimately constitute case evidence.

Central to democratic evaluation as a strategy for achieving critical distance and dialogue among those who participate in defining, shaping and mediating practice in schools and classrooms is the role of external 'evaluators' in the construction of case studies. They are responsible for gathering information and brokering its exchange via the medium of the case study report. It is this role which demarcates democratic evaluation from the kind of participatory/action research described by O'Hanlon, Brennan and Noffke, and Somekh. Both forms of research focus on problems of educational change in particular school contexts, and involve the gathering of information from a diversity of perspectives as a basis for an informed dialogue between those involved as participants in defining and shaping practice. The difference lies in differing beliefs about the feasibility of participants achieving the critical distance necessary for the processes of information gathering and exchange. Strategically, the difference between action research and democratic evaluation might best be characterized in terms currently employed by the UK Teacher Training Agency (TTA) in its attempts to develop teaching as an evidence-based profession. The TTA makes a distinction between engaging teachers in research and engaging them with research. It is asking whether teachers need to engage in research in order to engage with it. Those committed to action research may assume 'yes', while the democratic evaluator may assume 'no' to be the answer. My own position is that the answer should depend on the context and that the two 'paradigms' are not mutually exclusive as educational change strategies; the latter may well establish the conditions for the former to become feasible.

Given the insecurity and dependency of trainee teachers confronted with their *practicum* and already partly socialized through their experience as school students, Groundwater Smith and Walker's strategy of getting them to achieve critical distance by constructing case narratives from a case record documenting the complexities of practice in a school is an intelligible one, as they explain below.

> *Susan:* What students were being asked to do was to become researchers of these case records and develop a portrayal of curriculum in action. I wanted them to see that curriculum is a far more complex construct than they had originally thought. They tended to believe that curriculum was just the specified syllabus to be taught in classrooms: they came to see that curriculum is the interactions between all the players and the media used. We talked about that as the curriculum *text,* they were made to see this in a curriculum *context,* from the local school through to state policy, and then we intersected that with curriculum *pretexts,* the reasonings which lay behind why people made choices given that they were in a particular context . . .
>
> Sometimes people ask why I did not require students to collect the data if I was so keen to embed the notion of research in this process. My argument was that they would need to engage in so much barrier breaking first, so much negotiation, that they would find it difficult to get to the actual questions . . .
>
> So the students started to identify, but not yet name, some issues such as 'the hidden curriculum'. They started to ask questions like 'what's being learned here, besides the substance of the lesson?' They started to raise issues with respect to ethnicity, culture, social class and so on and how these things influenced what was happening . . .
>
> *Rob:* I think that goes back to Barry's original ideas about case study, that the purpose was to defer judgement in order to create space, because if you rush to judgement too quickly, you close off ways of understanding which can lead to other ways of acting.

However, it is important to recognize that the trainees engaged with the case record prior to their *practicum,* presumably in the hope that it created the conditions for maintaining critical distance and self-reflexive inquiry within the *practicum* itself.

To what extent is the scepticism about the capacity of participants to achieve critical distance and enter into mutually educative relationships without the assistance of an external researcher or information broker justified in the context of the continuing professional development of teachers? Brennan and Noffke acknowledge this sceptical challenge to their own projects.

> Many of those involved in outside evaluation were sceptical of the possibility that ordinary school communities, now placed in a position of greater responsibility for meeting the curriculum and learning needs of their local students, would be able to engage in the development of informed judgement.

Their accounts of the two projects suggest that the school communities involved indeed had problems in achieving critical distance and mutually educative relations through a participant or action research approach, and that a form of external intervention was significant in overcoming these problems. However, within the participant or action research mode the role of the outsider appears to differ from the role of MacDonald's researcher in gathering information and 'brokering' its exchange as a basis for mutual education. Within the context of Brennan and Noffke's participant or action research projects the idea of the outsider as evidence gatherer and information broker is replaced by the idea of the outsider as critical friend posing questions and raising issues about evidence gathered and supplied by the participants.

> But these reworkings of the concepts were not accomplished by outside forums in which such matters were debated and explored, and new action was formulated, with input from all those involved. Rather, officials and support staff, and outside critical friends, played an important role in raising issues which might have been too difficult to address without assistance, or which might have remained among the taken-for-granted operational shibboleths of a group immersed in its own practice.

O'Hanlon's detailed account of her role as an academic supervisor of a group of participant or action researchers undertaking their PhDs corroborates this view of the outsider as critical friend, but conceptualizes the role more broadly as a 'process facilitator' exercising responsibility for the organization of enlightenment as a social process of mutual education.

> Teachers gather evidence from their practice which supports their educational argument and then deconstruct the evidence in dialogue with colleagues to find the contradictions and disparities which inevitably arise. In this process they learn to reveal the concealed factors which reproduce the educational culture. The process of deconstruction occurs with the input of peers.

Of course, the outsider as facilitator needs to engage in, or at least with, research into the complexities of his or her own practices, but this second-order reflexivity, of which O'Hanlon's chapter itself might be considered an example, must be distinguished from the research role of the democratic evaluator. It is especially significant in the light of the fact that external facilitators of participant or action research tend to be academics operating from a higher education base, and there will be a tendency, as O'Hanlon suggests, for certain basic assumptions embedded in the traditional academic culture to be reproduced within their own 'facilitation' practices, thereby distorting the relationship between theory and practice within an authentic process of action research.

> Abstraction of knowledge in the form of theory is viewed as academically valuable, whereas practical knowledge is often translated into 'description and commentary' on practice which has little academic value without critique.

Although O'Hanlon interprets her role as an outsider very differently from that of the democratic evaluator, she does share much of the latter's belief about the lack of space within the established culture of schooling for teachers to achieve critical distance from the practices it defines and shapes. Constructing a physical and territorial space which is distanced from the workplace culture of the participant researchers, and the site for their evidence gathering, is, she argues, an important condition for enabling teachers to achieve 'critical distance'. She writes:

> for teachers to understand the underlying influences in the general culture and practice of their profession they must step beyond the everyday milieu of the school and into a space deliberately organized to provide them with the opportunity to practise critical reasoning about what they are doing, why they are doing it and how they can successfully achieve their educational aims.

If contemporary social change is challenging schools to transform their cultures in ways which are more consistent with educating all young people for active and responsible citizenship in a rapidly evolving liberal democratic global social order, then we need to reconstruct the role of higher education in supporting the processes which will enable teachers, and others, involved in defining and shaping schools' practices to meet those challenges. The current debates in a number of countries about how to engage them in and with educational research as a basis for school development is fundamental to this reconstruction. It is also fundamental to the reconstruction of teaching as a profession in a context where it is prone to continuous destabilization by the 'shifting sands' created by numerous, frequently contradictory, policy interventions.

Ingvarson's contribution (Chapter 13) highlights an important implication of teachers' engagement in and with research; namely, its potential as a basis for enabling them to generate their own professional standards, as opposed to having these externally defined and imposed by government and its agents. By having a role in shaping what is to count as valid knowledge about their practices, teachers become positioned for a generative role in professional standards setting. Ingvarson argues that the process has already begun with the kinds of projects we have involved teachers in at the Centre for Applied Research in Education; and, I would add, as illustrated by such contributors to this volume as Brennan, Noffke, O'Hanlon, Somekh, Groundwater Smith and Walker. Through such projects, Ingvarson argues:

> Professional development . . . was the result of engagement by teachers in networks and communities with a mutual desire to learn how to bring their values closer to their practice. By documenting this experience . . . teachers extended current knowledge about pedagogy, and this knowledge in turn provided a framework for the professional development of other teachers. CARE's research showed how the agenda for professional development could be driven by relatively stable professional knowledge and values, not merely swings in government policies and priorities.
>
> Although the people involved would not have used the term, CARE projects showed how professional development could be organized around teaching standards. CARE's action research was essentially standards-guided curriculum evaluation and professional learning.

Ingvarson is referring to standards here in a very different sense from that employed in the so-called 'standards debate', where the term refers to externally defined and standardized learning outcomes as opposed to professionally defined 'indicators' of professional aims and values which are evidenced in the pedagogical processes themselves. Such indicators may vary across different pedagogical contexts and will be open to continuous revision in the light of teachers' engagement with and in pedagogical research. Ingvarson warns us against assuming that the application of standards to practice implies the standardization of practice. Standardization would debilitate professional standards-setting as a dynamic process which involves the exercise of judgement in context, rather than a static one directed towards fixing educational practice in 'tablets of stone'. Ingvarson's use of the term 'standards' is quite consistent with what I referred to earlier as pedagogically driven change.

For Ingvarson it is not sufficient that action research and self-evaluation projects should contribute only to the professional development of the teachers involved in them. The professional knowledge they generate needs to be formalized and systematized for the profession as a whole to access, test and use as a resource in developing their own pedagogical practices. Only in this way can the 'prevailing attitude in teacher culture' be overcome; namely, that what counts as good teaching is a 'private' matter for individuals to determine rather than a question for teachers as a corporate professional body to address. Ingvarson argues that the formalization of the pedagogical knowledge generated through teachers' action research, and its use for the purpose of professional standards setting, empowers the teaching profession to influence national policy debates and 'to counter policies designed to deprofessionalise their work'. However, for Ingvarson teachers need incentives if they are to participate in the development and use of a professional knowledge base on any scale. This, he believes, will depend on the extent to which the activities of generating professional knowledge and 'standards setting' are 'locked into' a wider professional development system consisting of the following additional elements:

- the development of staged career paths that provide practitioners with incentives to achieve the specified standards and recognition for those that do;
- an infrastructure for professional learning to gain the knowledge and skills embodied in the standards;
- a credible system of professional certification.

The emergence of such a system, Ingvarson argues, would be complementary to, rather than a replacement for, in-service training that is specifically targeted at supporting reforms initiated by government. However, it constitutes 'an acknowledgement that, as in any profession, professional development is more than keeping up with changes initiated by government.' It would also contain the rise of managerialism in schools in which 'the goals for professional development are in danger of narrowing to school charters and duties based teacher appraisal schemes' and 'leave teachers and their professional associations outside debates about standards and expertise in teaching.'

In this concluding chapter I have attempted to highlight the significance of the contributions in this volume for reconstructing the relationship between educational research and practice in a context where the educational system at the beginning of the twenty-first century is facing the challenge of profound changes taking place in advanced industrial societies. In my view, we need more mutually educative debates both within the educational research community and between researchers and educational practitioners, which cut across the traditional boundaries between research paradigms and between the domains of 'theory' and practice; debates which need to be grounded in case studies and records of educational research-in-action.

References

Beck, U. (1992) *The Risk Society: towards a New Modernity*. London: Sage.

Fukuyama, F. (1992) *The End of History and the Last Man*. Harmondsworth: Penguin.

Giddens, A. (1994) *Beyond Left and Right*. Cambridge: Polity Press.

MacDonald, B. (1976) Evaluation and the control of education. In D. Tawney (ed.) *Curriculum Evaluation Today: Trends and Implications*. London: Macmillan and Schools Council.

MacDonald, B. (1984) Teacher education and curriculum reform: some English errors. Address to Spanish teacher trainers, Valencia.

Munroe, R. G. (1992) A case study of school-based training systems in New Zealand secondary schools. In J. Elliott (ed.) *Reconstructing Teacher Education*. London: Falmer Press.

Posch, P. (1991) Environment and school initiatives: background and basic premises of the project. In *Environment, Schools and Active Learning*. Paris: OECD.

Posch, P. (1994a) Changes in the culture of teaching and learning and implications for teaching and learning. *Education Action Research*, 1(2), 153–61.

Posch, P. (1994b) Networking in environmental education. In M. Pettigrew and B. Somekh (eds) *Evaluating Innovation in Environmental Education*. Paris: OECD/CERI.

Posch, P. (1996) Professional development in environmental education, networking and infrastructure. Synthesis report (draft), part 3. University of Klagenfurt, Austria.

Stenhouse, L. (1970) *The Humanities Project: and Introduction*. London: Heinemann Educational.

Stenhouse, L. (1975) *An Introduction to Curriculum Research and Development*. London: Heinemann Educational.

Index